ESSAYS ON BERKELEY

Essays on Berkeley

A TERCENTENNIAL
CELEBRATION

EDITED BY

JOHN FOSTER

AND

HOWARD ROBINSON

CLARENDON PRESS · OXFORD
1985

Oxford University Press, Walton Street, Oxford OX2 6DP

Oxford New York Toronto
Delhi Bombay Calcutta Madras Karachi
Kuala Lumpur Singapore Hong Kong Tokyo
Nairobi Dar es Salaam Cape Town
Melbourne Auckland
and associated companies in
Beirut Berlin Ibadan Nicosia

Oxford is a trade mark of Oxford University Press

Published in the United States
by Oxford University Press, New York

British Library Cataloguing in Publication Data

Essays on Berkeley: a tercentennial celebration.
1. Berkeley, George
I. Foster, John   II. Robinson, Howard
III. Berkeley, George
192   B1348
ISBN 0-19-824734-6

Library of Congress Cataloging-in-Publication Data

Main entry under title:
Essays on Berkeley.
Includes index.
Contents: Imagination, experience, and possibility /
Christopher Peacocke — Berkeley's central argument
against material substance / A.D. Smith — Berkeley's
master stroke / Ernest Sosa — [etc.]
1. Berkeley, George, 1685–1753 — Addresses, essays,
lectures.   I.   Foster, John, 1941– .   II. Robinson,
Howard.
B1348.E73   1985   192   85-15567
ISBN 0-19-824734-6

Printed in Great Britain by
The Alden Press Ltd,
Oxford

GEORGE BERKELEY
1685–1753

CONTENTS

LIST OF CONTRIBUTORS

STEPHEN R. L. CLARK, Professor of Philosophy, University of Liverpool.

JOHN FOSTER, Fellow of Brasenose College, Oxford.

A. C. LLOYD, Emeritus Professor of Philosophy, University of Liverpool.

W. H. NEWTON-SMITH, Fellow of Balliol College, Oxford.

CHRISTOPHER PEACOCKE, Fellow of New College, Oxford.

HOWARD ROBINSON, Senior Lecturer in Philosophy, University of Liverpool.

A. D. SMITH, Lecturer in Philosophy, University of Essex.

ERNEST SOSA, Professor of Philosphy, Brown University.

C. C. W. TAYLOR, Fellow of Corpus Christi College, Oxford.

J. O. URMSON, Emeritus Fellow of Corpus Christi College, Oxford.

R. C. S. WALKER, Fellow of Magdalen College, Oxford.

MARGARET D. WILSON, Professor of Philosophy, Princeton University.

ABBREVIATIONS

The following abbreviations have been employed throughout the text:

Works	*The Works of George Berkeley Bishop of Cloyne*, ed. A. A. Luce and T. E. Jessop, 9 vols. (Thomas Nelson, Edinburgh, 1948–57).
PC	*Philosophical Commentaries* (*Works*, vol. i).
Principles	*The Principles of Human Knowledge*, Part I (*Works*, ii).
Principles, Intro.	Introduction to *The Principles of Human Knowledge* (*Works*, ii).
Dialogues	*Three Dialogues between Hylas and Philonous* (*Works*, ii).
Alc.	*Alciphron or the Minute Philosopher* (*Works*, iii).

References to *PC* are by entry number; to *Principles*, *De Motu* (*Works*, iv), and *Siris* (*Works*, v), by section number; to *Dialogues* and *Alc.*, by page number. Other references to *Works* are by volume and page number.

CHAPTER I

INTRODUCTION

JOHN FOSTER AND HOWARD ROBINSON

BERKELEY'S principal objective was to defend religion and common sense against the modern corpuscularian philosophy. This philosophy threatened religion by representing the physical world as a great machine, which worked according to its own self-contained and deterministic laws. Such a mechanistic view was hostile to the religious outlook, and in particular to that of Christianity, in at least three ways. First, it implied that if God was causally involved in nature it was only at its boundary, as the creator of the fundamental ingredients (space, time, and matter), the laws, and (if the universe had a beginning) the initial conditions. Granted the initial creation, everything that subsequently happened in the physical realm could be causally explained in purely physical and mechanistic terms, without appeal to God or any other type of rational or purposive agency. There was no provision for the traditional conception of a causally immanent God, 'upholding all things by the word of his power' and 'in whom we live, and move, and have our being'. Secondly, by pushing God back to the boundary of nature, the mechanistic view called in question the need to postulate his existence at all. If all that happens within the physical realm can be causally explained in purely physical terms, why not simply take the physical realm as the terminus of explanation? Why not suppose that the physical universe has always existed and that anything which calls for explanation is fully explained by the way in which the state of the universe at any time is causally determined by the state which precedes it? Why should we think that the universe as a whole depends for its existence on some non-physical being or purposive agency beyond it? Thirdly, the mechanistic view conflicted with the religious conception of man. For, if all physical events are causally determined by prior physical conditions, we are forced to accept either a materialist or an epiphenomenalist account of the human mind—the former allowing the mind to have a causal influence on the physical world, but only as

itself part of the physical machine, the latter allowing the mind a life
of its own, but one which has no influence on physical events. Both
these positions are alien to any religious view, which sees man as
endowed with an intellect and spirituality which both transcend the
physical realm and, through their expression in action, have the
power to affect it.

If the corpuscularian philosophy conflicted with traditional religion by its mechanistic account of nature, it conflicted with common
sense, or at least the common sense of the 'ordinary man', by its
representative theory of perception and its distinction between
primary and secondary qualities. Prior to philosophical reflection, we
assume that, through sensory experience, we directly perceive items in
the physical world. And, while we allow for some modest distinction
between appearance and reality, we also assume that, in normal
circumstances, the things we perceive are (more or less) as they
sensibly appear, subject to the perspective of our viewpoint. Both
these assumptions were rejected by corpuscularians. They held that
we only perceive physical objects indirectly, by the mediating
perception of ideas which represent them. And they also held that,
with respect to the so-called secondary qualities, the representation
was systematically and fundamentally erroneous: physical objects
did not have any colour, temperature, flavour, odour, or sound save
in the form of powers to produce certain kinds of sensation in us—
powers which depended on nothing more than the primary qualities
(shape, size, configuration, and motion) of the material particles and
the laws of nature. Berkeley found these doctrines objectionable, not
only because they were contrary to common sense, but also because
he saw them as the thin end of a sceptical wedge which promised to
undermine the foundations of knowledge altogether. He believed
that once we had surrendered our common-sense epistemology to the
new learning, we would be powerless to defend ourselves against a
more radical scepticism, which claimed that any rational belief about
the physical world was unattainable. Such a sceptical position was, of
course, doubly offensive to Berkeley. For, in undermining our
knowledge of the physical world, it would inevitably bring down
religion too.

The fact that a doctrine is unpalatable does not, as such, provide
one with any grounds for rejecting it. Nor did Berkeley suppose that it
did. He realized that, to defeat the corpuscularian philosophy, he
would have to demonstrate its error and that he could not do this,

without begging the question, by simply reasserting the religious and common-sense doctrines which the corpuscularians denied. Moreover, he knew, as well as anyone, that, *prima facie*, the corpuscularian theory was supported by the empirical evidence. Even though it conflicted with common sense, it seemed to be what common sense itself inevitably leads one to through rational reflection on the empirical data. His problem was how to preserve the common-sense baby while discarding the corpuscular bath-water. As Russell nicely posed the dilemma some two centuries later: 'Naive realism leads to physics, and physics, if true, shows that naive realism is false.'[1]

Yet in one important respect, Berkeley himself was prepared to discard the baby. For in moving against the corpuscularians, he began by rejecting a fundamental aspect of the common-sense position.

It is indeed an opinion strangely prevailing amongst men, that houses, mountains, rivers, and in a word all sensible objects have an existence natural or real, distinct from their being perceived by the understanding. But with how great an assurance and acquiescence soever this principle may be entertained in the world; yet whoever shall find in his heart to call it in question, may, if I mistake not, perceive it to involve a manifest contradiction. (*Principles* 4).

Thus Berkeley sides with the ordinary man in accepting the directness and veracity of our perception of the physical world; but, while the ordinary man takes the objects he perceives to be external to the mind, Berkeley insists that they have no existence distinct from their being perceived. He thinks that any denial of this involves 'a manifest contradiction' and one which plays into the hands of the corpuscularians. The epistemology of common sense is correct, but its metaphysics are incoherent; and it is only by abandoning the latter that we can preserve the former.

It is not entirely clear what Berkeley takes the 'manifest contradiction' in the common-sense metaphysics to be. At times, he seems to be arguing that the existence of a sensible object cannot be separated from its being perceived because it is impossible to conceive of a sensible object which is unperceived. But this latter claim is itself open to different interpretations and it is not easy to find an interpretation which leaves the claim both plausible and adequate for Berkeley's

[1] Russell, *An Inquiry into Meaning and Truth* (George Allen and Unwin, London, 1940), 13.

purposes. If we construe conception as a species of perception (and Berkeley sometimes uses 'perceives' in this broad sense) and if we interpret the claim as equivalent to 'it is impossibe for there to be any sensible object which is both conceived and unperceived', the claim is clearly true, but utterly trivial. On the other hand, if we take Berkeley to be claiming that we cannot conceive of there being a sensible object which is unperceived, the claim is adequate for Berkeley's purposes, but hardly sómething which, without further argument, will command assent. Perhaps the most promising interpretation is one which falls in between these two extremes. On this new interpretation, we take Berkeley to be making two claims: first, that it is impossible to conceive of a sensible object (at least, in a way which reveals its sensible character) without imagining it; second, that it is impossible to imagine an object without imagining that one perceives it. Berkeley's point would then be that we cannot make sense of the supposition that there are unperceived sensible objects, since any attempt to form a concrete conception of something's being sensible but unperceived is self-defeating. To form a conception of the object we have to imagine ourselves perceiving it and thus its being perceived becomes part of the content of the conception. In all this, of course, we are using the term 'imagine' to signify something which involves, in part, the framing of a sensory image.

If this is Berkeley's argument, it is by no means uncontroversial. One point where it could be challenged (though not the only point) is over the correctness of the second claim. For even if imagination has to represent what is imagined as if from a certain perceptual viewpoint, why should we insist that this viewpoint is part of the imagined scene, rather than simply, as in the case of a film, an aspect of the mode of representation? On this issue, Christopher Peacocke comes to the defence of Berkeley's position. It is true that 'the viewpoint of the camera . . . need not be the point of view of anyone in the film'[2] and thus need not be part of what is represented. But, argues Peacocke, imagination is not analogous. For 'it is in the nature of the sensory imaginings with which we are concerned that to imagine something is, in part, to imagine an experience from the inside'.[3] For this reason, the perceptual viewpoint is part of what the imagination represents, and in this sense, according to Peacocke, Berkeley is correct in claiming that we cannot imagine an unperceived object. Whether he is also correct in concluding that the very notion of an unperceived sensible object is incoherent is, of course, another matter. And on this larger issue Peacocke offers Berkeley no support beyond the fact that those who wish to demonstrate the coherence of this notion cannot do so by an appeal to imagination.

If the incoherence of this notion is not immediately established by the unimaginability of an unperceived object, nor is it immediately established by the truth of the sense-datum theory, which claims that the sensible objects of which we are directly aware are ideas or impressions in the mind. For the sense-datum theory can be combined with a representative theory of perception, which holds that the mind-dependent entities of which we are directly aware are representations of external objects with a similarly sensible character. It is true, as Howard Robinson (echoing Hume) points out, that the only thing which tempts us to suppose that such external sensible objects exist is that, outside the context of philosophical reflection, we automatically interpret the sensible objects of immediate awareness as external—so that, from the standpoint of the sense-datum theory, the temptation rests on a mistake. But, of course, it does not follow from this that, as Berkeley thought, the notion of an external (mind-independent) sensible object is incoherent.

None the less, the sense-datum theory could still serve as a crucial step towards establishing the incoherence claim. And it is clear that Berkeley thought that it did.

> ... an idea can be like nothing but an idea ... Again, I ask whether those supposed originals or external things, of which our ideas are the pictures or representations, be themselves perceivable or no? If they are, then they are ideas, and we have gained our point; but if you say they are not, I appeal to anyone whether it be sense, to assert a colour is like something which is invisible; hard or soft, like something which is intangible; and so of the rest. (*Principles*, 8).

Berkeley's point is that the phenomenal character of the sensible qualities is part of their essential nature. If by 'red' and 'hard' we mean to signify certain *sensible* qualities—qualities which can feature in the content of sensory awareness—we cannot logically separate the qualities themselves from their modes of sensual appearance. And consequently, we cannot coherently attribute these qualities to objects external to the mind, since such objects are inaccessible to sensory awareness. In effect, it would be as absurd to suppose that there are external instances of sensible redness and hardness, or any other sensible quality, as to suppose that there are external instances of pain.

This is closely connected with the point stressed by David Smith, that, on the Berkeleian account of sense-experience, as on other orthodox versions of the sense-datum theory, the sensible qualities play a dual role, furnishing both the immediate objects of experience (or the elements of those objects) and the intrinsic features of the experiences themselves. As Smith puts it: 'One and the same sensory item is . . . both the object of awareness and the material reality of the state of awareness.'[4] The upshot is that the qualities cannot be abstracted from their sensory context, since it is precisely in the realization of the qualities that sensory awareness consists. Just as any realization of a pain-quale yields a pain sensation, so any realization of a sensible colour yields a colour sensation. To suppose that there are external instances of the sensible qualities is tantamount to supposing that sensations can exist outside the mind.[5]

Even if this conclusion follows from Berkeley's account of sense-experience, the latter itself, of course, could still be challenged. For the claim that the immediate objects of sensory awareness are internal to the mind is by no means uncontroversial. Traditionally, the acceptance of this claim has been based on the so-called Argument from Illusion: we are forced to acknowledge internal objects in the case of illusion, and, since, for any veridical perception, there could be an illusion of exactly the same experiential character, we are forced to acknowledge them quite generally. One way (though by no means the only way) in which this argument could be challenged is by pressing a distinction between the subjective character of an experience and its intrinsic character. It may be that, if I have a hallucination of seeing a dagger, my experience is subjectively indistinguishable from my actually seeing a dagger. But that does not entail that the two experiences are of the same intrinsic type. For perhaps in the one case I am directly aware of a sense-datum, which exists only in my mind, while in the other I am directly aware of a physical object, which exists outside my mind. If so, then the experiences would be of different intrinsic types (having immediate objects of different ontological types); but they could still be

---

4 *Below*, p. 55.
5 Cf. John Foster, *The Case for Idealism* (Routledge, London, 1982), ch. 6.

subjectively indistinguishable, if their immediate objects coincide in their sensible appearance.

This suggestion is one which Robinson attacks by appealing to the principle of 'same proximate cause, same immediate effect'. His point is that in the case where the veridical and illusory experiences are directly caused by brain processes of exactly the same kind—in one case the process being caused in the normal way, in the other being artificially induced—it would be highly implausible to suppose that the experiential effects differ in their intrinsic character, according to how the brain processes themselves have been brought about. Of course, the causal origins of the brain process make a difference to whether the resulting experience qualifies as a genuine perception of a physical object. But it would be very odd if they affected the experience's internal character. As Robinson puts it, 'it would be as if the brain knew that when it was being activated artificially it needed to provide subjective content for the experience, whereas when activated normally it knew that the external world would perform that task for it!'[6]

If Berkeley can establish that the sensible qualities have no realization outside the mind, he has made some progress in his battle with the corpuscularians, but he has not yet achieved a decisive victory. What he has done, in effect, is to undermine the corpuscularian distinction between primary and secondary qualities. The corpuscularians had claimed that, while the secondary qualities of physical objects, such as colour and temperature, were merely powers to produce certain kinds of sensation in us, their primary qualities, such as figure and extension, genuinely resembled their sensory representations. If Berkeley is right, this claim must be abandoned. If sensible qualities are confined to the mind, then external objects are deprived of *any* sensible character. The only form of resemblance between such objects and their sensory representations is in terms of abstract (formally and mathematically specifiable) structure. But what Berkeley has yet to show is that the corpuscularians cannot adapt to this position. Why should it be crucial to their theory that the primary qualities of bodies be of a sensible kind?

Berkeley's answer is that unless external objects do have sensible qualities, we cannot form any positive conception of their intrinsic nature—of what, beyond their abstract structure and nomological organization, such objects are like in themselves. It is not just that

[6] *Below*, p. 177.

their intrinsic nature is something which corpuscular science does not reveal; it is also that, unless this nature is composed of sensible qualities, we cannot even conceive of what it might be. However, as John Foster points out, it is far from clear why the corpuscularian need feel embarrassed by this. Provided he has the general notions of object and property, he can make sense of the supposition of there being external objects with natures beyond the scope of human conception. And presumably he can then, given our experiential data, hope to justify this supposition (together with some more specific theory of the structural and nomological character of the external reality) by an inference to the best explanation.

However, Berkeley's objections to the postulation of external objects do not stop here. In the first place, he denies that we can have any general notions of object and property of the required sort. And here the point is not just that we cannot frame an abstract image of object-in-general or of property-in-general—in the way we cannot frame an abstract image of a colour without spatial extension or of a colour patch without determinate colour and shape. The point is, more crucially, that our whole understanding of what it is for an object to have a property is tied to our perceptual grasp of what it is for a sensible object to have a sensible quality and our introspective grasp of what it is for a spirit to be in a mental state. We cannot make sense of the suggestion that there are external objects with non-sensible properties, since we can never detach our notions of object and property from their perceptual and introspective fields of application. Indeed, according to Ernest Sosa, property-instantiation has no place at all in the ultimate reality, as Berkeley conceives it. For something to have a property is always reducible to the perceptual, intellectual, or volitional activities of some mind or minds. Thus Sosa formulates Berkeley's basic metaphysical principle as

the denial of any nexus or copula or true relation other than perceiving (understanding or conceiving), and willing, both of which relate a mind to qualities or combinations of qualities, or in turn to a mind's being thus related to such. Everything that exists fundamentally does so as a term of one of these relations; and anything that obtains fundamentally is either a mind's standing in one of these relations to an idea, or a mind's standing in one of these relations to a mind's standing in one of these relations to an idea, and so on.[7]

As Sosa sees, this has what are, even from a Berkeleian standpoint,

[7] *Below*, pp. 69–70.

some very strange consequences, such as that a spirit's being a spirit and a quality's being a quality are not fundamental, but derivative from the way in which minds are related to ideas (or related to their being thus related) in one or more of the specified ways. But he thinks that Berkeley cannot abandon the general metaphysical principle and retain any rationale for his *a priori* rejection of objects outside the mind. This, perhaps, is somewhat controversial.

Even if the supposition of external objects makes sense, Berkeley has a further objection to the role in which they are cast by the corpuscularian theory. For he denies that such objects could exert any causal influence on each other or on anything else. Once again, the underlying point is the inseparability of a certain notion from the context in terms of which it is empirically grasped. The only way we can experience causal agency is by our introspective awareness of our own volitional acts, and, according to Berkeley, the kind of causation thus revealed is not something which we can detach from its volitional setting and envisage as operating in some external, non-mental world. This claim, of course, is controversial and Berkeley's defence of it is far from conclusive. But if it is right, it automatically excludes the kind of physical world which the corpuscularians postulate, in which objects are held to interact causally and causally to induce sensations in us. And it further means that we have no rational grounds for postulating an external world at all. For if such a world is causally inert, its postulation does not help to explain the course of human experience, and thus cannot be justified by an explanatory inference. In short, the external world becomes, from our standpoint, not only incomprehensible, but also superfluous. Or as Berkeley puts it, through the mouth of Philonous: 'Do you not at length perceive, that in all these different acceptations of *matter*, you have been only supposing you know not what, for no manner of reason, and to no kind of use?' (*Dialogues*, 220.)

This insistence that all causation is volitional not only delivers the *coup de grâce* against the corpuscularian philosophy, but also provides Berkeley with a way of bringing God into the story. For he now feels justified in concluding that our sense-experiences are directly caused by divine volition and that their orderly character is explained by the consistency of God's volitional policies. This restores the traditional doctrine of a causally immanent God, in opposition to the mechanistic view, and also gives us grounds, by an explanatory inference, for believing that such a God exists.

The main problem now is that, while Berkeley has justified the postulation of a causally immanent God, he seems to have made no provision for a physical world for us to inhabit and for God to control. Since there are no objects external to the mind, Berkeley's universe consists of no more than God and finite spirits, together with all that exists or occurs within them. The physical world, it seems, has vanished altogether. This would be an intolerable consequence for Berkeley, who is (minus its metaphysical aspect) aiming to defend the common-sense position.

Berkeley now has two options if he wants to retain the physical world in the framework of his mentalistic metaphysic. One option would be to identify the physical world with some portion of the ultimate mental reality. The other would be to exclude the physical world from the ultimate reality, but construe it as something whose existence is logically sustained by, and thus in a broad sense reducible to, the ultimate facts. How Berkeley's position stands with respect to these options is not entirely clear, partly because he never fully appreciated the distinction and partly because his own remarks were often inconsistent or equivocal. But, on the most natural interpretation, the predominant position in the *Dialogues* is of the first or 'realist' kind, while that in the earlier *Principles* is of the second or 'reductive' kind. More specifically, the *Dialogues* position seems to be one in which the physical world is identified with a complex idea in God's mind; and the *Principles* position seems to be a form of phenomenalism, in which the existence of the physical world is reduced to the organization which, by his volitional strategy, God imposes on human experience.

In locating the physical world in God's mind, Berkeley would, of course, be restoring one aspect of the common-sense metaphysic at the cost of discarding one aspect of the common-sense epistemology. For such a world, while not external to *all* minds, would be external to *our* minds; and thus it would be something with which we have perceptual contact only through the mediation of representational ideas. This itself makes the *Dialogues* proposal out of keeping with Berkeley's basic ideology. Moreover, according to Foster, the proposal can be faulted in a more fundamental way. For he argues that Berkeley does not have any rational grounds for postulating a physical world of this kind. Even if Berkeley is entitled to suppose that God has a conception of a certain kind of physical world, in terms of which he frames his volitional strategy, he is not, claims

Foster, entitled to suppose that this conception has an internal object which could serve as the actual physical world. If this is so, it seems that Berkeley would have done better to retain his earlier, phenomenalist account, though this too, as we shall see, is open to certain objections.

A question which now arises is what place (if any), in his theory of the physical world, Berkeley is willing or able to accord to corpuscular science. And this, of course, divides into two questions, one concerning his phenomenalist account and the other his realist account.

From the standpoint of his phenomenalism, corpuscular science is obviously false (indeed, incoherent) as a description of how things ultimately are. But it would still be possible for Berkeley to recognize it as true as a description of how things physically are. For, by extending his reductive account to science, he could say that the organization of experience logically sustains the truth of the corpuscularian theories in the same way as it sustains the truth of physical statements of the common-sense kind. The admission of corpuscular science on these phenomenalistic terms would pose no threat to either religion or common sense (ignoring, of course, any threat to either from phenomenalism itself). The explanatory role of God would remain in full force. And the sensible world of our ordinary beliefs—the world which is as it sensibly appears—would be preserved as a product of the cruder but more overt aspects of the sensory organization which science more deeply explores and more finely specifies.

There are passages where Berkeley seems to endorse this reductive account of science. But, as W. H. Newton-Smith points out, it is also possible to interpret him as holding an alternative and subtly different view. On this alternative view, scientific theories are construed not as factual assertions, which are either true or false, but as convenient tools for observational prediction. Newton-Smith labels this position 'semantical instrumentalism'; and because he assumes that any reductive account would be of a strong analytical form, requiring the translation of scientific statements into experiential statements, and because he also thinks (surely correctly) that such translations are not available, he considers this instrumentalist position to be Berkeley's best option. What is particularly interesting is the way in which Newton-Smith sees Berkeley as arguing for semantical instrumentalism on the basis of a belief in the 'underdetermination of theory by data'—a belief that, for any scientific theory, there is an alternative and (construed assertorically) incompatible theory which has the same observational consequences and fares equally well in respect of all other evidential considerations. Given Berkeley's anti-realist stance, Newton-Smith regards the inference from the underdetermination-thesis to the instrumentalist conclusion as sound. For since the rival theories cannot be distinguished at the level of the ultimate (experiential) facts, it is impossible for them to have different truth-values; and this means that neither of them can be true, since, taken as factual assertions, they are incompatible. Whether the underdetermination-thesis is in fact correct is another matter, and Newton-Smith regards it as entirely speculative. He also sees difficulties for Berkeley in squaring his instrumentalist construal of science with the rest of his phenomenalist system.

The second question we have to consider concerns the place of corpuscular science in Berkeley's realist account. If the physical world is identified with some complex idea in God's mind, we want to know whether it is the world of common sense or the world of scientific theory or perhaps (if this is possible) a combination of the two. On the face of it, the first of these options is the one which Berkeley intends, with corpuscular science being only admissible on phenomenalistic or instrumentalist terms. But Berkeley could be in difficulties here. For if (as Berkeley clearly intends) God's idea is to serve as the blueprint for his volitional strategy, and if science comes closer than common sense to specifying the sensory organization and thus revealing the content of that strategy, it seems that the idea would have to embody the scientific perspective. Admittedly, there are two respects in which it could not preserve this perspective exactly. In the first place, its components would be causally inert, so that any supposed causation between physical events, or from physical events to human experience, would have to be construed occasionalistically. Secondly, if it were to have the concrete character required for its identification with the physical world, it would have to be determinate in respect of those aspects of the world (like the intrinsic nature of the fundamental particles) which science does not and cannot reveal.

Interestingly, as Margaret Wilson points out, there is a passage in the *Principles* (60–6) where Berkeley might be taken as endorsing a realistic construal of corpuscular mechanisms. But this passage immediately follows one (concerning the motion of the earth) in which Berkeley explicitly endorses a phenomenalist position. And Wilson rightly argues that Berkeley's acknowledgement of the minute 'clockwork of Nature', much of which is so 'fine and subtle, as scarce to be discerned by the best microscope', refers to the fine grain of the sensory organization rather than to corpuscular structures which are ultimately real. She also argues that it would be very difficult for Berkeley to reconcile corpuscular realism with the rest of his system, though many of the difficulties here concern *any* attempt to equate the physical world (whatever its character) with a complex idea in God's mind.

If there are general difficulties for Berkeley's realist position, there are general difficulties for his phenomenalist position too. Perhaps the chief difficulty is that, unless the physical world is assigned some place in the ultimate reality, the role of Berkeley's God seems uncomfortably close to that of Descartes's demon. For to say that there is a physical world, but one whose existence is wholly sustained by the organization of human experience, seems to be only an alternative and euphemistic way of saying that there is no physical world, but our experiences are organized as if there were. The phenomenalist might reply that statements about the physical world turn out, on conceptual analysis, to be equivalent to statements about the sensory organization, so that it is implicitly self-contradictory to concede that the appropriate organization obtains but deny the existence of such a world. But this claim is plainly false. Whatever the nature of the ultimate reality, the physical language has its own distinctive ontological perspective which cannot be simply analysed away. So it remains unclear how Berkeley can deny the ultimacy of the physical world without rejecting its existence altogether.

Berkeley's position would be easier if, like Kant, he could accord a synthetic *a priori* status to the basic principles by which we interpret our experiences in physical terms. For this would mean that, while the inference from the sensory organization to the physical world could not be justified by mere conceptual analysis, the basic ontological structure of our physical beliefs (e.g. the acceptance of space and time, and spatio-temporal objects) would be furnished and validated by human understanding alone, leaving only the details of the physical world to be discovered by empirical means. But, as Ralph Walker stresses, while this may allow a form of idealism, it would not be compatible with the radically empiricist form which Berkeley is trying to defend. The only synthetic *a priori* principles which Berkeley can employ are the 'regulative' principles of induction and inference to the best explanation; and, while these may help to justify beliefs about the sensory organization and its theistic origin, they do nothing to legitimize the ontological perspective of the physical theory. And Walker thinks that even the employment of these principles is, from the standpoint of Berkeley's empiricism, problematic. For either they will be left without any further justification, or else they will be justified by transcendental arguments of a kind which, by justifying the additional 'constitutive' principles, would oblige acceptance of a Kantian, rather than a Berkeleian, account of the physical world. How problematic it would be for Berkeley to leave the regulative principles without any further justification is perhaps debatable.

With respect to the main problem, Berkeley's best response might be to appeal to Foster's distinction between 'prospective' and 'retrospective' sustainment. He would then concede that, given the 'conceptual autonomy' of the physical language (i.e. the impossibility of simply *analysing* the physical ontology away), there is no valid *a priori* inference from the sensory organization to the existence of a physical world. But, at the same time, he would insist that, given our knowledge that there is a physical world, we can then establish, by *a priori* philosophical argument, that it is the underlying sensory organization by which its existence is logically (or, as some would say, metaphysically) sustained. This would mean, of course, that Berkeley could not employ his phenomenalism as a way of defeating scepticism about the physical world. But since, in practice, we rely on our physical knowledge to obtain most of our information about the sensory organization, this line against the sceptic would not be available anyway.

Whether or not Berkeley can provide a satisfactory account of the physical world, there is also the question of whether he has a satisfactory account of the human mind and of its place in nature. In broad outline, Berkeley's conception of the mind is similar to that of Descartes. Like Descartes, he thinks that each person is, in a certain sense, directly aware of himself, though this self-awareness is provided not by an introspective *idea*, but by the person's engagement in mental activity. Again, like Descartes, he speaks of the self as a spiritual substance and clearly rejects the Humean view, which sees the mind as a bundle of mental events unified by no more than the relations in which they stand to one another. However, as A. C. Lloyd interprets him, Berkeley's position also differs from the Cartesian one in two crucial respects. For while Descartes took the essence of the self to consist in thinking (i.e. mental activity in a broad sense), Berkeley takes it to consist, more narrowly, in volition. And while Descartes took the self to be a substance in the strict metaphysical sense—something of which thinking is the essential attribute— Berkeley equates it with the volitional activity itself. Lloyd supports this interpretation by citing entries in the Notebooks (e.g. 'It should be said nothing but a Will, a being which wills being unintelligible' (*PC*, 599a) and 'Substance of a Spirit is . . . to act, cause, will, operate' (*PC*, 829)) and also by showing its conformity with Berkeley's empiricist and nominalist theory of meaning.

Perhaps the two most serious difficulties for this account of the self are: first, how to allow for the occurrence of sense-perception, in which, as it seems, the self is entirely passive; and second, how to make provision for the persistence of the self without falling back on a Humean theory. According to Lloyd, Berkeley's answer to the first difficulty is that even in sense-perception there is an active element of acquiescence (or attention), and his answer to the second is that the self is a single volitional act which derives its persistence from the succession of ideas in which it is actively involved. This second answer leads Berkeley to say in his Notebooks (*PC*, 651): 'In sleep and trances the mind exists not there is no time no succession of Ideas.' Whether this conclusion is objectionable, and whether it could be avoided without abandoning the core of Berkeley's theory, are matters for further investigation.

If Berkeley equated the self with volitional activity, he also held that this activity was 'free'. And as Stephen Clark sees it, these two doctrines are closely linked. 'If our soul was an entity with a definable nature, it might be possible to argue that being so it could not but will the way it did. But the soul, for Berkeley, "is the will properly speaking" . . . There is no substantial entity that has any prior existence of a kind that could determine what sort of effects it could will.'[8] The kind of determination which Clark is here excluding is, presumably, of a logical (or metaphysical) rather than a causal kind. For the restriction of causal agency to volitional agency is already secure in Berkeley's system, irrespective of how he construes the self. The only way in which a volition might be *causally* determined is by another volition (e.g. by an earlier volition of the same subject or by a volition of God). Berkeley would doubtless have excluded this

---

[8] *Below*, p. 238.

possibility by arguing that the supposed effect would, by being an effect, be deprived of its inherently active character and thus would forfeit its volitional status. In other words, he would say that for something to qualify as a volitional act, it has to be of an intrinsic kind which logically precludes its being caused by anything else. It has to be, as one might term it, 'intrinsically autonomous'.

What remains unclear is how Berkeley is to allow the free volitional self to make any impact on the physical world. It is part of both the religious and the common-sense view of man that the human mind not only transcends the physical realm, but can also act upon it. Having disposed of the corpuscularian philosophy, Berkeley has protected this view from the threat of physical determinism. But it can still be objected that his own philosophy undermines it in another way. Clark hints at the objection when he speaks of the 'real difficulty . . . for Berkeley's understanding of the relations between God's agency and ours.'[9] And Christopher Taylor, who examines the objection in some detail, sees it as exposing a fundamental weakness in Berkeley's position.

The problem is that, whether we think of the physical world as an idea in God's mind or as the product of the sensory organization, everything that takes place in it falls under the direct volitional control of God. It follows that if we are to have any causal influence on the physical world it must be by causally influencing God's volitions. But this, of course, is ruled out on Berkeley's theory. For God is a purely active being, not subject to any kind of external influence. So with respect to the physical world, the human mind is causally redundant. I can decide to move my body and will that this should happen, but the decision and volition do not causally affect the outcome. As Taylor puts it, echoing Davidson: 'All we ever do is move our wills: the rest is up to God.'[10] Taylor thinks that this restriction on the scope of human agency is a consequence which Berkeley cannot afford to accept.

It might be replied that Berkeley can secure the requisite links between the human mind and the physical world in an occasionalistic manner. Human volition, while not *causally* affecting God, may serve as an occasion, or reason, for divine volition; and provided God pursues consistent volitional policies (which we discern as psychophysical laws), there seems to be enough here to allow the human

---

9 *Below*, p. 238.
10 *Below*, p. 211.

subject to qualify, in some decent sense, as the agent of the physical action. Taylor counters that if the events which prompt God's volitions are thought of as directions or reminders, then even occasionalism is incompatible with God's autonomous sovereignty, though he concedes that occasionalism need not be construed in this way. He also objects, more strongly, that any form of occasionalism gives God a share in the moral guilt for sinful human action. As he puts it, 'God is the ruffian who carries out the wicked designs we are helpless to execute.'[11] But perhaps this could be answered by appealing to the 'principle of double effect'. God's intention, in executing our designs, is to make us occasionalistically efficacious agents rather than to promote evil. At all events, there seems to be some morally crucial difference between God's role in sustaining a natural order which provides for the fulfilment of our (sometimes wicked) intentions and the role of a hired assassin.

Of course, any form of theism which represents God as both omnipotent and benevolent is bound to encounter the more general problem of evil in some form. And it is as foolish to suppose that there is a simple solution as to conclude, on this basis alone, that theism is discredited. Characteristically, Berkeley's own response combines faith with good sense:

We ought not therefore to repine at the dispensations of providence, or charge god foolishly. I say it becomes us with thankfulness to use the good things we receive from the hand of God, and patiently to abide the evil, which when thoroughly considered and understood may perhaps appear to be good, it being no sure sign that a thing is good, because we desire, or evil, because we are displeased with it. (*Works*, vii. 134.)

As Clark aptly comments, 'the cultivation of that moral temper, in ourselves and in society, was Berkeley's goal, and, in some measure, his own achievement'.[12]

---

[11] *Below*, p. 224.
[12] *Below*, p. 253.

CHAPTER 2

IMAGINATION, EXPERIENCE, AND POSSIBILITY: A BERKELEIAN VIEW DEFENDED[1]

CHRISTOPHER PEACOCKE

BISHOP BERKELEY had a gift for making clear, crisp statements of doctrines that are also unbelievable. His doctrine that it is impossible to imagine an unperceived tree is often taken as a prime example of this gift. I will argue here that, on the contrary, there is an important sense in which the doctrine is true. It is a consequence of a more general account of the relations between imagination, experience, and possibility. Much of what I have to say will be an outline of this more general account; but we can begin with three simple questions.

The first of these questions can be introduced by examples. Imagine a suitcase. If you succeeded, now imagine a suitcase with a cat wholly obscured behind it. It seems that the same conscious, subjective image will serve to meet both requests, even though in one sense what is imagined in each case can be different: in the second case, in the imagined world there is a cat behind the suitcase, whereas that may be left open in the imagined world of the first case. A rather different family of cases could equally lead to the same conclusion. Compare: imagining being at the helm of a yacht; imagining from the inside an experience as of being at the helm of a yacht; and imagining from the inside what it would be like if a brain surgeon were causing you to have an experience as of being at the helm of a yacht. Again, we may have the same image (in the sense of a type image) fulfilling

[1] Earlier versions of this paper were read to a seminar given jointly with Jennifer Hornsby in Oxford in 1979 and to the Brasenose College Philosophy Society in 1982. In addition to the discussion on those occasions, I have been helped more recently by the comments of Roger Scruton, Kendall Walton, and the editors. I had the opportunity to prepare the text for publication when I was a Fellow of the Center for Advanced Study in the Behavioral Sciences. I am grateful for support from the Center, from the National Science Foundation (grant BNS 76-22943) and from the British Academy.

each request, while what is true in each of the imagined worlds varies. Our first question then is the nature of this distinction between what is in the image and what, in the same imaginative project, is imagined. Let us call this 'the question of the image/imagination distinction'. The second question emerges from an example of Wittgenstein's.[2] If a man says 'I am imagining King's College on fire', it seems absurd for his friend to respond 'How do you know it is King's College you are imagining? Are you aware that there is a precise replica of it on a film set in Los Angeles? May you not be imagining *it*?' We will want to know what it is that makes one singular content rather than another a component of what is being imagined; and we will want to know why it seems there is a sense in which it is absurd to suppose the imaginer might be mistaken about the identity of that content. We will include both these questions under the label 'the question of the content'. Corresponding questions could equally be formulated about the content's predicative components.

The third question is whether one can imagine an unperceived tree. Berkeley's claim that we cannot seems, as Williams remarks, 'to have something in it which is not utterly implausible'.[3]

The English word 'imagine' is sometimes used in the sense of 'suppose' or 'suppose falsely', as in 'The President supposes that there is some well-established economic theory which justifies his policies'. Supposition and false supposition are not the concerns of this paper: I will be concerned rather with a phenomenologically distinctive state of imagination whose presence is not guaranteed by any supposition alone. Thus a newly deaf man seated in a concert hall may imagine in the sense of supposing falsely that the orchestra in front of him is playing Mozart's Linz Symphony; it does not follow that he is auditorily imagining a performance of that Symphony by the presented orchestra or by any other. Henceforth I will use 'imagine' only for the phenomenologically distinctive state.

We can start on answering our questions by formulating this plausible General Hypothesis:

---

[2] *The Blue and Brown Books* (Harper, New York, 1965), p. 39. Wittgenstein's own answer is hinted at on the same page where he writes: 'For saying "There's no doubt I imagine King's College and no other building" is like writing the words "Portrait of Mr. So-and-so" under a picture.'

[3] 'Imagination and the Self', repr. in *Studies in the Philosophy of Thought and Action* (OUP, Oxford, 1968), ed. P. F. Strawson, at p. 193; later page references are also to this reprinting.

to imagine something is always at least to imagine,
from the inside, being in some conscious state.

The General Hypothesis is not to be read just as the necessitation of a conditional: it makes a constitutive claim about what it is to imagine something.

The General Hypothesis is too general for our purposes, and we will need a specialization of it. But already the General Hypothesis can help to explain a principle which links imagination with the first-person way of thinking of oneself. It seems that for each person, his imaginings always in a sense involve imagining something about himself. The sense in which this is so needs careful delineation. You may imagine what it is like for someone who sits in the front row watching you give a lecture. Here you imagine something about yourself in the sense that you yourself are seen from the point of view imagined; and certainly not all your imaginings need to be like that. The sense in which your imaginings always involve yourself is rather this: imagining always involves imagining from the inside a certain (type of) viewpoint, and someone with that viewpoint could, in the imagined world, knowledgeably judge '*I'm* thus-and-so', where the thus-and-so gives details of the viewpoint.

This condition does not merely relate each imaginer x to the object x. In addition it relates all imaginers to a single first-person (type of) way of thinking.[4] The condition seems to be a conceptual truth. It is not just a reflection of each person's egocentricity, for it seems that the least egocentric person's imaginings could not fail in this sense to be about himself. The condition is a consequence of two conceptual truths: one of them is the General Hypothesis, and the other is that for each thinker, the content 'I am not the person with *these* conscious states' is not epistemically possible. (Here '*these* conscious states' invokes a way of thinking of certain conscious states made available to the thinker by his actually being in those states.) Various different substantive theories of the first-person way of thinking may ensure this second truth, and any one of them in combination with the General Hypothesis will be capable of explaining the truth of the condition. The explanation is simply that according to the General Hypothesis, imagining is always imagining from the inside being in some conscious state (ϕ, say), and someone in such a state is in a

---

[4] This first-person type of way of thinking is labelled '[self]' in Chapter Five of my *Sense and Content* (OUP, Oxford, 1983).

position knowledgeably to judge 'The person with these conscious states is ϕ', and thus knowledgeably to judge '*I'm ϕ*'.

The points of the last two paragraphs could be made *pari passu* for the pure present-tense type of way of thinking ([now]). In one sense, not all your imaginings need be about the present: you may imagine, from the inside, features of the daily life of a Bostonian in 1776. But someone with a viewpoint of the type imagined could, in the imagined circumstances, knowledgeably judge contents of the form 'Such-and-such is the case *now*'. An analogous explanation of the phenomenon would invoke the epistemic impossibility, whatever its source, for each thinker of the content 'Now is not the time at which *these* conscious states are occurring'.

The range of conscious states within the scope of the General Hypothesis is wider than our main concerns. There are, for instance, conscious, subjective components of intentional action. Imagining playing the Waldstein sonata is different from imagining the sonata auditorily and seeing one's hands, mysteriously, hitting the right notes. Indeed there is a sense in which one cannot imagine playing the sonata if one has no idea how to play it: even though in that situation one could still imagine the sounds and seeing one's hands move.

We will want to be concerned more specifically with sensory imagination: these are imaginings describable pre-theoretically as visualizations, hearings in one's head, or their analogues in other modalities. For these we can formulate the more specific Experiential Hypothesis:

> to imagine being ϕ in these cases is always at least to imagine from the inside an experience as of being ϕ.[5]

Again, this is intended as a constitutive hypothesis. It may seem

---

[5] Phrases which are allowed to replace 'ϕ' here are restricted to those which specify the objective properties and relations of a person, rather than his subjective, experiential state. So 'at the controls of a plane', 'on the operating table being injected', 'over eight foot tall' are all allowable substitutions: 'in the state of having an experience as of Waterloo Bridge' is not allowed. This restriction is required if we are not to be committed to false instances which iterate 'experience as of': without the restriction, the Experiential Hypothesis would have as an instance that to imagine being in the state of having an experience as of Waterloo Bridge is at least to imagine from the inside an experience as of being in the state of having an experience as of Waterloo Bridge. Imagining having an experience of a given kind is *just* imagining having an experience of that kind. That is already enough to verify the General Hypothesis for these cases: we do not need to add an extra layer of 'experience as of'. For comments prompting this qualification, I thank W. D. Hart and Colin McGinn.

uncontroversial: but I shall, in developing from it answers to our three questions, argue that it can be used in defence of Berkeley's doctrine about unperceived trees and in criticism of some received philosophical views on imagination. It should be emphasized that the Experiential Hypothesis is a hypothesis about the concepts of what Dennett would call personal-level folk psychology, rather than subpersonal cognitive, in particular information-processing, psychology.[6] An information-processing psychology, could, though, help to explain how we can use a concept of imagination of which the Experiential Hypothesis is true: it could do this by explaining the similarity or even overlap of the underlying information-processing mechanisms in imagination and in perception.

According to the Experiential Hypothesis, to imagine being seated on a horse is always at least to imagine from the inside an experience of being seated on a horse, and similarly for other replacements for the schematic 'ϕ'. If the reader is one who hears the phrase 'imagining being seated on a horse' as ambiguous—between the case in which he has the point of view of the rider and that in which he has the point of view of someone seeing another (the imaginer) seated on a horse—he should still accept the Experiential Hypothesis: in both cases, some possible experience is imagined from the inside. Similarly, for such forms as 'imagining a valley', we can say that to imagine an F is always at least to imagine from the inside an experience as of an F (or more weakly, an experience of a sort which might be enjoyed in perception of an F). The Experiential Hypothesis does not attempt to eliminate imagination or to reduce it to something else: it seeks only to elucidate a connection between imagination and experience. It does not say that imagining and experiencing are phenomenologically close to each other.[7] What is imagined is not of course a fully determinate type of experience: it is rather a kind of type (a type of

---

[6] See his *Content and Consciousness* (Routledge, London, 1969); *Brainstorms* (Bradford, Vermont, 1978); and 'Three Kinds of Intentional Psychology', in *Reduction, Time and Reality* (CUP, Cambridge, 1981), ed. R. Healey.

[7] It is sometimes said that the experiments of Perky ('An Experimental Study of Imagination', *American Journal of Psychology* 21 (1910)) show that in some cases visual imagining and visual experience—even visual perception—are indistinguishable by the subject. But careful investigation would be needed to establish that it is not the case that a faint physical image projected on to a smoked glass screen causes the subject to imagine something which matches it. If that were the correct description, the subjects need not be mistaking perception for imagination. They would, though, be likely to be making a different mistake—that of supposing that the shape of the imagined objects and their movement is independent of what is in their immediate environment.

types), and this is something which allows for indeterminacies in the image which could not be present in a real experience of that type.

I THE QUESTION OF THE IMAGE/IMAGINATION DISTINCTION

The Experiential Hypothesis explains some features of the examples of the suitcase and the yacht. When the same image can serve two different imaginative projects, that is because the imagined experience fulfilling each project can be the same. An experience of a suitcase and an experience of a suitcase with a cat wholly obscured behind it may be of the same type; the same applies to the imagined experiences in the yacht example. The Experiental Hypothesis also accounts for some other familiar features of imagination. The images which serve in the fulfilment of a request to imagine a chiliagon (a thousand-sided figure) and in the fulfilment of a request to imagine a 999-sided figure may match: for an experience produced by a chiliagon and an experience produced by a 999-sided figure are not, for us, discriminably different. Wittgenstein's remark that the same description or even a picture can give the content of seeing or of imagination is also accounted for: a description or a picture does either of these things by specifying the content of a possible experience. Again, imagining material objects being a certain way is always imagining a state of affairs from a certain point of view because perceptual experience is always from a point of view.

The Experiential Hypothesis also has negative consequences for some theoretical proposals. It entails that it would not be right to try to elucidate seeing-as in terms of imagination, at least if seeing-as is so understood that, for instance, a table is commonly seen as a table.[8] Such an elucidation would invert the true order of things, if the Experiential Hypothesis is right: for imagining has to be explained in part as imagining an experience from the inside, and an experience may already represent things in the environment *as* being of certain

---

[8] The phrase 'seeing as' has sometimes, mistakenly, been used for what Wollheim calls 'seeing in', or sometimes 'representational seeing': for insistence on avoiding this error, see R. Wollheim, *Art and its objects*, 2nd edn. (CUP, Cambridge, 1980) supplementary essay V, 'Seeing-as, seeing-in and pictorial representation'. I use 'seeing as' correlatively with the use of 'representational content' in my *Sense and Content* (OUP, Oxford, 1983): so that if someone sees something as an *F*, he has an experience which, were he to take it at face value, would lead him to judge that there is an *F* in the vicinity. In this sense a picture of a tiger is not normally seen as a tiger.

kinds (it may already have a representational content). Another negative consequence is for Ryle's suggestion that to imagine Helvellyn is to think how Helvellyn would look.[9] A person who thinks that Helvellyn would look asymmetrical, or would look challenging, may be described as thinking how Helvellyn would look: but he could think these things without imagining anything at all. It would not meet this to restrict the properties attributed in thought to Helvellyn to the visually observational: to think that Helvellyn is rounded is still not necessarily to imagine anything. Ryle's 'think how' would have to be understood as 'imagine how' to make his claim true.

We need to introduce some apparatus for describing the differences between imaginings which, though having a common image, still differ. In the three examples which involve imagining being at the helm of a yacht, the differences result from different conditions which the imagined experience is imagined to fulfil. In one case it is imagined that the experience is perceptual; in the second it is left open; in the third, it is imagined that it is produced by an intervening brain surgeon. I shall say that these are differences in which conditions are *S-imagined* to hold. 'S' is for 'suppose': although S-imagining is not literally supposing, it shares with supposition the property that what is S-imagined is not determined by the subject's images, his imagined experiences.[10]

It may be tempting to press a parallel between the image/S-imagining distinction and the remembering/remembering-that distinction. One can remember that one has been vaccinated against polio without remembering being vaccinated. But S-imagining has additional properties not reflected in this limited analogy. The world

---

[9] *The Concept of Mind* (Penguin, London, 1963), p. 255. Ryle writes 'should' instead of 'would'.

[10] In *The Language of Thought* (Crowell, New York, 1975), Fodor uses the notion of 'an image under a description'. (The passages are reprinted in *Imagery* (MIT Press, Cambridge, Mass., 1981), ed. N. Block.) The descriptions of Fodor's usage should not be confused with my S-imagined conditions. Rather, Fodor's descriptions coincide with what, in *Sense and Content*, I called the representational as opposed to the sensational properties of the imagined experience. This applies in the case in which Fodor says that an image given by a hexagonal array of crossing, bounded lines may be experienced either under the description 'a pinwheel sort of thing' or under the description 'cube from such-and-such angle': the corresponding visual experiences have the same sensational properties, but different representational properties. Correlatively with this, my use of 'image' is wider than Fodor's. If these terminological matters are kept straight, nothing in the present paper conflicts with Fodor's position in that work.

in which an S-imagined condition is imagined to hold is always one in which there is an experience which the subject imagines having from the inside. Thus although there is no mention of an experience in the S-imagined condition that there is a cat behind the suitcase, that suitcase is thought of as the one which is seen in the imagined experience of a suitcase. Were there not ultimately some such connection with the imagined experience, we would have not a case of S-imagining, but a case of pure supposing or entertaining of a thought.

II THE QUESTION OF THE CONTENT

It is sometimes said that the reason it is absurd to suppose that an imaginer might be mistaken about what he is imagining is that imagining is done intentionally, and in general we have non-inferential knowledge of our intentions.[11] But we have to distinguish sharply between the intention to imagine something and the success of that intention. Special knowledge about the content of an intention does not necessarily lead to special knowledge about the result of executing that intention. An absent-minded speaker may intend to refer to St Paul as St Paul, but come out with the name 'Aristotle'. Not only is there no absurdity in asking him whether he really did refer to St Paul: there is no absurdity either in asking him whether he referred to him as St Paul. By contrast, the question 'Are you really sure that you have succeeded in imagining something as King's College?' is still absurd. The appeal to intention fails to meet up with the phenomenon to be explained, which is an absurdity in the question about what is (often) the result of an intention, rather than about the intention itself. In fact it is a common experience for visual or auditory imaginings to come to a thinker wholly unbidden—they may even interrupt his thinking. In such cases, it is still absurd to ask 'How do you know it is this rather than that you are imagining?': but here the appeal to intentions is unavailable.

An image may be of an object in a sense which is partially causal. My image of New College garden is causally of New College garden: that garden, rather than any other garden or place, plays a distinctive causal role in the explanation of the properties of my image. The spatial layout and the properties of plants in that garden help to

¹¹ H. Ishiguro, 'Imagination', in *British Analytical Philosophy* (Routledge, London, 1966), ed. A. Montefiore and B. Williams, p. 162.

explain causally the layout and properties represented in my image. The correct way of specifying the causal relations needed for the image to be of the garden needs further investigation, but will not matter for present purposes. Even if an image is produced intentionally, the intended object need not be identical with the object which stands in this causal relation. The tourist to whom New College is introduced as Hertford College may well, when he is asked to imagine Hertford College in the winter, form an image which is causally of New College. (A similar point applies to pictures.) For this reason, the relation of being causally of an object is no answer to the Question of the Content: since subjects can easily be mistaken about which object their image is causally of, there is no absurdity in asking questions which presuppose that they might be mistaken.

The question which it *is* absurd to ask is whether the subject may not be mistaken about which content it is that he is *S-imagining*. (Since this content is at the level of mode of presentation, rather than at the level of the object *tout seul*, the relation 'is causally of' could not have been the solution of the Question of the Content.) Our misinformed tourist may be struck, quite unintentionally, by a visual image of what he takes to be Hertford College in the winter: he S-imagines that the visual experience he is imagining from the inside is produced by Hertford College, and he is right about which object he is S-imagining to produce it. S-imaginings as well as the imagined experience may also come unbidden. Rather than being a special case of knowledge of our own intentions, knowledge of what we are S-imagining is a special case of knowing what we are, in a broad sense, thinking.[12]

III   THE QUESTION OF THE IMAGINABILITY OF UNPERCEIVED OBJECTS

Can one visually imagine an unperceived object—imagine it *as* unperceived? Berkeley's contention that one cannot has been criti-

---

[12] If we are to be strict, we should recognize an additional layer of complexity here. It is not sufficient for an ordinary case of imagining New College that the subject have an image which is both causally of New College and matches it, and also S-imagines that the imagined experience is a perception of New College. For this subject too might have been misinformed: someone may have pointed to New College in his presence, and called it 'Hertford'. This subject may have an image which is both causally of New College and matches it, and S-imagines that his experience is perceptual: but he also S-imagines (as he would put it) 'New College looks as Hertford actually does'. We must add for the standard case that the subject is not imagining New College to be different from the way he takes it actually to be.

cized by Bernard Williams in a justly famous paper.[13] But the position for which I have been arguing supports Berkeley, for the following reason. In being asked to imagine an unperceived tree, we are asked not just to imagine the sort of experience one has when one sees a tree, but to imagine a *tree*, really there in front of us. What this last involves, I have argued, is that the imaginer not merely imagine from the inside an experience as of a tree, but also that he S-imagine as a condition on the same imagined world that the experience is a perception of a tree. So when he imagines a tree, the S-imagined conditions entail that, in the imagined world, some tree is perceived. To combine this with the supposition that in that imagined world no tree is perceived is to place inconsistent conditions on the imagined world: and that was precisely Berkeley's conclusion.[14]

Williams offers two positive reasons in favour of the opposite claim. The first is that when one visualizes some object or state of affairs, that the state of affairs is being seen need not be an element *in* the imagined scene, in the way that a woman is an element of the visualized scene when I am asked to imagine a bath and happen to imagine a bath containing a woman. This is Williams's formulation and example.[15] His second reason lies in an analogy with the representational arts:

even if visualizing is in some sense thinking of myself seeing . . . from a perceptual point of view, there can be no reason at all for insisting that that point of view is of one *within* the world of what is visualized; any more than

---

[13] 'Imagination and the Self'.

[14] But was it also Berkeley's argument for his conclusion? It would be very difficult to defend such an interpretation. Berkeley does not, to my knowledge, give any specific treatment of imagination, which has to be done if the argument is to get off the ground. Mackie (*Problems from Locke* (OUP, Oxford, 1976) pp. 53–4), following a style of approach suggested by Prior, regards Berkeley as having misused a self-refutation argument. On Mackie's reading, Berkeley aimed to show that it cannot be that someone thinks truly that there is something not thought about, while in fact his reasoning can carry him only as far as the conclusion that there cannot be something of which someone truly thinks that *it* is not thought about. There is some support for Mackie's reading: in the First Dialogue, Philonous is made to say 'Is it not . . . a contradiction to talk of *conceiving* a thing which is *unconceived*?' (*Dialogues*, 200). But it may be that an even cruder, and totally indefensible, argument was influencing Berkeley: the argument that conceiving of an unperceived tree requires having an idea of a tree, and perceiving a tree is no more than having an idea of a tree. Cp. Hylas's response, after he has accepted Philonous's arguments for saying one cannot imagine an unperceived tree, 'But now I plainly see, that all I can do is to frame ideas in my own mind' (ibid.) and the passages from the *Philosophical Commentaries* noted by Urmson in his *Berkeley* (OUP, Oxford, 1982), p. 41.

[15] 'Imagination and the Self', p. 202.

our view of Othello is a view had by one in Othello's context, or the cinematic point of view is necessarily that of one stealing around the characters. We can, then, even visualize the unseen.[16]

The first argument uses the notion of being an 'element of the imagined scene'. On the natural reading of this notion, for something to be an element of the imagined scene is for it to be represented in the image, the imagined experience. The woman in the bath is so represented. For a case in which seeing is an element of the imagined scene in this sense, one has to turn to cases in which, for instance, one imagines a doctor examining a patient. In this sense, seeing indeed need not be an element of the imagined scene when one imagines a tree. But this notion of being an element of the imagined scene is not the one used in the argument for Berkeley's conclusion. One can equally be committed to claims about the imagined world by the content of the S-imagined conditions which go beyond the image, and the argument was that it is these that make for inconsistency in imagining a tree as unseen. This means that the weight of Williams's case must rest on his second, analogical argument.

Williams is surely right in saying that the viewpoint of the camera or of the audience need not be the point of view of anyone in the film or play. So why is it, on my view, that cinematographic and theatrical representation are so different from imagination? It is because it is in the nature of the sensory imaginings with which we are concerned that to imagine something is, in part, to imagine an experience from the inside; while it is not in the nature of theatrical representation that to represent something theatrically is, in part, to represent an experience from the inside. Because that is not in the nature of theatrical or cinematographic representation, as Williams's examples show, the director has a degree of freedom which the imaginer lacks; the director may intend the spectator to appreciate that an experience of the type he enjoys is to be taken as occurring in the represented world, and may equally intend him to appreciate that no such experience occurs.[17]

[16] Ibid., p. 205.
[17] This explanation of the difference should be contrasted with a modal explanation, which might be put forward. The modal explanation would seek to account for the difference by saying this: 'The state which gives access to the represented world in the representational arts, i.e. visual experience, is a state which can be enjoyed without there being any represented or depicted world, whereas for imagination, the corresponding claim is false: if an attempt to imagine succeeds, something non-trivial must be true in the imagined world.' This modal condition, however, is not a necessary condition for an absence of parallelism with imagination. In the case of perception of a

Imagination is to be distinguished from conception, make-believe and supposition. In defending Berkeley's claim, I am not denying that one can imagine an array of physical objects and then make-believe that it is unperceived, or then conceive of it as existing unperceived, or make the supposition that it was, will, or might be unperceived. One may even imagine a tree and then, in a second imaginative project, imagine a world in which no one sees *that* tree. What I am asserting is only that if what is imagined is a physical object, then the imagined experience of the object is, in the initial imagined world, a perception.

Suppose there is a machine with visible cogs, rods, and crankshafts. This machine is linked with sensors to detect whether there is anyone in the room: if there is someone there, the machine automatically adjusts itself, and works in a different way. A mechanic may surely try to work out in imagination how the machine operates when no one is looking at it. It may be queried whether the present account leaves any room for this possibility. It seems to underdescribe the situation to say just that the mechanic is imagining a sequence of experiences as of a machine working: he is trying to work out in imagination how it actually operates. Yet it could be equally wrong to say that he is imagining how it would look if he were watching it operate: he may know perfectly well that it would operate differently were he in front of it. It may be said that if we allowed imagination of the machine without perception of it in the imagined world, this difficulty would vanish. But we do not need to give up our account to accommodate the case. The correct description of this case is: there is some way in which the machine operates when no one looks at it, and our mechanic is imagining it operating that way. All the case shows is that, unsurprisingly, that wide scope quantification over ways is not equivalent to this narrow scope condition: the mechanic imagines the way it would operate if he were there.[18]

painting, *some* notion of representation (not necessarily one involving an agent) has to be used embedded in a specification of the visual experience characteristically produced: certain regions of paint are seen as representations of objects, events, and states of affairs. Even if this notion of representation is very weak, in the sense that it can be explained without reference to *practices* of representation and depiction, it cannot prevent the coherent introduction of a correlative notion of the represented world. Such representation then fails the modal condition, but is still not parallel to imagination: in the world depicted in the painting, no one need be perceiving the scene portrayed.

[18] In some cases, one imagines one thing by imagining something else. A meteorologist may imagine the effects of stronger westerly winds across the Atlantic by using in imagination Mercator's projection of the globe. There is no point of view, even for an astronaut, from which the earth looks as Mercator's projection depicts it.

The limited argument I have been offering for Berkeley's conclusion gives no support to his or any other form of idealism. If it is impossible consistently to imagine an unperceived material object, all that follows is that the possibility of unperceived material objects cannot be established by appeal to what can be imagined. It could still be established by some other route. The suggested pro-Berkeleian argument is effective only against an opponent who, like the imagined objector in *The Principles of Human Knowledge*, is trying to establish the possibility of unperceived objects from considerations of imaginability.[19]

This last point matters in the assessment of a rejoinder Williams might give. Williams might say: 'I agree that imagining is always at least imagining an experience from the inside. But one should not immediately move from this to the claim that the imagined experience must exist in the imagined world. You do hold that it must—let us call your (Peacocke's) notion of imagination P-imagination. My notion, W-imagination, is related to yours thus: what I say is W-imagined is the type of objective state of affairs presented as obtaining in the imagined experience, such as King's College being on fire. Now there is no obstacle of inconsistency to our adding to the specification of a W-imagined world that the state of affairs of the given type is unperceived.'

A minor point about this rejoinder is that W-imagination does not align closely with the intuitive concept of imagination, since W-imagination does not allow room for imagining a pain in one's foot: here there is no objective state of affairs which may obtain independently of whether it is experienced. Some minor revision could perhaps accommodate this. The major point is that to use W-imagination in criticism of Berkeley's argument is to ignore the dialectical situation of the opponent Berkeley is envisaging. Since this opponent is hoping to argue from imaginability to possibility, he needs a concept for which it is independently plausible to hold that what is imaginable is possible. That *is* plausible for imagination as characterized in this paper: the plausibility rests on the two ideas that what can be experienced is possible, and that experiences that can be imagined are possible.[20] But if the opponent uses the idea that what is

---

[19] Section 23.
[20] The first idea would certainly need qualification to take account of experiences as of impossible objects. It should at least be restricted to cases in which the representational content of the experience is not internally a priori incoherent. None of

W-imagined is possible, and further may be consistently conjoined with the supposition that what is W-imagined is unperceived, then it is being taken for granted that material objects that can be experienced can also exist unperceived. Of course *I* would not dispute that! The point is rather that 'Material objects that exist experienced can also exist unperceived' has not then been established by considerations of imaginability; and indeed what would establish it— a proper account of the notion of a physical object and its relation to experience—may well make any appeal to imagination superfluous. What still stands after the introduction of W-imagination is this Berkeleian claim: there is no notion of imagination on which one can consistently imagine a physical object as unperceived and on which, taking imaginability here as sufficient for possibility, it is arguable that what is imaginable is possible. Even someone totally unsympathetic to Berkeley's metaphysics and theory of the mind can regard this conclusion as an important, if negative, contribution to an account of the nature of our grasp of the possibility of unperceived objects.

I proceed now to consider whether by using the materials developed in the course of this argument in defence of a Berkeleian claim we can generalize to reach conclusions about other areas.

IV   GENERALIZATION AND APPLICATION

Are there general limitations on the role that imagination could play in our grasp of certain possibilities? Whenever someone says that imagination has some distinctive role in our grasp of a particular range of possibilities, we should always ask this question: does his point survive the application to his case of the distinction between the imagined experience and what is S-imagined? If it does not, his account will be unacceptable. (The significance of that unacceptability will of course depend upon whether there is no candidate other than imagination for allowing us grasp of the possibility in question.) I will give two cases in which application of the distinction between the imagined experience and what is S-imagined undermines a natural account of the relation between imagination and understanding. Each of these cases concerns a massive topic which deserves extended separate treatment: my aim here is just to indicate the point

the examples in question are excluded by this restriction. Further restriction would be needed to handle contents which are a posteriori impossible. But this would by no means exclude all the cases of the kind needed for the argument of the text.

at which these considerations about imagination may be brought to bear.

The first case concerns our conception of other minds, on which each of us grasps the possibility that other subjects may have experiences in exactly the same sense and experiences of exactly the same type as himself. It is natural to suggest, and has been suggested, that each of us grasps this because he is capable of imagining from the inside someone else being in a particular conscious state: 'It is this general faculty of sympathetic subjective imagination that takes us on the first step outside of ourselves in the acquisition of an objective concept of mind, and that enables each person to place himself among the contents of the world.'[21] It is certainly true that we can imagine what it is like for someone else who is in pain. Suppose your injured friend Paul is on the other side of the room. You may imagine a pain from the inside, and imagine that the pain is Paul's: you may even add in imagination visual experiences of the kind he would be expected to enjoy from his location. This already shows that the case is not precisely on a par with imagining an unperceived tree; for that was argued to be incoherent, while there is no evident incoherence in your most recent imaginative project involving Paul's pain.

The problem for the envisaged theorist is not impossibility, but circularity. That the imagined experience is imagined to be that of someone other than the subject who is imagining is not something that could be inferred from the nature of the imagined experience: on the contrary, the imagined experience would be the same if the subject were imagining himself having a similar pain and a similar view on the world. That the imagined experience is that of another is wholly captured in the *S-imagined* conditions, which include the condition that the imagined experience is that of that person who is (actually) over there, the other side of the room. But this condition is intelligible only to, or is graspable only by, those who already have the conception that there may be many subjects all of whom have experiences in exactly the same sense. If someone does not already have the conception of many minds, such S-imaginings are unavailable to him; if he does, S-imagining takes for granted too much of that

[21] T. Nagel 'The Limits of Objectivity' in *The Tanner Lectures on Human Values I 1980* (CUP, Utah and Cambridge, 1980), p. 85. Nagel also gives an analogy on which our earlier discussion bears: 'To represent an experience from outside by imagining it subjectively is the analogue of representing an objective spatial configuration by imagining it visually' (p. 86).

conception to be a suitable means of explaining what is involved in possessing it. If alternatively it is said that what is imagined is a *type*, and the proposal is just that we can conceive that this type is enjoyed by others, the content of the conceiving again just presupposes possession of the notions possession of which was to be explained.[22]

The other case is that of radical and absolutely undetectable intersubjective inversion of the colour spectrum (or some other secondary quality sensory dimension). This is the case in which it is said that it is really possible that things another sees as green, you see as red, and conversely. This example, or some other, is to be spelled out in such a way that the ordering relations between experienced qualities under the inversion mapping are preserved, and similarly for aesthetic preferences and anything else which might result in detectability of the inversion. It is sometimes said in favour of such inversion being a genuine possibility that we know perfectly well what it is for it to obtain because we can imagine the other's experience were it to be true. Let us apply to this our tactic of asking how the claim fares when we apply the distinction between the imagined experience and what is S-imagined. The experience we imagine from the inside when we imagine the other's experience, is, for example, an experience as of red grass and of green fire engines. Now that the content of *that* experience is one which really could obtain not many would want to dispute: there could be red grass and green fire engines. What the defender of the possibility of radical undetectable intersubjective inversion requires is the possibility of the *S-imagined* conditions: the possibility that the imagined experience is, undetectably, the type which is enjoyed by the other when he looks at green grass and red fire engines. That we can imagine red grass and green fire engines cannot show that to be possible: again, it corresponds to nothing in the image, the imagined experience. If such intersubjective inversion is a genuine possibility, that will have to be established by appeal to something other than imagination.

The cases I have considered are very different from one another. Few would doubt that there can be unperceived trees, or that there is some coherent conception of many minds, however hard it is to

---

[22] Is it in any case really necessary for having the concept of a certain type of conscious state that one be capable of imagining it? Many people cannot imagine the experience of nausea which may be caused on a sea voyage: but they have the ability to judge that they have it when they do have it. This ability, with whatever it brings in its train, seems enough for possession of the concept, be the imaginative abilities of the thinker as they may.

elaborate. The possibility of radical and undetectable intersubjective inversion, on the other hand, remains problematic in the extreme. But there is one conclusion which both cases highlight, and with which Berkeley and Williams would agree: in respect of possibility and understanding, even less can be squeezed out of imaginability than we might have supposed.

CHAPTER 3

BERKELEY'S CENTRAL ARGUMENT AGAINST MATERIAL SUBSTANCE

A. D. SMITH

ONE of the most striking sentences in Berkeley's work is the following: 'From what has been said, it follows, there is not any other substance than *spirit*, or that which perceives.' (7)[1] This sentence is striking not for the undiluted metaphysical idealism which it propounds—for such assertions of course abound in Berkeley's work; what is really striking about the sentence is that it occurs in section *seven* of the *Principles*. That is to say that, leaving aside the introduction to that work, Berkeley feels that he is in a position to refute all alternatives to his form of idealism after just six short paragraphs! Now no doubt it is true that elsewhere in his writings Berkeley presents other arguments and considerations favouring idealism; but the argument alluded to here both takes pride of place at the beginning of Berkeley's major work, and dominates all his subsequent discussions. It is therefore this argument that I shall intend when I speak of Berkeley's Central Argument—henceforth abbreviated to BCA.[2]

Given the centrality of the argument in question, it is astonishing how many commentators on Berkeley have either overlooked or paid scant attention to the argument. But more significantly for our present purposes, those writers who have paid attention to BCA have almost universally treated it as an egregious howler. In this paper I wish to give BCA the closer attention and seriousness that its focal position in Berkeley's thought surely warrants. In fact, on closer inspection, BCA can be seen as involving a number of fundamental and difficult issues in what is now commonly known as 'cognitive science'—issues that must be carefully considered before BCA is consigned to the waste bin.

[1] References such as this are always to Berkeley's *Principles*, by section number.
[2] A. A. Luce rightly refers to the parallel sections of the *Philosophical Commentaries* (377–80) as 'the doctrinal climax of notebook B'—*Works*, i. 123.

Because Berkeley is separated from us by almost three hundred years of philosophical reflection, I intend to reveal the fundamental issues involved in BCA by discussing Berkeley's ideas in the context of his own philosophical contemporaries and predecessors—especially Descartes; but I trust that the 'contemporary relevance' of the issues thus highlighted will be quite apparent. Finally, I should like to add that this essay is not intended to be a historical reconstruction of the thinking that led Berkeley to BCA; rather am I concerned to present the issues, as understood from a seventeenth-century or early eighteenth-century perspective, that are objectively implicated in BCA.

I

Let us first of all look at BCA itself. Since some recent commentators have explicitly discussed the argument in question, this can be done briefly.[3] As the sentence quoted at the beginning indicates, Berkeley's target is the philosophical position that recognizes the existence of material (or unthinking) substance or substances. In the first six sections of the *Principles* Berkeley had not mentioned the distinctively philosophical notion of substance. There he was concerned to refute 'an opinion strangely prevailing amongst men' (4)—namely, that sensible objects have an existence independent of our perceptions of them. However, this common opinion was, at the time, typically filled out philosophically by the claim that such sensible objects consist of various accidents inhering in a material substance: a substance that was usually taken to be different by nature from the substance of thinking and perceiving beings. It is for this reason that Berkeley calls such material substance 'unthinking'—and sometimes even 'stupid'! It is on this philosophical notion of material substance that Berkeley directs his attack in section seven.

Material substance is defined, therefore, as that in which (at least) *sensible* qualities inhere. Such qualities are, of course, the features of objects that are perceived via the senses. But it is a commonplace from Descartes and others that such objects of perception or thought are *ideas*. Hence, by definition, material substance is that in which ideas inhere—or, equivalently, that which has ideas. But to have ideas is to perceive or think. Therefore the very notion of *material*

---

[3] See, for example, M. R. Ayers, 'Substance, Reality, and the Great Dead Philosophers', *American Philosophical Quarterly* 7 (1970), pp. 38–49.

substance as unthinking substance is incoherent. The only substance there is or can be is perceiving thinking substance, or what Berkeley calls *spirit*.[4]

The above argument is BCA in essence; and it is not difficult to see why no one has taken the argument seriously. Indeed, at first sight it seems simply sophistical. Leaving aside Berkeley's reliance on the traditional notions of substance and accident,[5] his argument seems to rely on a confused conflation of the object of perception and the perceiving of it, or of sensible qualities and 'sensations'. Now it is this very distinction that is at the heart of the issues I wish to explore in this essay. Can we really believe that Berkeley was unaware that such a distinction has repeatedly been made in philosophy, or that he confusedly overlooked it? If so, then he must have been one of the greatest fools in the history of philosophy, and it is not then clear why we should bother to read him at all. In fact the truth is, as Michael Ayers has expressed it, that Berkeley's 'examples and arguments show that he is so well aware of the sensation/quality distinction that he can consciously make it his target . . .'.[6] Before rejecting BCA, therefore, we should carefully consider what is involved in making such a distinction, and what grounds there might be for rejecting it. As I have said, I intend to investigate these issues by considering the philosophical framework, deriving from Descartes, which was handed down to Berkeley, and against which he was consciously reacting.

II

I want to begin the substantive consideration of the issues implicated in BCA by considering the concept of a *representation*. Until fairly recently this term would probably have suggested to a philosopher the so-called representative theory of perception (or of cognition

---

[4] Berkeley also adds, against those who would suggest that at least something *like* ideas can inhere in material substance, the principle that 'an idea can be like nothing but an idea' (8). Perhaps it is still worth emphasizing that Berkeley is absolutely committed to the strong position outlined: material substance is not problematic or redundant, but impossible and nonsensical. For clinching evidence on this point see sect. 22.

[5] It should be obvious, despite what some commentators have suggested, that Berkeley is far from questioning the substance-attribute metaphysic in the manner of a true phenomenalist. Sensible qualities *are* for him dependent items, requiring a substance in which to inhere. The point is that this substance must be Spirit.

[6] Ayers, 'Substance, Reality, and the Great Dead Philosophers', p. 40.

generally), where this is intended to be a theory according to which we are immediately conscious only of mental items in such a way as to lead to insuperable epistemological difficulties—the 'veil of perception' problem. Berkeley's predecessors, Locke and the Cartesians, were supposed to hold some such theory. As will emerge below, I see no good grounds for any such attribution; but in any case, for the present I wish to set aside any such associations as the term 'representation' may have. I intend, rather, to employ the term as it has come to be used almost universally in cognitive science since the breakdown of behaviourism. As one recent writer has said: 'The first point, then, is that human behaviour has proven to be of such a nature that the only satisfactory theories will be those in which inner *representations* play a role (though not necessarily a role that is not eliminable at another level of theory). Diehard peripheralist behaviourists may still wish to deny this, but that is of concern to historians of science, not us.'[7] And it is indeed difficult to see, at least at first sight, how we can dispense with some such notion, given that when I, for instance, perceive a rose, I do not become the rose, nor does the rose itself physically enter my mind—whatever that might mean.[8] To borrow a term from R. W. Sellars, we need to recognize the *epistemological dualism* involved in the perception of physical objects: I remain ontologically distinct from the objects I perceive, and my perception takes place in me, not in the object perceived.[9] Or, to approach the point from a slightly different angle: it seems clear that a perceiver of an environment must be a registerer of *information* about that environment, and such registering of information is just what is meant by speaking of a perceiver as representing that environment.[10] Now it may be that ultimately we shall have to question the usefulness for theories of cognition of the concept of a representation; but initially it seems to have a lot going for it.

We are now beginning to touch on that feature of conscious life

[7] Daniel Dennett, 'Brain Writing and Mind Reading', reprinted in his *Brainstorms* (Montgomery, Vermont, 1978), p. 41.

[8] We may be reminded here of Locke's (rather unsympathetic) reaction to John Sergeant's robust defence of this Aristotelian way of speaking in *Solid Philosophy Asserted* (London, 1697). For Locke's reaction, see John Yolton's *John Locke and the Way of Ideas* (London, 1956), esp. p. 109.

[9] See Sellars's contribution to Durant Drake *et al.*, *Essays in Critical Realism* (London, 1920), p. 190.

[10] For a good recent treatment of the concept of information by a philosopher, see Fred I. Dretske, *Knowledge and the Flow of Information* (Basil Blackwell, Oxford, 1981).

that has come to be known as *intentionality*: all (or at least most) conscious states are essentially states in which we are conscious *of* something or other as a distinct object of awareness. As Husserl wrote: 'What forms the materials into intentional experiences and brings in the specific element of intentionality is the same as that which gives its specific meaning to our use of the term "consciousness", in accordance with which consciousness points *eo ipso* to something of which it is the consciousness.'[11] This emphasis on intentionality is hardly peculiar to Brentano, Husserl, and their followers; it was, in fact, a commonplace in the Cartesian tradition.[12] Thus, for example, we find Arnauld writing: 'Comme donc il est clair que je pense, il est clair aussi que je pense à quelche chose. . . . Car la pensée est essentiellement cela'; and again: '. . . je soutiens qu'il est clair, à quiconque fait reflexion sur ce qui passe dans son esprit, que toutes nos perceptions sont des modalités essentiellement représentatives'.[13]

The key seventeenth-century term for expressing this directedness of thought was, of course, *idea*. As Descartes says: 'Of my thoughts some are, so to speak, images of the things, and to these alone is the title "idea" properly applied.'[14] So ideas are a subclass of thoughts; but if we are interested in cognition, or thought as it has been contrasted with volition, then ideas are our sole concern: to think and to perceive is simply to have ideas, the having of ideas is the constitutive activity of cognizing consciousness.[15]

Now although to think or to perceive is to have ideas, these ideas are not, in one sense, the objects perceived or thought about, at least usually.[16] I say 'in one sense', because in another sense, involving no

---

[11] *Ideas*, tr. W. R. Boyce Gibson (London, 1931), p. 249.

[12] And, of course, also in the earlier Scholastic tradition. For an excellent and concise account of St Thomas's theory of intentionality, see A. Marras, 'Scholastic Roots of Brentano's Conception of Intentionality', in *The Philosophy of Brentano*, ed. Linda L. McAlister (Duckworth, London, 1976), pp. 128–39.

[13] *Des Vraies et des Fausses Idées* (Rouen, 1723), pp. 10 and 40 respectively.

[14] *The Philosophical Works of Descartes*, trs. E. S. Haldane and G. R. T. Ross, (Cambridge, 1972), 2 vols., vol. i, p. 159. (Hereafter abbreviated as follows: H&R, i. 156.)

[15] The Cartesians also, of course, spoke of *perceiving* ideas, but I shall forgo this usage as it has misleading connotations for a modern reader.

[16] The Cartesians did hold, however, that all awareness necessarily involves reflexive awareness that one is aware; and so when I am aware of something by having an idea, that idea will in some way be an object of reflexive awareness: 'For does anyone who understands something not perceive that he does so?'—H&R, ii. 73. For a Cartesian such self-conscious awareness is not something added to thought or which

epistemological dangers, ideas *are* the things thought about, since in this sense ideas are the things thought about in so far as they are thought about or are 'in the mind'. This important and suggestive ambiguity in the term 'idea' is also found in such related expressions as 'what is in the mind.'[17] In one sense, when I am thinking of a particular rose, what is 'in my mind' is of course the rose itself, the *physical* rose, though of course it is not physically in my mind. In another sense, what is in my mind is a thought of that rose. This ambiguity is expressed in the Cartesian tradition by the distinction between the objective and the formal (or, sometimes, material) reality of ideas.

The Cartesians took the notion of an object being in the mind with an ontological seriousness of which we are today rightly suspicious. When I think of that rose, according to them, the rose itself really does have a mode of existence in my mind; we are not dealing here with a mere *façon de parler*. But, of course, the rose does not exist in my mind the way it exists in a vase, formally, but objectively, or as known. Arnauld sums up the position concisely:

l'idée du soleil est le soleil même, entant qu'il est objectivement dans mon esprit. Et ce qu'on appelle *être objectivement dans l'esprit* n'est pas seulement être l'objet, qui est le terme de ma pensée, mais c'est être dans mon esprit *intelligiblement*, comme les objets sont accoutumés d'être: et l'idée du soleil *est le soleil, entant qu'il est dans mon esprit*, non formellement comme il est dans le ciel, mais objectivement.[18]

supervenes on it—it is of the very essence of fully *conscious* awareness. Descartes tries to do justice to this rich sense of consciousness by claiming that apperceptive awareness does not involve a second level of ideas representing first-level thoughts: 'For we cannot will anything without knowing that we will it, nor could we know this without an idea; but I do not claim that the idea is different from the action itself'— *Philosophical Letters*, tr. A. Kenny (Clarendon Press, Oxford, 1970), p. 93—hereafter abbreviated as 'Kenny'. And elsewhere he explicitly says that the volition and the perception of it are 'really one and the same thing'—H&R, i. 341. Arnauld calls this omnipresent awareness of our thoughts a 'reflexion virtuelle' and contrasts it with a more self-conscious kind of self-awareness which is 'plus expresse, par laquelle nous examinons notre perception par une autre perception'—*Des Vraies et des Fausses Idées*, pp. 49–50. This issue is fundamental for interpreting Cartesian thought, and especially its views on 'sensation', which I shall discuss below.

  [17] '. . . cette chose, quoique unique, a deux rapports: l'un à l'âme qu'elle modifie: l'autre à la chose aperçue, entant qu'elle est objectivement dans l'âme; et . . . le mot de *perception* marque plus directement le premier rapport, et celui de *Idée* le dernier'— Arnauld, *Des Vraies et des Fausses Idées*, p. 39.
  [18] Ibid., pp. 41–2. Initially Descartes did not express himself in precisely this way, though he did speak of 'this mode of being by which a thing is objectively (or by representation) in the understanding by its idea'—H&R, i, 163. However, in his reply

Arnauld then goes on to draw out the implication of this ontological view of objects being in the mind that was crucial for Descartes's proof of God's existence in the Third Meditation: he says that the objective being of the sun in my mind, when I think of it, is 'une manière d'être beaucoup plus imparfait, que n'est celle par laquelle le soleil est réellement, mais qu'on ne peut pas dire néanmoins n'être rien, et n'avoir pas besoin de cause'.[19] So the intentionality of thought is construed by the Cartesians in terms of the positive objective existence of objects in the mind. What lies behind this account, of course, as Arnauld's use of the word 'intelligiblement' clearly indicates, is the Scholastic notion of *species*. Following Aristotle, in their own way, the Scholastics held that knowledge of an object involves the reception by the knower of the form of the object known.[20] Physical objects are composites of form and matter, but matter, though the *principium individuationis*, is of itself unintelligible—objects are known only *qua* possessors of forms. Now if, when I perceive a rose, I came to possess the form of the rose in the way that the rose possesses that form, I, or my sense organ, would *become* a rose. Knowledge arises because of the *immaterial* reception of forms.[21] Such an immaterial reception of form is present even in sensory knowledge, where the received form or species is a *phantasm*, even though this operation takes place in our sense faculties which are *corporeal*.[22] Such sensory knowledge is only of particulars; we attain genuinely intellective knowledge of objects as being of certain kinds when the *agent intellect* abstracts the pure form or *intelligible species* from the particular material conditions of the known object as embodied in the phantasm.[23] Even this barest of outlines of the

to the First Set of Objections, Descartes says: 'Now I have written somewhere *an idea is the thing thought of itself, in so far as it is objectively in the understanding'*—H&R, ii. 9. I do not know which passage Descartes has in mind: it is certainly not to be found in the *Meditations*. Perhaps Descartes came to endorse Arnauld's mode of expression as a result of reflecting on the latter's own set of Objections—see H&R, ii. 87 and 106.

[19] *Des Vraies et des Fausses Idées*, p. 42. Cf. H&R, i. 163.

[20] 'We have actual sensation or actual knowledge because our intellect or our senses are informed by the species or likeness of the sensible or intelligible object'—St. Thomas Aquinas, *Summa Theologica* (London, 1963–81). 1a, 14, 2.

[21] 'The form of a thing is limited by its matter to one thing. Therefore it is evident that the nature of knowledge is opposite to the nature of materiality. Thus things that receive forms only in a material way are non-knowers, for instance, plants'—ibid., 1a, 84, 2.

[22] 'Sense images (phantasmata) . . . are likenesses of individuals and exist in corporeal organs'—ibid., 1a, 85, 2, ad 3. Cf. 1a, 75, 5 and 1a, 78, 4.

[23] 'Now in sense-knowledge the knowledge-form (*species sensibilis*) is the likeness of one individual only; so by means of it only one individual can be known. But the

Scholastic account of cognition should indicate a certain congruence between the Cartesian and Peripatetic traditions. Both attempt to do justice to the intentional directedness of the mind towards objects by postulating the reception by a cognizer of some aspect of the being of the objects cognized, the reception in both cases being viewed as in some way immaterial. In the light of this it is astonishing that the Cartesians have been saddled with a sense-datum theory and a veil of perception problem. I can only think that such wild attributions have been made because of the besetting sin of historians of philosophy: namely, that of reading history backwards, from one's own viewpoint. Nevertheless, despite the congruence, there are important differences between the Cartesians and the Scholastics. For one thing, Descartes regarded the notion of *species* as intimately bound up with such notions as *real accident* and *substantial form*, which were the main targets of the new philosophy. For another, and more importantly for our purposes, a Cartesian could only find the idea of the *immaterial* reception of form in a *corporeal* organ unintelligible. I shall deal with this point more fully below.

III

In order fully to appreciate the force of BCA we need to consider one more aspect of the Cartesian philosophy. Many commentators on Descartes have, with some justification, equated Cartesian thoughts with *consciousness*. It is a commonplace to point out that Descartes extended the application of the term *cogitatio*. One aspect of the extension is that the term now covers volitions; another is that it also covers what came to be known as 'sensations', perceptual as well as somatic. The problem with such an assertion, however, is that it easily leads one to suppose that our use of the term 'sensation', informed as it is by writings on philosophical psychology over the last two hundred years, corresponds precisely to some Cartesian concept— which it does not. And at the very least this line of interpretation skates over what was clearly a very difficult subject for Descartes: the relation of the senses and sense experience to 'pure thought': a difficult and *central* subject, since it involves, in a Cartesian context, the fundamental issue of the relationship between mind and matter.

knowledge-likeness in our intellect (*species intelligibilis*) is the likeness of the thing in its specific nature, which can be shared by an unlimited number of individuals'—ibid., 1a, 14, 12.

Against the many passages where Descartes seems clearly to count sensory awareness as a form of thinking,[24] we must bear in mind the following facts. First, Descartes typically separates off imagination and sensation from the other 'pure' cognitive acts in his repeated inventory of thoughts: 'What is a thing which thinks? It is a thing which doubts, understands, [conceives], affirms, denies, wills, refuses, *which also* imagines and feels.' (H&R i. 153)[25] Second, there are many passages where Descartes is quite insistent that the senses and the imagination, unlike pure thought, are inessential to a person: '. . . this power of imagination which is in one, inasmuch as it differs from the power of understanding, is in no wise a necessary element in my nature, or in [my essence, that is to say, in] the essence of my mind' (H&R, i. 186). And from this he draws the natural conclusion that we shall not possess sensory awareness in our post-mortem existence (Kenny, 256).

The reason behind these facts, and the reason why Descartes treats the senses and the imagination together, is that both these forms of awareness require a corporeal organ for their exercise—in particular the *common sense* centring on the pineal gland. We are concerned here with 'a genuine part of the body, of sufficient size to allow its different parts to assume various figures . . .' (H&R, i. 38). The difference between sensory awareness and imagination is that in the first case figures are impressed on the imaginative faculty as a result of the operation of external objects, and in the second case these figures are formed as a result of our volitions: 'Quando objecta externa agunt in sensus meos, et in iis pingunt sui ideam seu potius figuram, tum mens, quando ad eas imagines quae in glandula inde pinguntur advertit, *sentire* dicitur; cum vero illae imagines in glandula non pinguntur ab ipsis rebus externis, sed ab ipsa mente, quae, rebus externis absentibus, eas in cerebro effingit et format, tum *imaginatio* est.'[26] So sensory and imaginative awareness are inessential to us since they essentially involve corporeal activity (unlike pure thought), and we are but contingently embodied.

Anscombe and Geach, in notes to their translation of Descartes's writings, suggest that there is no problem here. 'Sensation' is

[24] e.g. H&R, i. 153.

[25] Emphasis mine. There is hardly a single instance of such a list of thoughts in Descartes's writing that fails to exhibit this feature.

[26] *Œuvres de Descartes*, eds. Ch. Adam and P. Tannery (Paris, 1957–), vol. v, p. 162. (Hereafter abbreviated to 'AT'.)

sometimes used to mean a purely physical activity in sense organs, and sometimes 'a mere species of consciousness'.[27] And, indeed, there are many passages in Descartes to support this interpretation; and it doubtless does justice to one strand in Descartes's thinking. Thus, for example, he writes: 'The sense in which I include imaginations in the definition of *cogitatio* or thought differs from the sense in which I exclude them. *The forms or corporeal impressions which must be in the brain for us to imagine anything are not thoughts; but when the mind imagines or turns towards those impressions, its operation is a thought.*' (Kenny, p. 100.) Moreover, this topic has as a parallel the fact that whereas early in his career Descartes had called the figures impressed in the brain 'ideas', he later explicitly discarded this usage—compare H&R i. 38 and AT xi. 176–7 with H&R ii. 52.

However I believe that this interpretation ignores the complexities, and even tensions, in Descartes's theory. To regard sensory awareness as 'a mere species of consciousness' is to underplay the significance of Descartes's repeated assertion that it is a species of consciousness *internally related to corporeal activity*, possible for us only while embodied: sensations do not pertain to our mind 'in so far as it is a thinking thing but only in so far as it is united to another thing, extended and mobile, which is called the human body' (H&R, i. 255). Such an underplaying of the complexities of Descartes's position seems to arise from the fact that Anscombe and Geach (and, it may be added, the majority of commentators) are working with a distinctively post-Cartesian conception of a sensation—one which, as we shall see, Berkeley played no small part in fashioning.

I have sometimes heard it objected that Descartes could not have thought that a body was essential for sensory awareness, since he claims to possess apodeictic certainty that he senses, quite as fully as that he has pure thoughts, and that therefore his argument for dualism, based on the *Cogito*, goes through for sensations in so far as they are a species of thought. This line of thought, however, relies on the view that Descartes regarded what has come to be known as 'the argument from differential certainty' as the sufficient basis for dualism; and I trust that it is no longer necessary to stress that this simply is not the case. The move from the *Cogito* to the embracing of dualism is mediated by the claim that we know the essence of pure thought and the essence of the corporeal; the argument will not go through for sensations, therefore, since Descartes was quite frank in

[27] *Descartes Philosophical Writings* (London, 1970), p. 69 n. 1.

admitting that he did *not* comprehend the nature of sensation.[28] Relatedly, it might be objected that if my interpretation is correct, then it is not clear why, at the beginning of the Sixth Meditation, Descartes forgoes an argument for the existence of the body based on the indubitable fact of sensory awareness. The answer to this point is that the very unclarity about the nature of sensory awareness does not allow Descartes an incorrigible inference to the existence of body which independently is still problematic. In other words, to employ Kripke's distinction, the non-existence of body, even given the fact of sensory awareness, is, at that stage of Descartes's argument, an *epistemic* possibility; but, of course, it does not follow from this that it is (nor that Descartes thought it was) a *metaphysical* possibility—that the corporeal imagination is not of the essence of sensory awareness.

A more interesting objection might be based on Descartes's answer to Henry More's question whether angels have sensations. Descartes replied: 'the human mind separated from the body does not have sensation strictly so called; but it is not clear by natural reason whether Angels are created like minds distinct from bodies, or like minds united to bodies' (Kenny, p. 256). This passage suggests that, for all we know, it is possible for a creature to be created by God who enjoys sensory experiences without being embodied. The important point, however, is that despite this admission, Descartes still confidently declares that human beings at least will *not* enjoy sensory experiences after the dissolution of the body. And this is because such an angel would be a different kind of soul from a human soul, for the latter, unlike the former, has been so designed as to be fit for uniting with a body in 'a real and substantial manner' (Kenny, p. 127). 'For if an angel were in a human body, he would not have sensations as we do, but would simply perceive the motions which are caused by external objects, and in this way would differ from a real man.' (Kenny, p. 128)

It might, finally, be argued that although Descartes regarded the functioning of corporeal organs as *causally* necessary for the occurrence of sensations, the former is not a part of the *essence* of the latter. But this is to interpret Descartes, once again, in the light of a post-Cartesian understanding: this time, in terms of a distinctively Humean conception of causality—one which is hardly likely to have been embraced by one who wrote that 'if we ask what the effect is, we

---

[28] Though it must be admitted that Descartes's claim to clear and distinct knowledge of pure thought is but weakly supported.

must first know the cause and not conversely' (H&R i. 16; *cf.* i. 229).
The correct way to view Descartes's account of sensation is as a
development, under the influence of his form of dualism, of the
Scholastic position already outlined. It will be recalled that for a
Scholastic sensory awareness is the function of bodily sense organs; it
constitutes genuine knowledge or awareness because these organs
receive the forms of objects immaterially. Hence it was quite natural
for a seventeenth-century writer to believe that what is sensory is *in
some sense* essentially corporeal. The important point is that a basic
shift of metaphysical perspective altered the understanding of what it
is to be corporeal. Matter, after Descartes, was no longer viewed as
either an unintelligible potentiality or a composite of this and a
corporeal form, but as an intelligible simple nature with an intelligible, because merely mechanical, *modus operandi*. No genuine
awareness is possible at this level of mere physical action; for that we
must turn to a substance with a different and essentially cognitive
nature—mind. Nevertheless, the traditional equation of the sensory
with the corporeal lived on, with the result that a *materialist* account
of sensations, though not of pure thought, was widespread in the
seventeenth century, especially among those writers who were
strongly influenced by both the Peripatetic and Cartesian traditions.
Thus, for example, John Sergeant regards sensations as purely
corporeal phantasms in the brain, and yet refers to them as 'gay florid
pictures' and 'obvious and familiar . . . appearance[s]'.[29] One upshot
of this view is that animals, whom no one wished to credit with
immaterial and hence immortal souls, were purely mechanical
contrivances.[30]

Now the quotation from Sergeant, above, indicates that for him
animals, though purely mechanical contrivances, were at least
sentient. Descartes, however, seems not to have had such a conception of sentiency as a state of awareness below that of full
consciousness of objects. To echo a phrase of John McDowell's: with
animals all is dark within, for Descartes. At this point it is worth
remembering that Descartes believed that a purely mechanical
account could be given of a *person's* behaviour when that person's

---

[29] *Solid Philosophy Asserted*, Preface, sect. 19 and Preliminary Discourse I, sect. 12
respectively.

[30] Thus Sir Kenelme Digby, a self-styled Aristotelian who had a considerable
influence on Sergeant, refers to animals as 'automatons' and 'engines', and endorses
Descartes's mechanical account of the senses with but a minor qualification: *Two
Treatises* (London, 1645), 1. 23. 6. Cf. Sergeant, Preliminary Discourse I, sect. 8.

mind is not on what they are doing: '. . . animals do not see as we do when we are aware that we see, but only as we do when our mind is elsewhere' (Kenny, p. 36; cf. ibid., p. 206). Here again we notice Descartes's insistence on the necessarily apperceptive dimension to all awareness, and also his distance from more modern understandings of sensation. For later thinkers *unnoticed sensations* are genuinely mental items, not 'merely' material states. For Descartes this idea of an unnoticed mental item did not make sense: the mental enters the picture not before the level of such noticing.

Given this radical distinction between conscious mind and 'full' matter,[31] in order to do justice to the essential corporeal element in sensory awareness Descartes had to replace the Scholastic notion of immaterial reception of form in a corporeal organ with a joint contribution from mind and matter. In sense experience I 'turn towards' the corporeal figures in the imagination. Descartes indifferently employs a number of terms to express this operation: *intueor*, *adverto*, *inspicio*, *converto*, etc. It is precisely in this operation involving both mind and matter that sensory awareness consists; but Descartes was incapable of giving a clear account of it. This is not only because it involves the nature of the mind's interaction with the body, but, more importantly, from a later viewpoint it attempts to locate paradigmatically mental qualia at the point of this unintelligible interaction.

It should be clear from this brief account how very different is Descartes's dualism from its present-day successor. Descartes agreed with the Scholastics (and, indeed, with the Platonic tradition) that what was essential to and distinctive of man was the power of abstract discursive thought. This was the power which pertains uniquely to an immaterial soul. The senses brought in at least a relation to what is material. At the present time, however, the issue between materialists and their opponents is principally fought over the nature of sensations.[32] Perhaps the cognitive dimension to human awareness can be spelled out in topic-neutral or functionalist terms; but what about raw feels? So whereas tradition has argued to the immateriality of the soul from our ability to understand the universe, modern dualists attempt to argue thus from our ability to feel pains, twinges, and tickles!

---

[31] The allusion, here, is, of course, to Sartre.

[32] Wilfrid Sellars is a particularly good example of a modern materialist who regards the identification of sensations with material processes as the most difficult part of the materialist programme.

IV

Having noted the difficulties Descartes faced in giving an account of sensory awareness, let us, before returning to BCA, finally consider those thoughts which Descartes both took himself fully to comprehend and took (together with volitions) to constitute the essence of the mind: those *pure thoughts* which arise when 'the mind employs itself alone' (H&R, ii. 229). Now it will be recalled that, in an attempt to do justice to the fact that such thoughts are both states *of a subject* and yet also *intentional* states of a subject, Descartes introduces the distinction between the objective and the formal reality of the ideas which constitute such thoughts. This distinction may remind us of the following often noted fact about representations—a fact which, it seems to me, *we cannot ignore if we are to employ the notion of representation at all* in order to cast light on the nature of thought. In order for representing to take place we must have an item that fulfils the representing function—what I shall call the *representans*—and an (at least purported) item that is represented—what I shall call the *representatum*. Typically the *representans* and the *representatum* are distinct individuals: the portrait is one thing, the sitter portrayed another. Occasionally one *aspect* of an individual can serve to represent another aspect of the same individual: we might so construct an object that its colour accurately represented changes in that thing's temperature. But even here, though the distinction between *representans* and *representatum* is not a distinction between different individuals, there is still, and necessarily, a distinction of features. That absolutely one and the same thing should represent itself is unintelligible. A picture can certainly depict another picture; but if an artist informed us that his picture represented itself, this would be a joke—a bit of self-conscious *élan*.

It follows from the above that a representing item must possess its own nature as a concrete item in the world. The whole nature of a *representans* cannot simply consist in its representing something, in its simply being a representation. A picture, for example, must have, in its own right, a certain location, size, distribution of pigments, etc. I shall call these the *material* attributes of a *representans*—though they may, as yet, be non-physical if they are attributes of a non-physical individual. And once again, these material attributes must be ontologically distinct from the attributes of what is represented. Even when, as we might say, the universal materially instantiated by the *representans* is identical with a universal instantiated by the *represen-tatum*—as when the blue pigment in a portrait is qualitatively identical with the blueness of the coat worn by the sitter—there are two distinct instantiations of the universal. If a thought or idea is taken to be a representative item, the previous points will hold here too. Of course, as has often been said, thoughts do not represent in anything like the way that pictures do; thoughts are, we might say, intrinsically representational. Still, if the employment of the term 'representation' is not to be wholly useless and misleading in cognitive science, the above points must be admitted.

We have now come to the crucial question for Descartes: what are the material features of a pure Cartesian thought? Descartes claims that our knowledge of the nature of such thoughts is about as clear and distinct as anything is;[33] but let us pursue the matter. Suppose you are thinking of a triangle. Let us allow that you have a perfect understanding of the nature of a triangle. Still, this understanding is not of the material nature of that thought, but of its object; so what is your understanding of the thought itself as a state of or process in your mind—as *representans*? It is, perhaps, somewhat odd to ask after the material features of a thought in a Cartesian context, since a thought is itself not an individual but a mode of a substance. Still, we do require an account of the material nature of such modes.

In order to see how serious this problem is for Descartes, just recall how pure Cartesian thoughts are: they must be *wholly* devoid of anything sensory. Think of something. But do not represent it iconically in any way: image no colours or sounds or shapes. Banish from your mind anything at all relating to somatic and kinaesthetic sensations. And finally do not entertain any word or symbol in your mind, for these too are of the imagination.[34] What did you succeed in thinking of?[35] Berkeley's answer is, of course, *Nothing*. The very idea of having a thought of *such* purity is nonsensical. And this Berkeley took to be a *reductio ad absurdum* of Cartesianism. In the very area where Descartes believes himself to have clearest knowledge of the nature of the mental, he presents us with a psychological impossibi-

[33] See, for example, the end of the Second Meditation.

[34] 'Purely intellectual things are not strictly remembered; they are no less thought of the first time they come to mind than the second. Of course, they are commonly associated with names, and these are corporeal, and so can be remembered'—Kenny, p. 112.

[35] For the time being, we should restrict our inquiry to thoughts about 'external' objects. I shall discuss the importance of this restriction below.

lity. Moreover, even if, *per impossibile*, one succeeded in having such a pure thought, the search for the material features of such thoughts through self-conscious awareness will be clearly futile. One's mind is a substance; therefore it needs attributes; these attributes are thoughts—but considered materially. Cartesianism both fails necessarily, contrary to its essential project, to give any account of such attributes, and also presents us with a preposterously empty phenomenology of thinking.[36]

V

Berkeley found the solution to the Cartesian problem of mental representation in the very area which, as we have seen, gave Descartes such problems—sensation. For it is precisely sensations that are the sought for material features of the mind as thinking representing substance. This solution of Berkeley's of course requires him to present a new conception of sensation; and this is precisely what he does by rejecting the strong traditional conception of sensation as essentially bound up with the operation of corporeal organs. Sensations, rather than being operations in corporeal organs, as with the Scholastics, or the dubious products of the mind's interaction with essentially alien matter, as with Descartes, are, for Berkeley, the mental items *par excellence*. There can be no sensations that are not wholly in the mind as a distinct individual substance, and no mind without sensations—for then it would be a bare substance. There can be no thought or cognition without sensation or sensory images, for without these we should not even be conscious. The 'higher' cognitive processes are no longer viewed, as they were by Descartes, as occurring in splendid intellective isolation, but as constituted by functions centring on the indispensable core of any conscious state— sensations. Let us term this account of mind Psychological Empiricism. It was by propounding this view that Berkeley gave impetus to Hume and the whole Sensationalist school of nineteenth-century psychology that has so shaped our modern understanding of the term 'sensation'.

I have been moving towards Berkeley's radical metaphysical position as enshrined in BCA via a consideration of issues pertaining to cognition. But it may be thought that the development away from

---

[36] The identification of the material features of thoughts with physical features of the brain was, of course, not open to anyone in the Cartesian tradition.

the Cartesian account of thought is simply effected by an injection of distinctively *empiricist* theses into the Cartesian framework. However, if this is anywhere near the truth, why have I expounded this development in relation to Berkeley—for surely the empiricist 'corrective' was effected at least as early as Locke? How, then, can such a development within cognitive theory be interestingly related to Berkeley's metaphysical position when it is also present in Locke's robust scientific realism?

In fact it seems to me that, especially in the area we are considering, Locke holds a position intermediate between that of Descartes and of Berkeley. Locke neither would have wished to arrive, nor could he have arrived, at the metaphysical conclusions of Berkeley, because he cannot be fully credited with following through the development in cognitive theory I have been tracing in connection with Berkeley. This fact can perhaps best be appreciated in the following way. I said above that for Berkeley sensory ideas become mental items *par excellence*. Not only is this true for Locke; but there is also a sense in which for Locke ideas are 'more mental' than the mind itself! For it will be recalled that Locke holds that we lack a priori knowledge that what thinks in us is something other than material substance. He holds this principally because he believed that we have no good grounds for denying to an all-powerful creator the ability to endow suitably contrived physical systems with the power to think.[37] This view is intimately related to Locke's claim that 'the perception of ideas [is] . . . to the soul what motion is to the body: not its essence, but one of its operations'.[38] If thoughts and perceptions are operations of the soul, the soul must have what I have been calling a material nature, the operations of which constitute such cognitive activities; and perhaps these material features really are *material*! If so, then the soul which thinks in us would be fundamentally physical; it would be deemed mental, not in virtue of its essence, but in virtue of its being fit for operating cognitively—for producing ideas. Thus it is that ideas are the primary mental items for Locke, such that even the

---

[37] *An Essay Concerning Human Understanding*, 4. 3. 6. Locke seems to have embraced this position under the influence of Newton: '. . . et plusieurs personnes qui ont beaucoup vécu avec Locke m'ont assuré que Newton avait avoué à Locke que "nous n'avons pas assez de connaissance de la nature pour oser prononcer qu'il soit impossible à Dieu d'ajouter le don de la pensée à un être étendu quelconque"'— *Éléments de la Philosophie de Newton*, Pt. I, Ch. 7 in Voltaire's *Œuvres Complètes* (Paris, 1828), vol. ii, p. 632.

[38] *Essay*, 2. 1. 10.

mind might be truly described as mental only in a derivative sense. Now of course Locke is actually strongly inclined to the view that what thinks in us is non-physical. But what this means is that Locke is left without any possible means of specifying the material features of mental representations. Now whatever the intrinsic merits of this position, two points should be noticed. First, in the context of the development of thought about thought that we have been following, Locke's position coincides with one aspect of Descartes's theory: for although, by embracing Psychological Empiricism, he escapes the criticism of believing in wholly empty Cartesian thoughts, he shares Descartes's radical inability to say anything constructive about the material aspects of mental representations. The chief difference is that whereas Descartes claims to have clear and distinct knowledge of the nature of his thoughts, Locke acknowledges his complete ignorance in this matter. Secondly, Locke was unperturbed by this situation because he rejected the central Cartesian claim that apperceptive awareness puts us in a position to identify the essence of the mental. Berkeley, however, shared this Cartesian outlook. He can uphold the claim to have knowledge of the essence of the mind by doing away with any operations underlying thought. Such underlying operations are otiose when the material features of thoughts are identified with sensations. Locke, therefore, stands apart from the development of a theory of cognition we have been following. BCA is a reaction against a more orthodox Cartesian heritage.[39]

VI

Having noted Berkeley's move whereby sensations are taken to be the material features of mental representations, we must now ask the question: what are such representations representations *of*? The occurrence of such sensory items in the mind accounts for the material reality of mental representations; but what of their objective reality, their *representata*? In a sense, of course, Berkeley will answer that the *representata* of thoughts and perceptions are simply all the things we ever think of or perceive—since he is giving an account of human cognition as it actually exists, in all its variety. But a more illuminating answer is that cognitions, since they are sensory states,

---

[39] Locke's departure from the Cartesian tradition is reflected, of course, in his rejection of the view, endorsed by both Descartes and Berkeley, that the soul *always* *thinks*.

can only be states of awareness of sensory qualities as perceived, as phenomenally present to a conscious subject. Every 'abstract' thought must be ultimately constituted out of such sensible objects. (We recall here Berkeley's heated polemic against abstract ideas, based on the contention, central to his theory, that the content of every thought must be as determinate as the content of actual perception.[40] This view is central to his theory because a straightforward implication of taking sensory ideas to be the necessary material features of any cognition.) Hence Berkeley can agree nominally with Descartes in classing together thoughts and perceptions as ideas; but whereas for Descartes this was because both sensory awareness and thought (whether iconic or not) involve the exercise of the intellect without which there is no consciousness, for Berkeley it is because both sense perception and iconic thought (there is no other) are sensory, for without sensory character there is no cognition, since sensations constitute the material reality of mental representations.

What more can we say of these sensible qualities that are the *representata* of cognitions? Clearly, the answer, as we have seen, must at least involve the thesis that they are what we are immediately *aware of* in perception or in the thoughts which such perception conditions. And it will take some weighty argument to show that what we are thus aware of in perception is anything other than, for example, the manifest colours of objects, sounds with their phenomenal characteristics—in short, the perceptible qualities of *physical objects*. When I open my eyes, for example, and see a ripe tomato, it is absurd, Berkeley would insist, to abstract away the tomato itself as ultimate object of awareness from the glowing redness that I perceive there. This perceived redness is an attribute of the object of which I am aware in this perception. In the traditional realist framework, this means that such an attribute inheres in a material substance. But this last claim now presents us with a serious problem, because the development away from the Cartesian account of cognition essentially involved the claim that the very sensory elements just alluded to furnish the material features of mental representations—i.e. they are fundamentally and necessarily *mental* attributes inhering in the mind as representing substance. One and the same sensory item is, then, both the object of awareness and the material reality of the state of awareness. Berkeley agrees that these sensory items are dependent

---

[40] On closer inspection, however, it turns out that Locke's own theory of 'abstraction' is not very different from Berkeley's account.

entities requiring a substance in which to inhere. But material substance cannot intelligibly be introduced to fulfil this substantial role, for we have already seen that these sensory items inhere in mental substance in so far as they are the material features of cognitions. Thus the vague metaphysical relation of *inhering in* is now grasped more clearly as the epistemic relation of *perceived by*. The only intelligible notion of substance is perceiving thinking substance.

In the context of the far from unthinking development away from Cartesianism, this last metaphysical turn in Berkeley's system is a matter of sheer consistency. But what has happened in the course of this development is that the central notion of representation, from which we started, has been completely subverted. For remember that the essence of representation is the ontological distinction between *representans* and *representatum*. In our search for the material features of mental *representantia* we hit upon sensations; but on closer investigation these were seen also to be the features of *representata*. Hence the whole system of representationalism has collapsed. Mental states are no longer intrinsically representational, but *presentational*.

VII

Viewed in context, I think BCA appears in its true light as an interesting and significant move in the history of philosophy. It successfully highlights and then dissolves genuine difficulties in a tradition informed by two intimately related theses: that apperceptive awareness puts us in immediate contact with the essence of the mind, and that therefore we have an adequate, because inner, understanding of genuinely cognitive activities. This is clearly not the place to essay an assessment of the objective soundness of Berkeley's position—a procedure which should certainly focus on the two theses just mentioned. But it is perhaps worth pointing out a possible source of criticism locatable *within* Berkeley's overall theory.

The Psychological Empiricist claim that sensory ideas are necess-

---

[41] But not wholly uncontroversial either. The theoretical possibility of wholly non-sensory awareness is embodied in Thomas Reid's theory of cognition—a philosopher who continues to exercise a considerable influence on modern writers. It is also arguable that the phenomenon commonly known as 'blind sight' suggests that we may be dealing here with more than a mere theoretical possibility: see, for example, L. Weiskrantz *et al.*, 'Visual Capacity in the Hemianopic Field Following a Restricted Occipital Oblation', *Brain* 97 (1974).

ary and sufficient for awareness can be understood in a weak and a strong sense. Understood merely as the claim that, if we are to be aware of anything at a time, we must have some kind of sensory awareness at that time, it is not wholly implausible.[41] But understood as the claim that each act of awareness is an act of sensory awareness, the thesis is not only wildly implausible, but one rejected by Berkeley himself. For we should not forget Berkeley's insistence that we are aware of neither ourselves as active willing beings nor relations by an idea—an insistence signalled in the second edition of the *Principles* by the introduction of the term *notion*.[42] Berkeley himself, therefore, recognizes forms of cognitive activity that cannot be accounted for simply by the perception of sensory ideas by Spirit. And it is instructive to recall that Descartes, when offering examples of pure thoughts, typically mentions the ideas we have of ourselves as thinking beings (in addition to mathematical and transcendental ideas). Once this is fully recognized, the possibility then arises—one fully exploited by Descartes, of course—that even when we are sensorily aware of sensible objects, more is involved in the total cognitive situation than the mere having of sensations. If we follow through this line of thought, while yet embracing Psychological Empiricism in its weaker form, we find ourselves in an intellectual environment very different from that of Descartes and Berkeley: namely, that of the Kantian tradition, with its emphasis on the *dual* determination of awareness by both sensibility and understanding. The problem of working out this basic Kantian insight is still a philosophical task for us—as is amply indicated by, for example, the current controversy concerning qualia and functionalism.[43]

[42] See, for example, sect. 89. Notoriously, Berkeley fails to elucidate the concept of a notion, except to say that we have a notion of something when we possess an understanding that is not constituted by perceiving an idea.

[43] See, for example, S. Shoemaker, 'Functionalism and Qualia', *Philosophical Studies* 27 (1975) and 'Absent Qualia are Impossible—A Reply to Block', *Philosophical Review* 90 (1981); N. Block, 'Are Absent Qualia Impossible?', ibid. 89 (1980) and 'Troubles with Functionalism' in *Minnesota Studies in the Philosophy of Science*, vol. 9; W. Seager, 'Functionalism, Qualia and Causation', *Mind* 92 (1983).

CHAPTER 4

BERKELEY'S MASTER STROKE

ERNEST SOSA

I

First Scene: On a wintry morning a child S sits on his back steps and views a snowball O in good light on the ground before him. In virtue of some of its qualities—its whiteness and its roundness, though not its coldness—object O aided by circumstances (light, S's open eyes, etc.) causes a visual experience in S. S has a visual experience of something white and round before him, involving an image of something white and round in his visual field. And S believes that the round thing before him is white.

Second Scene: S closes his eyes and imagines something white and round before him by forming (causing) a visual image of such a thing.

Third Scene (a short while later): Asked whether he has just seen something white and round, S assents, now quickly and with no corresponding image, but understanding the question quite well, and well aware of what he is assenting to and of the qualities involved.

Fourth Scene: Snowball O remains in the back yard but unperceived by anyone now that S has left.

(For the theist there is of course a further presence throughout, namely that of God, who causes and sustains the whole scenario and each of its scenes.)

An ontological analysis of such a scenario prima facie requires at least the following elements:

1. On the side of object O (the snowball):
   (*a*) The qualities that O has: whiteness, roundness, etc., and combinations of these.
   (*b*) The stuff (snow matter) of O, which unlike O itself would apparently survive squashing.

(c) O itself.

(d) The having of *a* by *c*: singular states of affairs such as the state
with regard to O of *its being spherical.*

(e) General states of affairs derivative from *d* in the way *there
being something spherical* is derivative from the state with regard
to O of *its being spherical.*

2. On the side of subject S (the person):

(a) The qualities and combinations of qualities that S experiences:
whiteness, roundness, etc., and combinations of these.

(b) The states that S experiences: there being something white
(before him), etc.

(c) The images formed by S: e.g., his image of something white and
round.

(d) S himself.

(e) The experiencing of *a* and *b* by *d*.

(f) The forming (causing) of *c* by *d*.

(g) The experiencing of *c* by *d*.

(h) The imagining of *a* and *b* by *d*.

(i) The willing of *h* by *d*.

(j) The thinking (understanding, conceiving, entertaining) of *a*
and *b* by *d*.

(k) The intrinsic character of S himself: his actual monadic
properties, his virtues, vices, faculties, etc.

3. Spanning O and S:

(a) The causing of experiences and images in S by O.

(b) The resemblance between image I in S and object O.

4. For the theist there are also:

(a) God.

(b) The causing (willing) by God of items under each of 1, 2, and 3
above.

(c) God's understanding or conceiving of various qualities and
combinations of qualities.

II

Relevant to that scenario, here are four propositions whose truth is
important in Berkeley's philosophy:

a. Snowballs (along with houses, mountains, etc.) are things we perceive with the senses.
b. What we perceive with the senses can be nothing but our own ideas or sensations.
c. Our ideas or sensations cannot exist unperceived.
d. Snowballs (houses, mountains, etc.) cannot exist unperceived.

These form the argument of *Principles*, section 4. Clearly d follows from a–c. So it all goes back to the premisses. And Berkeley does marshal supplementary arguments in support of a, b, and c. Concerning c, compare sections 3 and 4, where it is held that the existence of a sound, a smell, a colour, etc., obviously entails the existence of a perceiver. Here Berkeley was in harmony with a widespread belief fostered by Locke, and he saw no need to argue in great detail. But Locke had distinguished between primary and secondary qualities, and had restricted his belief in matter to the former. Berkeley finds an inconsistency here. For Berkeley the arguments that show the subjectivity of the secondary qualities equally show the subjectivity of the primary qualities. (Cf. sections 14 and 15.) Actually, Berkeley thought the arguments to show not so much that external objects could not have colour or extension as that we could not know their true colour or extension. (Cf. sect. 15. And compare entry 265 of the *Philosophical Commentaries*, according to which '. . . ffrom Lockes arguings it can't be prov'd that Colours, are not in Bodies'.)

The supplementary arguments for a and b are as follows. For one thing, Berkeley tries to show that there is nothing else we could possibly perceive, nor anything else that houses, mountains, etc., could possibly be except collections of ideas. In sects. 16 and 17 Berkeley argues that the very idea of matter is incomprehensible. What is matter? If we have no idea of its intrinsic nature, we need at least some notion of its relation to the colours, shapes, etc., that we know. Shall we say that matter *supports* sensible attributes? But what does this mean? Sect. 18 argues that even if matter were comprehensible it would be unknowable. We don't know that there is any matter by the senses, since what we sense directly is only ideas or sensations. And we don't know that there is any by reason, since there is no necessary connection between such matter and our ideas or sensations. (Cf. sects. 86 and 87.) Section 19 argues that even if matter were comprehensible, the postulation of existing matter would not help at all to explain how we come to have our ideas and sensations, since by hypothesis matter is inert.

Berkeley's main conclusion:

> (M) There is no conceivable notion of objective matter, nor can we really make sense of supposed thoughts about objectively material things of which we have no direct awareness.

III

Russell was pulled in that same direction by his Principle of Acquaintance:[1]

> (PA) Every proposition which we can understand must be composed wholly of constituents with which we are acquainted.

We are said to have '. . . *acquaintance* with anything of which we are directly aware, without the intermediary of any process of inference or any knowledge of truths' (46). We moreover

have acquaintance in sensation with the data of the outer senses, and in introspection with the data of what may be called the inner sense — thoughts, feelings, desires, etc.; we have acquaintance in memory with things which have been data either of the outer senses or of the inner sense. Further it is probable, though not certain, that we have acquaintance with Self, as that which is aware of things or has desires towards things. (51)

Consider the following reasoning:

> a. The Principle of Acquaintance (PA above).
> b. One cannot be directly aware of any (objective, material) round thing (e.g., of any snowball).
> c. The constituents of the proposition that the (objective, material) round thing (before me) is white are that round thing itself (the snowball) and the property of whiteness.
> d. Therefore, we cannot understand the proposition that the (objective, material) round thing (before me) is white.

Russell hence seems committed to this Berkeleian conclusion d, unless he can find a way to avoid one of a, b, or c. In *The Problems of Philosophy* he does wish to reject d and with it Berkeley's M. The

---

[1] Bertrand Russell, *The Problems of Philosophy*, (Oxford University Press, Oxford, 1959), p. 58. (First published in the Home University Library, 1912.)

premiss rejected by Russell is c, which runs afoul of his Theory of Descriptions.

According to Russell's Theory of Descriptions the proposition (P) *that the round thing (before me) is white* is analysed as the conjunction of the following three propositions:

   i. There is at least one round thing (before me).
  ii. There is at most one round thing (before me).
 iii. Whatever is a round thing (before me) is white.

If that is a correct analysis then it is an error to suppose that the round thing itself is a constituent of proposition P. For no such thing figures among the elements of the quite general propositions i–iii, which involve only properties and quantification (and oneself). Thus if the snowball itself is the subject of i, ii, and iii conjoined — of P — it is so only 'indirectly,' by being the one thing that satisfies i and ii. Russell may thus reject c and hence avoid the Berkeleian conclusion d.

But can anyone be directly aware of the property of being round (objectively, materially)? If not, our progress has been illusory and we are no closer to avoiding d. Here is the argument now:

   a. The Principle of Acquaintance (PA above).
  b′. One cannot be directly aware of the quality of (objective, material) roundness.
  c′. Among the constituents of the proposition that the (objective, material) round thing (before me) is white is the property of (objective, material) roundness.
  d. As before.

In chapter X Russell takes up our knowledge of properties or universals. Unfortunately, there is not in that chapter a clear, unequivocal answer to our question. In fact, we are told that, among universals, 'there seems to be no principle by which we can decide which can be known by acquaintance, but it is clear that among those that can be so known are sensible qualities, relations of space and time, similarity, and certain abstract logical universals'(109). But since no primary quality is listed among the examples of sensible qualities, the status of roundness is left ambiguous.

The key to a solution lies on p. 58:

Many universals, like many particulars, are only known to us by description. But here, as in the case of particulars, knowledge concerning what is known by description is ultimately reducible to knowledge concerning what is known by acquaintance.

If we could find a causal connection between external bodies and our sensations or ideas, Berkeley supposes, then '. . . it might be at least probable there are such things as bodies that excite their ideas in our minds' (*Principles*, 19). Since Berkeley infers his God as best explanation of the phenomena (see, e.g., *Principles*, 146, *Dialogues*, 215) he is in no position to reject explanatory induction.

Russell now needs a connection between the objective, material roundness of a physical snowball and our subjective visual experience of a certain sort (assuming we have direct acquaintance only with the qualities present in our experiences: e.g., the qualities of our visual images).

According to Russell's chapters II and III the connection is provided by causation. Thus the property of being objectively, materially round is for Russell a property whose exemplification by something bearing a certain spatio-temporal relation to one *causes* in one certain sense-data (visual and tactual). Here appeal is made only to causality, to certain qualities of our sense-data (those required for one to have experience as if one saw a round thing), and to certain relations of space or time. And for Russell, as we have seen, these universals are all known directly, except for causality. Very well then, so how *may* we attain an understanding of causality if not directly? Russell's answer is derivable from his famous 'On the Notion of Cause' (his Presidential Address to the Aristotelian Society in the year he published *The Problems of Philosophy*, 1912).[2] According to that essay, to the extent that there is something clear and useful in the common or philosophical notion of causality it is only the notion of natural or scientific law, and this involves nothing more than certain 'functional relations between certain events at certain times, which we call determinants, and other events at earlier or later times or at the same time' (201). Presumably, these functional relations involve only relations of space or time; and these, recall, are universals which for Russell we know directly. Russell can thus accept his empiricist Principle of Acquaintance and yet avoid Berkeley's radical M.

Russell's way of avoiding M is of course unavailable to Berkeley, who is 'unable to comprehend in what manner body can act upon spirit . . . [and who draws the obvious conclusion:] it is evident the

---

[2] *Proceedings of the Aristotelian Society*, 1912–13.

production of ideas or sensations in our minds, can be no reason why we should suppose Matter or corporeal substances' (*Principles*, 19).

IV

Not only does Russell offer materials whereby to avoid Berkeley's idealist M. He also joins Moore in charging Berkeley with a terrible confusion. Russell puts it thus:

Berkeley's view, that obviously the colour *must* be in the mind, seems to depend for its plausibility upon confusing the thing apprehended with the act of apprehension. Either of these might be called an 'idea'; probably either would have been called an idea by Berkeley. The act is undoubtedly in the mind; hence, when we are thinking of the act, we readily assent to the view that ideas must be in the mind. Then, forgetting that this was only true when ideas were taken as acts of apprehension, we transfer the proposition that 'ideas are in the mind' to ideas in the other sense, i.e. to the things apprehended by our acts of apprehension. Thus, by an unconscious equivocation, we arrive at the conclusion that whatever we can apprehend must be in our minds. This seems to be the true analysis of Berkeley's argument, and the ultimate fallacy on which it rests. (42)

On the contrary, it seems to me that Russell misses Berkeley's point, which is rather that sensible qualities are *present* only through being perceived or conceived, and not that their very *being* derives from their being perceived or conceived.[3] Certainly the very being of whiteness does not derive from *my* perceiving or conceiving whiteness. This could be said with some show of plausibility only of God and of no lesser spirit, provided no quality could ever be unconceived by God. Yet it remains open (and so far as I can tell undiscussed by Berkeley) that the very being of whiteness does not *derive* from its being conceived by God, *present* though it be to Him through his conceiving it (so that it 'exists in His mind').

Granted, Berkeley wavers on the status of *ideas* (see esp. *Principles*,

---

[3] Berkeley cannot be understood without a firm and constant grasp of this distinction. It helps explain for example his frequent emphasis on the point that if we are clear on the *meaning* of 'exists' we shall see it to be unintelligible that sensible qualities and things immediately perceived by sense could possibly exist unperceived. The point depends on the meaning of 'exist' because many opt for 'absolute' existence or exemplification without the mind, whereas deeper and closer attention shows that sensible qualities can be really present in reality only by being present to a mind, by being perceived. Deeper reflection reveals therefore presence to the mind or perception as the only meaning truly available for so-called 'existence' (leaving aside bare Being, to be discussed below).

140 and *Dialogues*, 247). But nearly always he does hold to a view of qualities as 'distinct from the mind' and of ideas as qualities or complexes of qualities viewed under the aspect of being perceived or conceived (at least by God).[4]

In his 'Refutation of Idealism' Moore falls into an error similar to Russell's, as follows.[5]

That reality is spiritual or mental is a central tenet of Idealism. Moore disputes not this but the Idealist argument for it. The arguments of some idealists for their central tenet rest on the claim that at least for entities other than perceivers *esse* is *percipi*. According to Moore, this claim stems from a faulty analysis of experience, particularly sensory experience.

If on a cloudless day you look at the sky and then at a lawn, your successive experiences must have something in common, since they both involve experience or consciousness of something. But they are also different in that one is experience of blue and the other of green. So it appears that in each case there are two elements present: the consciousness and the colour. How are these related?

Idealism is said to claim that the colour is part of the *content* of the consciousness or experience or awareness. And hence the colour is an essential part of the total experience. But if Moore is right, the only relevant sense of 'content' in which the blue could be part of the content of the experience is that in which red is part of the content of a red rose. As he further notes, perhaps in this sense blue is part of the content of an experience of blue, but it seems unlikely since the experience must then be literally blue. In any case, what we are sure of is *not* that the awareness is blue but that it is *of* blue, and this involves a relation between the subject and the blue, the same relation that is involved in anyone's awareness of anything.

Finally, Moore writes, if

we clearly recognize the nature of that peculiar relation which I have called

---

[4] A convincing case for this is made by A. A. Luce in 'Berkeley's Existence in the Mind', *Mind* 50 (1941); reprinted with minor corrections in C. B. Martin and D. M. Armstrong, *Locke and Berkeley* (Doubleday & Co., Garden City, NY, 1968) 284–96. Consider, just for an example or two, that 'qualities are in the mind only as they are perceived by it; that is, not by way of *mode* or *attribute*, but only by way of *idea*' (*Principles*, 49); also that the 'hardness or softness, the colour, taste, warmth, figure, and suchlike qualities, which combined together constitute the several sorts of victuals and apparel, have been shown to exist only in the mind that perceives them: and this is all that is meant by calling them *ideas*' (*Principles*, 38).

[5] G. E. Moore, *Philosophical Studies* (Littlefield, Adams & Co., Paterson, NJ, 1959), pp. 1–31 (first published by Routledge and Kegan Paul, London, in 1922).

'awareness of anything'; if we see that *this* is involved equally in the analysis of *every* experience — from the merest sensation to the most developed perception or reflexion, and that *this* is in fact the only essential element in an experience — the only thing which gives us reason to call any fact mental; if, further, we recognize that this awareness is and must be in all cases of such a nature that its object, when we are aware of it, is precisely what it would be, if we were not aware: then it becomes plain that the existence of a table in space is related to my experience of *it* in precisely the same way as the existence of my own experience is related to my experience of *that*. (29)

Moore is not content simply to deny that the *esse* of the snowball itself, and of Berkeley's houses, mountains, etc., is *percipi*. He denies it even of acts of or events in a mind. Not even the *esse* of itches, tickles, or after-images is *percipi*. Suppose while intent on your driving you have an after-image, or suppose you have a sensation of blue as you walk absorbed in your thoughts on a cloudless day. The after-image and the sensation may perhaps exist *unnoticed*. But can they exist unexperienced? Would this not be for them to exist detached, i.e. without anyone *having* them?

Besides, as seen already with regard to Russell, Berkeley is fundamentally concerned not with images or even with acts of imaging in a certain way, but rather with ideas as certain combinations of qualities. It is these whose *esse* is *percipi*. And their *esse* is *percipi* not necessarily in the sense that they derive their bare being from anyone's mental activity (though this *may* perhaps be true *anyhow*, through God's provision of such being to qualities and ideas by his volition). The *esse* of (whiteness and roundness), for example, does not derive from *my* perception of (whiteness and roundness) — as I view a snowball in good light — *not in the sense that the very being of such an idea derives from my perceiving it on that occasion*. Rather is the *esse* of (whiteness and roundness) *percipi* only in the sense that the *presence* of it in reality requires its being perceived, or at least conceived, and *not* the (presumed) absurdity of its 'absolutely' existing (being exemplified) 'without the mind', beyond anyone's ken.

V

The most directly evident, palpable, concrete presence of qualities in reality is *constituted* by their presence in experience or imagination. But qualities are never thus present except in certain minimal clusters. It is a fallacy to suppose a quality present in 'abstraction' from such a cluster. So one cannot find triangularity truly present to the mind (in experience or imagination) abstracted from every distribution of angle measures. Nor can one find triangularity (even with a specific distribution of angle measures) in abstraction from all colour contrast. It does not follow that there is no quality of triangularity, nor that it is never present in reality. If one visually experiences or imagines a red triangle, then the triangular shape would seem present along with the red colour: not that neither would seem present but rather that *both* would seem present *and* neither the shape nor the colour could be thus present without a conjoined colour or shape, respectively.

Berkeley complains about the concept of Being that it is the most abstract of all (further up yet than triangularity). By our present account of his position on abstraction, what that rules out is any possibility that pure Being be present in experience or imagination *detached from all other qualities* (or properties). But it is not ruled out that the qualities present to a spirit not only be perceived or willed (or both) but also *be* — and indeed *be* in virtue of being perceived or willed. And it is not ruled out that the spirit to whom the qualities are present not only perceive or will (or both) but also *be* — and indeed *be* in virtue of perceiving or willing. (Thus 'whoever shall go about to divide in his thoughts, or abstract the *existence* of a spirit from its *cogitation*, will, I believe, find it no easy task' (*Principles*, 98).)

Sometimes Berkeley's words do suggest his recognition of Being or Entity and of Unity as allowable notions or ideas, however impossible it may be to *abstract* them. Consider thus Philonous's challenge to Hylas: not just a challenge to conceive of Entity (period) but rather to 'frame a distinct idea of entity in general, prescinded from and exclusive of all thinking and corporeal beings, all particular things whatsoever' (*Dialogues*, 222; and compare *Principles*, 120). But elsewhere Berkeley opts for a nominalist treatment of Identity: see *Dialogues*, 247–8. And about spirits and ideas we are told that there is 'nothing alike or common in them' (*Principles*, 142) and that they 'have nothing common but the name' (*Principles*, 89) of 'Being' — not even Being, presumably. Besides, the 'general idea of being appeareth [to him] the most abstract and incomprehensible of all' (*Principles*, 17). And 'for any one to pretend to a *notion* of entity or existence, *abstracted* from *spirit* and *idea*, from perceiving and being perceived, is, [he suspects], a downright repugnancy and trifling with words' (*Principles*, 81; and cf. *Dialogues*, 222, esp. the first eight speeches). Elsewhere, moreover, he displays, underlined, the 'universally received maxim, that, *every thing which exists, is particular'* *(Dialogues* 192), which from the context he evidently interprets as: *everything truly present in reality is fully specific.* This of course rules out any possibility that Being be truly present in reality. And it even rules out that triangularity be thus present (accompanied or not). Only triangularity of a fully specific sort can be thus present. Is there then anything that can be present but is not abstractable (i.e., must be accompanied)? This depends on how we are to interpret particularity (i.e., specificity). Is *equilateral triangle* fully specific or is it not yet so since, e.g., it might be red or it might be blue? If it is, then it surely provides a case of the present in reality (in experience or imagination) though not abstractable (e.g., from accompanying colour). If however not even *equilateral triangle* is fully specific, then it is that much more difficult for Berkeley to escape algebraic manipulation of symbols for true thought in presence of ideas: true geometric thought, for example, will require imaging of specific shape and colour (and it is not quite clear what else besides).

VI

Let us return now to the ontological analysis of our wintry scenario at the outset above. It seems to me that Berkeley either does or can well simplify category 2 by recognizing at its foundation only distinct items *a, d, e, h, i,* and *j.* Everything else in 2 is either disallowed (*b, k*) or may be derived (*c, f,* and *g*): thus each of *c, f,* and *g* may be derived from *e* and *h.* And that leaves a category 2 containing just: qualities and their combinations into more complex ideas; subjects of experience, conception, and volition; and the experiencing and conceiving by subjects of ideas either passively or through their own volition.

Berkeley's true master stroke, however, is to remove all of category 1 and (consequently) all of 3: to 'remove' it all at least in the sense of not allowing it any fundamental status in his ontology. And his leading edge is, I contend,

> *the denial of any nexus or copula or true relation other than perceiving (understanding or conceiving), and willing,* both of which relate a mind to qualities or combinations of qualities, or in turn to a mind's being thus related to such.

Everything that exists fundamentally does so as a term of one of these relations; and anything that obtains fundamentally is either a mind's standing in one of these relations to an idea, or a mind's standing in one of these relations to a mind's standing in one of these relations to an idea, and so on.

Berkeley had supposed that *if* we could find a clear relation between, on one side, material substrata, and on the other side the qualities we sense directly, such as colours, *then* we could legitimately recognize such items, as well as thought about them. But if we are told that the snowball itself or its matter 'supports' the whiteness which we sense directly, what is such 'support'? It is not the support that a roof may derive from columns. And the question then stands: What 'support' is it? 'Exemplification' must be rejected, but not *ad hoc*: hence the global rejection of such a nexus as meaningless, a rejection self-evidently warranted to Berkeley, but defended anyhow, frequently and variously.

Everything in categories 1 and 3 is either rejected outright as a needless absurdity that explains nothing or else reduced to what involves fundamentally only categories 2 and 4.

One thereby gains several important advantages,[6] among which the following three deserve emphasis:

a. Avoiding any problem of how mind can interact with matter. (Though one does of course retain the question of how spirits can interact with 'bodies', with snowballs, for example, or with houses or mountains. We are still owed an explanation of what is really involved in *such* 'interaction'.)

b. Attaining a strikingly simple ontology that dispenses with what seems so hard to conceive clearly (material substrata), which even if somehow conceivable would anyhow be unknowable and theoretically useless (*Principles*, 18, 19).

c. Removing thus at a stroke a problem among the deepest and most intractable in all philosophy, one that bedevils subsequent philosophy to our own day: that of how to explain the possibility of our thought about the world (intentionality) in terms ultimately of how the world is in itself (the facts). Berkeley of course reverses the question, since for him reality is fundamentally thought, experience, and will, and it is the so-called objective (including the

---

[6] Several are listed at *Principles*, 85 and at *Dialogues*, 257–8. And see also *Principles*, 86 and *Principles*, 88 re scepticism.

natural) that needs explaining by reference to spirits and their perceiving or understanding of ideas, and their willing of such, etc.

VII

In proceeding thus Berkeley passes by a more moderate conception espoused by each of Russell and Bradley at least for a time. He passes by the relatively moderate conception according to which, although there are no substrata, and thus no exemplification of qualities by substrata, still there is a relation or nexus of co-exemplification or 'compresence' holding among qualities themselves. Russell, for example, develops[7] a

theory of qualities . . . according to which there are not 'instances' of hotness (or at any rate of any degree of hotness), but complexes of which hotness is an element. Space-time, on this view, depends upon qualities which are empirically unique, such as those used in defining latitude and longitude, and the complex 'hotness compresent with such-and-such a quality, or collection of qualities' takes the place of 'hotness in such-and-such a place' (218).

Russell holds as well

that the relation of compresence may hold outside of experience as well as within it; indeed, if there is the unexperienced world that physics supposes, its space-time will depend upon unexperienced compresence. (318)

And compare Bradley:[8]

We may take the familiar instance of a lump of sugar. . . . If we inquire what there can be in the thing beside its several qualities, we are baffled. . . . We can discover no real unity existing outside these qualities, or, again, existing within them . . .

Sugar is, of course, not the mere plurality of its different adjectives; but why should it be more than its properties in relation? When 'white', 'hard', 'sweet', and the rest coexist in a certain way, that is surely the secret of the thing. The qualities are, and are in relation. (16)

VIII

According to Berkeley's deepest view *nothing* is qualified *in any way*,

[7] In *Inquiry into Meaning and Truth* (Penguin Books, Baltimore, 1967); first published by Allen & Unwin in 1940.
[8] F. H. Bradley, *Appearance and Reality* (Oxford University Press, Oxford, 1955). First published in 1893.

not fundamentally anyhow. The appearance of things having qualities is to be explained in every case as derivative from the perceiving (understanding) or willing of spirits. These basic, true relations (and copulas) all involve acts of mind or spirit. Minds, in particular, therefore have no qualities, and in that sense no intrinsic natures. They only perceive (understand) or will. And qualities along with their combinations into ideas have no fundamental exemplars. They are only perceived or willed to be perceived.

Nor is there, according to Berkeley, any such compresence or coexistence as Russell and Bradley were willing to postulate, not outside experience anyhow. (Hylas suggests at *Dialogues*, 199 that 'each quality cannot singly subsist without the mind. Colour cannot without extension, neither can figure without some other sensible quality.' However, he then adds, 'as the several qualities united or blended together form entire sensible things, nothing hinders why such things may not be supposed to exist without the mind.' But this meets its inevitable refutation by Philonous in the next speech.)

Is Berkeley's view about qualities and their combinations into ideas to be extended to all properties of whatever sort or level? (By qualities here I mean *sensible, monadic* properties.) If so, then according to Berkeley not only is nothing *qualified* in any way but nothing is *propertied* in any way either. This is the really radical position, the one required for the most beautifully simple Berkeleian view. It is the one required for the 'leading edge' of his master stroke as presented above: that there is no nexus or copula whatever other than perception and volition. For if there is *anything* of whatever sort that is characterized in *any* way then its being so characterized will import a nexus of exemplification whereby the thing exemplifies the character and a copula of singular predication whereby the character may be attributed to the thing.

It seems to me that Berkeley sees the simple, radical solution, and wants it; but does he earn a right to it? It might be thought that the very perception of an idea by a spirit already refutes the radical view, since it involves the exemplification of the relation of perception by the spirit and the idea in that order. But what gives one the right to force exemplification on the scene in that way? Berkeley sees no need of such 'exemplification' beside his two true relations: perception (understanding) and volition.

What should concern us more seriously is rather that there *seem* to be many other cases of exemplification, at least prima facie. Being an idea would seem to be exemplified by each idea, being a quality by each quality, being a spirit by each spirit. Further, ideas may include constituent qualities. Is not complexity then exemplified by such ideas? Take a particular idea that combines roundness and whiteness. Is it not constituted in a certain way from roundness and whiteness? And is that not now a further relation beside perceiving and willing? This is not to be dismissed along with pseudo-relations like being-to-the-left-of, where one might visually experience something round and white to the left of something square and black. Being-to-the-left-of may be considered a pseudo-relation that does not really (fundamentally) relate anything, whose *esse* is *percipi*, and which combines with other such pseudo-relations and qualities to form larger and larger ideas. Such ideas are not fundamentally exemplified but only understood, perceived, or willed. The same may not be held with regard to the *constitution* relation that relates a complex idea to its constituent qualities (and pseudo-relations). Though such a relation cannot be borne by anything to anything outside the ken of God, and hence cannot possibly exist (be exemplified) outside the grasp of a Mind, the fact remains that there really are the idea and its constituent qualities and the former is really constituted from the latter, and hence it would seem the constitution relation is really exemplified, in a way that seems not to *derive* wholly from anyone's perception or conception. Or would Berkeley reply that God's handiwork may be found not only in spirits and ideas themselves but also in the relations between these and in the relation of constitution between ideas and their constituent qualities and in the being spiritual of spirits and in the being an idea of each idea, etc.? All then derives from the activity of the Divine Creator and Sustainer. Fair enough. But God's creation of snowballs, houses, and mountains with their various qualities is not fundamental but flows from his creation at a more basic level of spirits and their ideas, and his arranging for various spirits to have various ideas in various ways, etc. Such an answer is unavailable for our question about the constitution of ideas by qualities. Though qualities could not possibly constitute ideas unnoticed by God, we have no notion of a deeper level not including that constitution such that the constitution of ideas by qualities flows or supervenes somehow from what God creates at that deeper level. Ideas and qualities are already at the deepest level: if God brings about the constitution of the former by the latter he must do so directly, and hence what God thus creates would seem to be precisely the exemplification by qualities of the constitution relation with respect to ideas (or more complex qualities). And exemplification would hence after all remain even at the deepest level of Berkeley's ontology. It is not really clear, therefore, how Berkeley is to dispense with all exemplification at the foundation of his ontology: how he can explain the intellectual appearance of exemplification at more superficial levels by reference to the minding (perceiving or willing) of ideas by minds (as opposed to their exemplification by instances).

IX

If exemplification is left standing as a further fundamental relation in addition to perception and volition, however, that weakens Berkeley's position immeasurably. For he is no longer able to complain that the 'support' of a substratum (e.g., a material substratum) for its qualities is neither that which columns give a roof nor any other he can conceive. The obvious answer is now that the 'support' is simply exemplification and that it would be imperceptive or disingenuous to require a true definition, analysis, or reduction of what is fundamental. Just as each spirit exemplifies spirituality; each idea ideality; and each conjunctive idea conjunctive constitution with respect to its conjunct constituents; just so each (material) snowball could exemplify roundness and whiteness. Further, if we can form a ('relative') notion of spirit as that which *perceives* and *wills*; if 'by the word *spirit* we mean only that which thinks, wills, and perceives', if 'this, and this alone, constitutes the signification of that term' (*Principles*, 138); then by parity we could surely form an equally good (relative) notion of body as that which *exemplifies* colour and shape.

Berkeley could now complain that we have no direct acquaintance with any body, whereas we do with a spirit and with ideas. But the bearing of this is not obvious if we can now *understand* the notion of body (by its exemplification relation to colour and shape). And besides, given *understanding* of body, Berkeley would now owe us an *argument* that he is *not* acquainted with a body already in being acquainted with himself. (What rules out that he himself now be a body, an exemplifier of colour and shape?)

One could of course fall back on the arguments against objective secondary qualities and, by extension, against primary qualities as well. But these arguments seem subsidiary and mainly intended to rule out not really the *possibility* of qualities present without the mind so much as our *knowledge* of which qualities are thus present when and where. (*Principles*, 14 and 15 contrast such weaker arguments with the earlier demonstration from a truth 'so near and obvious to the mind, that a man need only open his eyes to see' it: namely, the inconceivability of supposed 'subsistence without a mind', as *Principles*, 6 has it.)

Yet Berkeley does need to hold firm against the possibility of exemplification as a fundamental nexus or true 'relation' along with perception and volition. Remove that keystone denial and his system collapses.[9] His best response is evidently to reject any such supposed properties as being an idea, being a spirit, being constituted by conjunction, and the like. They all must receive the treatment explicitly accorded their logical kin: Unity, Entity, Being, and Identity (see above). These are all viewed as nothing more than tokens in algebraic language, which stand on their own for nothing real or in any way present in reality.[10] (One may of course have one's doubts about such radical nominalism and about the imagist empiricism of thought on which it rests, but perhaps we see how Berkeley's rejection of exemplification is defensible by appeal to a large and independently introduced and supported feature of his philosophy.)

X

Just how does God bear up the Universe down to its most secret recess?

[9] No wonder that, as he affirms in the same words both in the *Principles* and in the *Dialogues*, he is 'content to put the whole upon this issue': whether there is any true 'existence' of sensible qualities and objects other than presence to the mind; or whether, instead, *esse est percipi* (*Principles*, 22; *Dialogues*, 200).

[10] And the like must perhaps be said of the doctrine 'that the intense heat immediately perceived, is nothing distinct from a particular sort of pain' (*Dialogues*, 176), and that 'sensible pain is nothing distinct from [certain] . . . sensations or ideas, in an intense degree' (*Dialogues*, 177). Either pain (or, perhaps, being painful) is a *determinable* of specific intense degrees of heat (among other things) or it is an alleged *property* of such degrees of heat. In either case Berkeley is firmly committed to denying it any real status. As a mere *determinable* pain would not be fully specific and hence would never be present fundamentally in reality (recall *Dialogues*, 192, and the discussion of it above): i.e., it would never be thus present in experience or imagination. As a basic *property* of intense degrees of heat it has to be even more repellent to Berkeley: allowing it as such would after all allow exemplification as a fundamental 'relation' of his ontology along with perception and volition. Must 'pain' and 'pleasure' hence join our list of algebraic counters devoid of independent meaning?

Not, apparently, by sensory perception of it all, since God strictly perceives nothing by sense (*Dialogues*, 240–1).

Nor is it rather by understanding (conceiving, considering) what we perceive and think, not at least *in the way we do so* since he lacks a spatio-temporal perspective. And that same lack would seem also to prevent Him from attaining an understanding of what we perceive or think in a way sometimes made accessible to others by their spatio-temporal perspectives related to ours (as by thinking 'It rained there then' my judgement may coincide with yours of yore that 'It rains here now'). Again, that is closed to Him by the fact that he is not ensconced at any particular place and time. (According to Philonous at *Dialogues*, 254, 'God is a being of transcendent and unlimited perfections', and though He is immediately said to have a nature 'incomprehensible to finite spirits', that does not prevent him from adding at 257 that God's 'spirituality, omnipresence, providence, omniscience, infinite power and goodness, are as conspicuous as the existence of sensible things, of which . . . there is no more reason to doubt, than of our being'.)

God rather, outside space and time, has presumably a (direct?) view of each spirit of whatever sort or power and of each (perspectival) quality and combination of qualities and he relates the latter to the former via relations of perceiving (by sense or understanding) in a coherent way (at least to a large extent, allowing of course for illusions, dreams, and the like), taking into account also the volitions by all lesser spirits (whether he causes these as well or not).[11]

Since God himself is not spatio-temporally located, he can consider perspectival ideas but he cannot veridically experience them or assent to them.

Actually, even for lesser spirits who are supposed 'spatio-temporally located' there remains a puzzle: Just how can the experience or thought of S 'correspond' to the experience or thought of S'? When S experiences or thinks himself to be seated, what (presumably perspectival) content of the experience or thought of S' makes the experience or thought of S 'correspond' to that of S'? If S_1 and S_2 think 'I am seated' and S_1' and S_2' think 'You are seated' what can

---

[11] What latitude and manner of freedom are allowed to lesser spirits? Having 'denied there are any other agents beside spirits' Berkeley adds that 'this is very consistent with allowing to thinking rational beings, in the production of motions, the use of limited powers, ultimately indeed derived from God, but immediately under the direction of their own wills, which is sufficient to entitle them to all the guilt of their actions' (*Dialogues*, 237). But this leaves our question standing.

make the thought of S1 correspond to that of S1′ but not to that of S2′, and the thought of S2 correspond to that of S2′ and not to that of S1′? In the absence of fundamental spatial relations Berkeley would seem restricted to causation as the only promising avenue to secure interspirit reference thus permitting S1′ to refer to S1 rather than to S2 with the thought 'You are sitting'. If so, he faces an apparently vicious regress of spirit interaction (which independent reasons lead to sooner or later anyhow), as follows.

How can I single out a spirit except by means of its relations to my experience? I might pick out a person as the one responsible for certain sounds and sights that I experience. But how can *he* be causing *me* to have these sounds or sights in my experience unless he has already singled me out? And is not his predicament just like mine to begin with? In other words: if either of S or S′ is to cause anything in the other (by means of volition, which is of course for Berkeley the only real causation) then he must *single out* the other so as to be able to focus on *him* (out of all possible such foci) and exert volition on that focus. But the only way for either S or S′ to single out the other would seem to be as the (*true*) causal source of certain experiences. And that presupposes interspirit causal action already effected. Not that there is an unavoidable regress here, since nothing logically precludes that each of S and S′ act causally on the other as early as either one does so. But that seems utterly implausible as an account of what actually happens.

Berkeley replies, at *Principles*, 147,

that in affecting other persons, the will of man hath no other object, than barely the motion of the limbs of his body; but that such a motion should be attended by, or excite any idea in the mind of another, depends wholly on the will of the Creator. He alone it is who *upholding all things by the Word of his Power*, maintains that intercourse between spirits, whereby they are able to perceive the existence of each other.

Our voluntary motions thus serve as occasions for God to cause corresponding ideas in suitably placed observers. But what is a 'suitably placed' observer? Since shared space *derives* from correspondence of ideas, it cannot be used to explain such correspondence. The 'placement' of observers must hence derive from something ontologically more basic. Suppose, again, there is no real interspirit causation among lesser spirits but only occasionalist causation, which itself derives from God's real causation of ideas in spirits systematically on the occasion of ideas present to the same or other spirits. But what determines *which* spirits it is the character of whose consciousness will serve as an occasion for God to affect a given spirit in corresponding ways? This may be just brute fact, or Divine Design opaque to human reason. There remains anyhow the mystery of how God Himself singles out any lesser spirit. That is quite puzzling since God causes lesser spirits to exist from their earliest moments and these are powerless to affect God via perception on His part (God being purely active and perceiving nothing by sense).

We might suppose that spirits are located spatially via their bodies, where a body B is the junction of certain sequences of experience and thought on the part of many perceivers or thinkers, God included. There is B as experienced in a first-person way by its subject and as experienced in a third-person way by various observers and as correctly understood by God to have all of these aspects to the various subjects involved, including its having the subjective aspect that it has to its subject. B is hence a confluence of various gappy sequences of ideas presented to various spirits. But what happens when it presents no idea perceptually to *any* spirit? How does God think of it then? Perhaps by its place in a spatio-temporal framework anchored via bodies $B_1, \ldots, Bn$ to spirits $S_1, \ldots, Sn$?

Once we can single out a body Bi we have an origin relative to which everything else falls into place. But how is Bi to be 'anchored' to Si? It seems not enough that Si have certain experiences 'corresponding' to Bi and fitting with the experience of spirits with suitably 'circumstanced' (nearby, etc.) bodies. For this whole combination may be repeated indefinitely many times by different groups of spirits. To object thus is however to miss Berkeley's commitment to spirits as basic ontological ground. The suitable experiences of $S_1, \ldots, Si, \ldots, Sn$ will determine a body Bi for Si different from body Bi' of Si' despite the qualitative identity between the relevant experiences of $S_1, \ldots, Si, \ldots, Sn$ and $S_1', \ldots, Si', \ldots, Sn'$ respectively. But if bodies are individuated thus by underlying spirits so that qualitative identity of bodies is no bar to diversity of corresponding spirits, then spirits are not to be singled out by their bodies and the question remains of how God is able to bring it off.

There is besides a further difficulty deriving from the principle that *diversity could not stand alone*, that there could never be two items that not only differed *solo numero*, and shared all properties, and entered into all the same relations with the same *sorts* of terms, but also between which there was no basic relation save diversity.

(If diversity *could* stand alone, then for example there could be indefinitely many books in your hands now all quite alike and interrelated only by diversity.) Perhaps Berkeley would appeal to a sort of identity of indiscernibles by postulating that no two spirits could possibly share lives identical in every respect of experience and thought. Thus God at least would be able to distinguish them.

Even if we do in some such way secure a derivative place within Berkeley's ontology for the body Bi of a spirit Si, however, the question yet remains as to the character and status of the 'unexperienced physical universe': the remote in space or time, the very small, the very large, etc. What determines the status of all such reality, however derivative it may turn out to be? There is a great temptation to draw from Berkeley that its status is secured by the experiential perception of God, even for all of it that remains forever unperceived by any lesser spirit. But that answer is ruled out since for Berkeley God perceives nothing by sense experience (*Dialogues*, 240–1).

Perhaps God will be thought the Atlas who bears up physical reality not through His (nonexistent) sensory perception but through his infinite Understanding and Thought.

Take then all lesser spirits ever and fix their lives of experience and thought to their most minute details. If infinitely much 'physical reality' can yet remain unobserved and even unconceived, what serves as *its* ground, if it cannot ground itself? 'God's thought', we are now told. But how can this be if there are infinitely many remaining physical possibilities *all* of which are compatible with what we have fixed in life content for all lesser spirits? Yet God must surely conceive all such physical possibilities, none thereby deriving any advantage in respect of actuality. But being alternative *incompatible* possibilities they cannot all be actual. So our question remains: What grounds the actuality of all physical reality that remains undetermined by the combined content of the lives of all lesser spirits?

It seems rather Divine Understanding and Will that in combination now offer the most promising avenue. By Divine Will night-experience and day-experience alternate (by and large), derivatively of course from the Divine Fiat that 'bodies' should present appearances conforming to Newtonian mechanics. Relatively general and fundamental volitions (Newtonian mechanics) hence limit more particular and superficial ones. Where these are not fully fixed, however, the Divine Will also fills the gap by determining which experiences *would* follow which on the part of *all* lesser spirits $S1, \ldots,$ Sn. And this would perhaps fix to the extent possible the 'existence' and 'features' of whatever 'bodies' there ever are: not only of those 'presenting' at least one 'facet' to at least one spirit, but even of those that never appear in any way to anyone.[12] (Perhaps the Divine Will would even fix which experiences would be had and in what order by spirits not in fact actual if there *were* such spirits satisfying certain conditions—conditions defined presumably by what is perceived, understood, or willed, since these are the only real conditions for spirits to satisfy.)[13]

Given that ideas can be shared through being multiply present in a plurality of minds, and given that their presence is tantamount to their volition (active understanding) or perception (passive understanding), it is at least easier to understand the possibility of a

[12] Thus 'when things before imperceptible to creatures, are by a decree of God, made perceptible to them; then are they said to begin a relative existence, with respect to created minds' (*Dialogues*, 252). Also, may we not understand the Creation 'to have been entirely in respect of finite spirits; so that things, with regard to us, may properly be said to begin their existence, or be created, when God decreed they should become *perceptible* [my emphasis] to intelligent creatures, in that order and manner which he then established, and we now call the laws of Nature? You may call this a *relative*, or *hypothetical existence* if you please. But . . . so long as you can assign no other sense or meaning in its stead; why should we reject this?' (*Dialogues*, 253) It is God's prescience and power that yields the strength, liveliness, distinctness, regularity, vividness, constancy, orderliness, and coherence, and the correlative passivity on our part, all of which are in combination constitutive of what 'are called *real things*' (*Principles*, 29–33).

[13] Important and prominent though it is, volition in Berkeley is rather puzzling. Volition is the source of the having of ideas: we are supposed to see this easily in our own free imagination and to extend the notion by analogy to God. But what is the logical form of the volition involved in our free imagination? Is it that of: *S wills X*? What then takes the place of X? Is it some situation (state, condition, event) constituted by S's perceiving certain ideas? Would not S then need some conception of X from the very moment when he begins to will it? But if he *already* has a conception of X which he needs for the willing, how can it be the willing that yields the conception. (The puzzle for Berkeley lies in his tendency to conflate conception with imagination: otherwise one could appeal to a pre-image conception effective in the formation of the image.) Perhaps the solution is to allow *two* basic forms of conception: active conception (volitional understanding) and passive conception (experiential understanding). God is always active; lesser spirits only sometimes. Perception of ideas may then occur either actively and volitionally, as it always does in God, or else passively and experientially, as it often does in us.

common world: for a start, ideas may be grasped in common, and the Divine source and ground of all existence may provide us with our sensory ideas by his willing us to have them (which requires that they be present to Him). But if ideas are qualities experienced by a plural public and not images or sensa private to a single subject, then it becomes puzzling why qualities cannot exist outside the mind (singly or in combination). Images and sensa are of course very plausibly regarded as ineluctably mental and private to their subjects. With qualities it seems quite otherwise. If whiteness and roundness may be perceived not only by me but also by you and by God (while yet remaining the same idea or combination of qualities), if it is not private to any one mind, why may it not also be *exemplified* by a snowball itself as a fundamental fact (requiring perhaps God's concurrence but no more so than any other fundamental fact, such as the perception of an idea by a spirit)? It is here that Berkeley strikes masterfully by denying explanatory value and even meaning to such a nexus in a true metaphysics.[14]

[14] I have used the excellent Berkeley commentaries: from Luce and Warnock to Tipton and Pitcher; and also the several fine collections available, including those edited by Martin and Armstrong and by Turbayne. Also helpful were J. A. Robles's 'Percepción e infinitesimales en Berkeley' *Dianoia* (part I in 1980 and part II in 1981); and the symposium on Berkeley in the first issue of *Analisis Filosofico* (1981), with papers by J. Rodriguez Larreta, A. Moretti, and E. Rabossi. I am not conscious of specific debts to the literature (other than those acknowledged in footnotes), but no doubt there are some if not more. For comments and discussion, my warm thanks to John W. Lenz, Philip L. Quinn, James Van Cleve, and especially to John Foster and Dan Garber.

CHAPTER 5

BERKELEY ON THE PHYSICAL WORLD

JOHN FOSTER

I

BERKELEY'S philosophy of the physical world is built around two central claims. The first is his claim that reality is ultimately purely mental, consisting solely of minds (spirits) and what exists or occurs within them. The second is his claim that there is a physical world and one which (more or less) answers to the specifications of our ordinary beliefs. These two claims appear to be incompatible: it seems that to accept the existence of a physical world, with its three-dimensional space and its solid extended occupants, is precisely to accept the existence of something outside the mind. But Berkeley believed that the two claims could be reconciled. He thought that the physical world itself is wholly constituted by the things which exist and the facts which obtain in the mental reality. It is the nature of this reconciliation which I want to explore in the present essay.

Before we look more closely at Berkeley's own position (or positions), it will be useful to distinguish two ways in which someone who accepts a mentalist doctrine of ultimate reality might try to preserve the existence of the physical world. On the one hand, he might claim that, while the ultimate reality is purely mental, the physical world itself is part of that reality—that it is, quite literally, composed of mental entities and mental facts. For example, he might take physical objects to be collections of minds and take the spatial arrangement of these particle-minds to consist in the qualitative relations between their experiential states.[1] On the other hand, he might concede that the ultimate mental reality is wholly non-physical, but claim that the facts which obtain in this reality in some way logically suffice for the existence of a physical world (and I am here using the term 'logically' in a broad sense to cover not only a

---

[1] For a specific version of this see my *The Case for Idealism* (Routledge and Kegan Paul, London, 1982) ch. 11.

priori but also, as some people term them, metaphysical necessities). For example, he might, following a phenomenalistic course, claim that, while physical objects are not as such mental, their existence and spatial arrangement is logically sustained by the organization of human sense-experience. Now these two ways in which a mentalist might try to preserve the existence of the physical world are quite different. The first way, which takes the physical world to be part of the ultimate reality, is a form of physical realism. It differs from our common-sense view of the physical world not in respect of the ontological status of physical entities, but only in respect of their intrinsic nature. It takes the physical world to be ultimately real, but to be mental in its substance and character. The second way, in contrast, is a form of reductionism. It concedes that at the level of ultimate reality the physical ontology disappears, but insists that statements about physical entities can still be counted as true in virtue of facts about minds. It preserves the physical world not by locating it within the ultimate mental reality, but by construing it as something derivative, which this ultimate reality sustains.

The distinction between these two approaches—between *mentalistic realism* and *mentalistic reductionism*—is not one which Berkeley himself explicitly drew, nor, I think, fully appreciated. But the distinction will help to put his philosophical views in a clearer perspective. In particular, it will help to clarify the difference between his accounts of the physical world in the *Principles* and the *Dialogues*. Neither of these accounts, it must be admitted, is internally consistent. But as I interpret them, Berkeley's true position in the *Principles* is a form of reductionism, while his true position in the subsequent *Dialogues* is a form of realism.

II

First and foremost, of course, Berkeley is a mentalist. On this he never wavers or equivocates, despite his varying accounts of the physical world. This mentalism stems directly from his doctrine of *esse est percipi*—the doctrine that, within the domain of unthinking things, to exist is to be perceived. In effect, the doctrine restricts the ultimate ontology to two sorts of entities, namely minds (spirits) and their ideas.

Berkeley accepts this restriction because he thinks that it is impossible to conceive of a counter-example. Thus suppose we try to conceive of some type of object which exists in the ultimate reality, but is neither a mind nor composed of ideas. To have any positive conception of the intrinsic nature of this object, we are, Berkeley thinks, forced to clothe it with sensible qualities—the kind of qualities, like colour and visual or tactual extension, which feature in the content of sense-experience. In other words, we are forced to conceive of the object either as a concretion of sensible qualities or as a substance in which such qualities inhere. But Berkeley thinks that it is both self-evident and demonstrable by a variety of further arguments that sensible qualities can have no ultimate realization except as the internal objects of perception, i.e. as ideas existing in the mind. So if we conceive of the object as a concretion of sensible qualities, we have to construe it as a collection of ideas. And if we conceive of it as a substance in which such qualities inhere, we have to construe it as a mind. Either way, we fail to achieve the conception we were seeking—of something which would serve as a counter-example to Berkeley's mentalist doctrine.

I think that Berkeley's reasoning here is basically sound, though at certain points his arguments need to be amended or supplemented.[2] Where I think he goes seriously wrong is in assuming that the conclusion of this reasoning is enough to vindicate his mentalist doctrine. What the reasoning establishes is that if the ultimate ontology is not confined to minds and ideas, the additional entities are ones of whose intrinsic natures we can form no positive conception. But it by no means follows from this that there are no such entities nor even that it would be irrational to postulate them. Where this becomes crucial, of course, is over the issue of the physical world. Berkeley's opponent—the 'materialist'—is claiming that physical objects are both ultimate and mind-independent, and Berkeley is challenging him to provide some positive and coherent account of what these objects are like in themselves. But it is far from clear why the materialist should feel obliged to meet this challenge. Why should he not be happy to concede that he can offer no positive specification of physical objects beyond a description of their structural, causal, and dispositional properties—a description which does not reveal their intrinsic content.[3] Of course, he can only be happy with this if he can also offer some reason for believing that such

---

[2] In effect, I have tried to provide an improved version of Berkeley's argument in *The Case for Idealism*, Part II.
[3] For a full discussion of this see my *The Case for Idealism*, chs. 4–5.

objects exist; and, clearly, if they have no sensible qualities, they are not directly perceptible. But the materialist will argue that the postulation of these insensible objects can be justified by an explanatory inference. Their postulation is justified because, together with the postulation of certain psychophysical laws, it best explains the orderly character of human sense-experience. In effect, it best explains why human experience is organized as if a physical world obtains.

If Berkeley was wrong to assume that the materialist need feel embarrassed over his incapacity to specify the intrinsic nature of these mind-independent objects, he also had an independent argument against the materialist's case for postulating them. The materialist claims that we can justify their postulation by an explanatory inference—an inference which takes us from observed experiential effects to their unobserved physical causes. But Berkeley argues that, even if there were such objects, they would be causally inert and thus incapable of playing the explanatory role which the materialist assigns to them. For he thinks that the only kind of causation which we can conceive of is that of which we have an introspective understanding through the exercise of our own volition—through such volitional activities as the framing of a mental image and the attempt to move some part of one's body. And he thinks that the kind of causation thus revealed to us is not something which we can abstract from its volitional setting and envisage as operating independently of the will. In short, Berkeley thinks that all causation is, and has to be, volitional, and that, consequently, we cannot make sense of the materialist's claim that our experiences are caused by external unthinking objects. And if we cannot make sense of this claim, then we cannot justify the postulation of such objects by their role in explaining experience.

In claiming that all causation is volitional, Berkeley is, of course, assuming that our concept of cause involves the notion of some genuine agency or necessitation. Thus if someone were to define causation in a Humean fashion, as mere constant conjunction in the perspective of our inductive propensities, Berkeley would consider this definition inaccurate, but happily concede that, thus defined, non-volitional causation is possible. His claims are simply that volition is the only form of genuine agency (or causal necessitation), that only by invoking such agency can we provide a genuine explanation of human sense-experience, and that only a theory which is genuinely explanatory can be rationally inferred from our experiential data. Whether these claims are correct is another matter, and certainly Berkeley does not provide anything approaching an adequate defence of them. The first claim is particularly controversial, and in two distinct ways. On the one hand, it is far from clear that we do not possess a coherent notion of non-volitional agency; on the other hand, it is questionable whether, in the case of volition, introspection reveals anything more than constant conjunction. However, for the purposes of our discussion, we must leave these issues on one side.

Berkeley's conclusion is not that human sense-experience has no explanation, but that it must be explained in terms of the causal agency of God. Clearly, our sense-experiences are not the product of our own volition (unlike the mental images we frame) and their orderly character is not of our own making. Berkeley concludes that these experiences are the product of divine volition and that their orderly character is the product of the consistent volitional policies which God adopts:

But whatever power I may have over my own thoughts, I find the ideas actually perceived by sense have not a like dependence on my will. . . . There is therefore some other will or spirit that produces them.

The ideas of sense . . . have likewise a steadiness, order, and coherence, and are not excited at random, . . . but in a regular train or series, the admirable connexion whereof sufficiently testifies the wisdom and benevolence of its Author. Now the set rules or established methods, wherein the mind we depend on excites in us the ideas of sense, are called the *Laws of Nature*: and these we learn by experience, which teaches us that such and such ideas are attended with such and such other ideas, in the ordinary course of things. (*Principles*, 29–30.)

Given his assumptions, I think that Berkeley's position here is basically well-founded. There is no denying that our sensory ideas do have a certain order and coherence—one which precisely accords with the hypothesis that we are the perceptive inhabitants of a certain kind of physical world. And, given that all causation has to be volitional, it is reasonable to account for this sensory order in terms of the volitional strategy of some controlling mind. In effect, it is reasonable to conclude that our experiences are directly caused by God and deliberately selected with the aim of making them conspicuously amenable to physical interpretation.

The only point where Berkeley goes astray here is in thinking (or so it seems) that the sensory order is reducible to certain phenomenal regularities in the ordinary sense, whereby, as he puts it, 'such and such ideas are attended with such and such other ideas, in the ordinary course of things'. In actual fact, the sensory order can only be adequately specified by reference to the physical theory which it prompts us to accept (or at least by reference to something which preserves the structure of that theory). It is not just that the order accords with the hypothesis that we are the perceptive inhabitants of a certain kind of physical world. It is also that the order can only be fully and exactly specified in terms of that hypothesis (or something isomorphic). The order consists, precisely and irreducibly, in the fact that our experiences are systematically as if that hypothesis were true. This presupposes, of course, that the hypothesis postulates a physical world which is conspicuously orderly in its own terms. For even if our experiences were purely random, they would match the specifications of *some* kind of physical world. What makes our experiences genuinely orderly is that they can be taken to reflect, in an orderly fashion, the character of an orderly world. It is in this sense that they are *conspicuously* amenable to physical interpretation.

The fact that the sensory order can only be fully and exactly specified by reference to some physical theory does not mean that it is wholly concealed at the phenomenal level—that, outside the perspective of its physical interpretation, human experience appears totally random. Clearly, this is not so, and, from an epistemological standpoint, it is important that it should not be. For presumably it is those aspects of the sensory order which we *can* discern at the phenomenal level which provide us with our entry into the physical theory. Presumably, it is only because there are at least some crude phenomenal regularities which are conspicuous in their own terms, but which invite physical interpretation, that we ever come to acquire any physical beliefs. But the point is that the order which we discern at the phenomenal level is only a fraction of the order which we come to discern in the perspective of the physical theory. And it is this latter order which must be taken as the expression of God's volitional strategy.

What this means, in effect, is that Berkeley's conception of God's selection procedures, with respect to the causation of human experience, was too atomistic. He recognized that God's overall aim was to make human experience conspicuously amenable to physical interpretation, but he wrongly supposed that this aim was implemented by the adoption of a set of specific volitional rules (revealed, from our viewpoint, as the laws of nature) ensuring certain regularities at the phenomenal level. The fact is that, just as the sensory order cannot be detached from the perspective of some physical (or strictly, psychophysical) theory with which our experiences accord, so God's selection procedures cannot be detached from his overall strategy of securing an accord with that theory.

In a sense, these points help to strengthen Berkeley's case. For if the sensory order could be fully specified in purely phenomenal terms, the need to explain it by appeal to some external reality would be diminished. Indeed, it might be possible to find a perfectly adequate explanation in terms of certain autonomous phenomenal laws, without having to postulate anything outside the realm of experience to explain the laws themselves. It is because the sensory order can only be specified by reference to some physical theory, so that the experiential realm is, as it were, nomologically unmanageable in its own terms, that there is a pressing need for an externalist explanation. And if the explanation has to be volitional, then Berkeley's theistic hypothesis is surely the most plausible. In another way, of course, these points only serve to increase the pressure on Berkeley to make good his basic assumptions. If human experience is organized as if a certain kind of physical world obtains, and if that is precisely how the organization is defined, then the most natural explanation is that such a world does obtain. Berkeley regards this explanation as doubly defective—both defective in its postulation of a mind-independent world and defective in its acceptance of non-volitional causation. But on neither point are his arguments compelling.

III

As a restriction on the composition of the ultimate ontology, Berkeley's doctrine of *esse est percipi* does not determine any particular theory of the physical world. Indeed, it leaves him, with respect to the status and nature of physical objects, with four options: (1) to construe such objects as minds or collections of minds; (2) to construe them as ideas or collections of ideas; (3) to deny that such objects feature in the ultimate reality, but admit them as things whose existence the ultimate facts in some way logically sustain; and (4) to deny that there are physical objects at all in any sense. Options (3) and (4) are respectively reductionism and nihilism. Options (1) and (2) are forms of physical realism, though constrained by the mentalistic metaphysic.

While all four options are available to him, Berkeley never seriously entertains either (1) or (4). He takes it for granted that our senses afford us adequate grounds for believing in the existence of a physical world and considers it a defect in a theory if it leads to scepticism. Likewise, he takes it for granted that physical objects are, by definition, unthinking: the suggestion that they are really collections of minds he would have dismissed as manifestly incoherent.[4] On both these points, of course, Berkeley's position is in line with common sense. This leaves him with a choice between (2) and (3). And on this issue, his position is less clear. Part of the difficulty is that, even in the course of a single work, he says things which are clearly inconsistent, some of them favouring (2) and others favouring (3). A further problem is that, by failing to appreciate the distinction between the realist and the reductive approaches, Berkeley never explicitly addresses himself to the issue as I have formulated it. This means that, in trying to determine his true position, so much is a matter of the implications of his remarks, rather than of what he actually says.

There can be no doubt that Berkeley's basic instinct—his disposition prior to any deep philosophical reflection—was to accept option (2), which takes physical objects to be ideas or collections of ideas in the mind. This position is the direct application of the doctrine of *esse est percipi* to the physical world: it construes physical objects as things whose existence is to be perceived. I shall henceforth call this the Simple View. There are many passages in both the *Principles* and the *Dialogues* where Berkeley explicitly endorses this view. A famous example occurs in section 6 of the *Principles*, where he claims the view to be self-evident:

Some truths there are so near and obvious to the mind, that a man need only open his eyes to see them. Such I take this important one to be, to wit, that all the choir of heaven and furniture of the earth, in a word all those bodies which compose the mighty frame of the world, have not any subsistence without a mind, that their being is to be perceived or known . . .

Berkeley's basic instinct to accept the Simple View was partly due to his failure to appreciate the distinction between the realist and the reductive approaches. Without an explicit recognition of the possibi-

---

[4] I think it *is* incoherent, but not manifestly so. See the reference in note 1.

lity of reductionism, he finds himself automatically moving from his mentalist doctrine of *esse est percipi* to its direct application to the physical world. Thus, in defence of his preceding remarks, section 6 concludes:

> To be convinced of which, the reader need only reflect and try to separate in his own thoughts the being of a sensible thing from its being perceived.

Whatever its merits, this argument is only directly relevant to the composition of the ultimate reality. There is no special difficulty in separating the being of a sensible thing from its being perceived, if the thing is accorded a lower ontological status—if it is taken to be, as I would put it, 'ontologically derivative' rather than 'ontologically primitive'.[5] The phenomenalist, for example, can allow the physical world to contain unperceived sensible objects, by reducing the existence of such objects to certain 'possibilities of sensation' or to other aspects of the way human experience is organized. That Berkeley feels able to apply the argument directly to physical objects shows that he has not taken the reductionist option into account, though, as we shall see, the theory which eventually emerges and predominates in the *Principles* is implicitly of a reductive kind.

If Berkeley was drawn to the Simple View partly through a failure to notice any alternative, it is also true that he found the view attractive in another respect—at least as he initially interpreted it. For he liked the way in which, in line with common sense, it made physical objects directly perceptible. It combined what philosophy had established about the nature of perceptual experience, namely that the immediate objects of perception are internal to the mind, with what we all accept prior to philosophical reflection, namely that we directly perceive portions and aspects of the physical world. Indeed, at the end of the *Dialogues*, Berkeley (through the mouth of Philonous) describes this combination as the summary of his whole position:

> My endeavours tend only to unite and place in a clearer light that truth, which was before shared between the vulgar and the philosophers: the former being of opinion, that *those things they immediately perceive are the real things*; and the latter, that *the things immediately perceived, are ideas which exist only in the mind*. Which two notions put together, do in effect constitute the substance of what I advance.[6]

---

[5] This is my terminology in *The Case for Idealism.*
[6] *Dialogues*, 262.

Berkeley liked this not only because it was (to the extent that his mentalism permitted) in line with common sense, but also because it put our knowledge of the physical world on a secure foundation. In this last respect, of course, the favourable contrast was not so much with reductive positions (at least not with those of a phenomenalistic kind) as with representative theories, which locate the physical world behind a 'veil of perception'. Ironically, as we shall see, it was precisely a representative theory, though of a very unusual kind, which Berkeley had developed in the preceding pages of the *Dialogues*.

Although it has this epistemological advantage, it seems that, even from Berkeley's standpoint, the Simple View is open to a number of objections. I shall begin by mentioning the three most fundamental.

In the first place, if the physical world is entirely composed of ideas, there seems to be no way in which the separate sensory elements fit together to form a unified whole—at least, not a whole which would qualify as a *physical world* in any recognizable sense. The reason, of course, is that the elements are not arranged in a common space. An individual idea may include a spatial field (as, for example, in the case of visual experience); but there is no enduring and intersubjective field in which the ideas of different subjects and ideas at different times are collectively located. And, consequently, the Simple View seems to dissolve the physical world into a collection of disconnected fragments. Secondly, it seems that even if all the fragments could be pieced together, they would only cover a fraction of the spatio-temporal whole which we actually believe to obtain. For there would be no provision for the existence of unperceived objects or for perceived objects with unperceived aspects. Thus we would apparently be forced to say that there was no physical world before there were humans (or animals) to perceive it, that oranges have nothing inside them until they are peeled, and that my desk is annihilated every time I leave my study and recreated on my return. All this is clearly contrary to what we actually believe. Thirdly, the Simple View seems to exclude any genuine distinction between veridical perception and illusion. For if there are no external objects for them to represent, there seems to be nothing with respect to which our sensory ideas can be accurate or inaccurate. The drunkard's 'pink rats' and Macbeth's visionary dagger have, it seems, as much claim to count as part of the furniture of the world as the desk and paper I currently perceive. In effect, the physical world would appear to have lost its objectivity.

To these three objections we should perhaps add a fourth, though even its prima facie force is less clear-cut. I am thinking of the objection that the Simple View makes it impossible for different subjects to perceive the same physical item and thus conflicts with our belief that physical objects are publicly observable. The basis of this objection is clear enough: each subject only directly perceives his own ideas and these ideas, which represent nothing external, exist in *his* mind alone. What is not clear is that this prevents physical objects from being publicly observable in any adequate sense. For if physical objects are *collections* of ideas, different subjects could perhaps be said to perceive the same physical object by perceiving ideas which are elements of the same collection. Of course, since ideas are not located in some common sensory space, there is still the problem of finding some non-arbitrary basis for grouping them into the relevant collections. But this problem is already covered by the first objection: it is a special case of the more general problem of how the separate sensory elements fit together to form a unified sensible world.

These prima facie objections to the Simple View are ones which Berkeley cannot afford to ignore. If he is to preserve the physical world in any recognizable sense, he has to preserve it as something unified, objective, and public, and as something vastly more extensive and internally rich than our actual perceptions cover. In effect, he needs to preserve the physical world in a form which, apart from the unavoidable conflict with his metaphysical doctrines (i.e. his mentalism and his insistence on volitional causation), accords with our ordinary beliefs. Berkeley is aware of this, and it is essentially in his attempt to meet these requirements that the conflict in his thought arises.

IV

In his *Three Dialogues*, Berkeley's solution is to identify the physical world with the internal object of God's perception—with a complex idea which exists in God's mind and which, in partial and piecemeal fashion, our sensory ideas represent.[7] This retains the Simple View, which equates the existence of a physical object with its being

---

[7] This at least is how I interpret the position developed in the *Second* and *Third Dialogues*. See especially pp. 211–15, 230–1, and 234–5.

perceived; but, by making the physical world external to human minds, it avoids the objections to which this view seemed vulnerable. Since God's perception is not fragmented by time or distributed across different minds, the physical world perceived has the requisite unity: it is not a collection of isolated ideas, but one complex idea, which contains all physical items in a single spatio-temporal field. Likewise, since God's perception is not subject to the limitations of human perception, the physical world can be as extensive and replete as we ordinarily believe: there is no problem in supposing that there were mountains and rivers before there were humans to perceive them or that my desk continues to exist when there is no one in my room. Moreover, since there are external items for our sensory ideas to represent, there is, with respect to human experience, a genuine distinction between veridical perception and illusion. And, in the same way, physical objects are rendered publicly observable, since different human ideas can represent the same item in God's idea.[8] In short, by locating the physical world in God's mind, it seems that Berkeley can solve all the problems at a stroke. He can retain the Simple View, but, at the same time, secure a physical world with a unity, objectivity, publicity, and repleteness to match the specifications of our ordinary beliefs.

Berkeley takes God to be a purely active being, not subject to any causal influence. Consequently, he thinks of God's perception of the physical world as an active conceiving rather than as a passive sense-experience;[9] and, to stress the contrast with sense-experience, he often uses the terms 'knows' and 'comprehends' in place of 'perceives'.[10] The fact that God's perception is not sensory does not, of course, mean that what he perceives is not a sensible world—a world composed of the kind of sensible qualities and relations which feature in the content of human sense-experience. And it is doubly crucial for Berkeley that the object of God's perception should be sensible in this way. For otherwise the physical world would not meet the specifications of our ordinary physical beliefs; nor, indeed, would it be something of which we could even form a positive conception, and so would be no more respectable, as an ingredient of the ultimate reality, than the mind-independent world of the materialist.

---

[8] See *Dialogues*, 248.

[9] See especially *Dialogues*, 240–1.

[10] Berkeley's varying terminology with respect to God's perception (i.e. conception) of the physical world is nicely set out and clarified by G. Pitcher in *Berkeley* (Routledge and Kegan Paul, London, 1977), pp. 175–9.

What remains puzzling about this is why Berkeley should suppose that a sensible quality, or complex of qualities, can achieve some genuine realization by being divinely *conceived*. It is one thing to accept a sense-datum account of ordinary perception, which claims that the quality-patterns which feature in the content of sense-experience are genuinely realized (as sense-data) by featuring in that content. It is another thing to claim that such patterns are also genuinely realized simply by being conceived. And certainly, in the human case, this claim seems wrong. Surely I do not create a real colour-patch or a real sound simply by thinking of one.

Berkeley's answer would be that I *do* create a real colour-patch and real sound (though not real in the sense of *physical*) if I conceive of them by the framing of an *image*. For in that case there is, he would claim, something (the image) which is the internal object of my conception and which instantiates the sensible qualities in question. This could be disputed (indeed I would dispute it myself), but let us, for the sake of argument, suppose it to be true. Berkeley could then claim that God's conception of the sensible world is a form of imaging or something analogous. One reason for allowing it to be merely *analogous* to imaging is obvious: we cannot expect God's psychological operations to be quite like ours. But there is also another and more subtle reason. It is arguable that to frame an image of something is to represent oneself as sense-perceiving it. And, presumably, if God cannot have sense-experiences, he cannot (or at least would not) represent himself as having them either. At all events, it seems safer for Berkeley to appeal to the case of human imagination, as an example of an active conception with a sensible object whose *esse* is *concipi*, and then merely claim that God's conception of the sensible world is like human imagination in *that* respect.

One of the most curious aspects of Berkeley's new position is that, while retaining the Simple View, it commits him to a representative theory of perception. As he originally interpreted it, the Simple View gave us direct perceptual access to the physical world, by equating our own sensory ideas with the physical items we perceive. This, indeed, was one of the reasons why he found the view attractive. But by locating the physical world in God's mind, Berkeley is now committed to saying that our access to it is only indirect. We perceive physical objects, but only by perceiving certain other objects, i.e. our own ideas, which represent them. Berkeley himself, strangely, seems to be only half-aware that his position has changed. For although, in elaborating the theory, he stresses the fact that the physical world is now external to human minds, and speaks of God's ideas as the 'archetypes' of which our sensory ideas are the secondary copies, he still feels able, in the end, to claim that his theory preserves the direct realism of common sense. For in effect, as we saw, he claims that it is precisely this direct realism, combined with the sense-datum theory, which constitutes 'the substance of what I advance'. No doubt this is what Berkeley had *wanted* to advance. But it was not the theory which actually emerged.

Part of what Berkeley liked about direct realism, as we noted, was that it puts our knowledge of the physical world on a firm foundation. For we can derive our physical knowledge from the character of our sense-experiences without having to make inferences to some external realm beyond what these experiences immediately present. This raises the question of whether physical knowledge is possible on Berkeley's new account. If the physical world is located in God's mind, do we have any way of discovering its character? Do we even have any reason to believe that such a world exists? Since Berkeley wants to avoid scepticism, it is essential to his project that these questions should be answered affirmatively.

Before we can deal with this epistemological issue, we need to get clearer about the relationship, as Berkeley conceives it, between our sensory ideas and the physical items in God's mind which they represent. On standard representative theories, a sensory idea is thought of as representing a particular physical object in virtue of two factors: first, a certain qualitative or structural resemblance between the idea and the object (or the object as it is projected onto the observer's viewpoint); and secondly, the fact that the physical object is, in some suitable way, causally involved in the production of the idea, with each represented object-feature having a special involvement in the production of the corresponding idea-feature. In Berkeley's theory, this second factor has to be replaced by something else, since he holds that volition is the only form of causal agency. What replaces it is the fact that, in the framework of God's volitional policies, the object, together with the 'circumstances' of the relevant human subject, serves as an occasion for God to cause the idea: 'there is an *omnipresent eternal Mind*, which knows and comprehends all things, and exhibits them to our view in such a manner, and according to such rules as he himself hath ordained, and are by us termed the

Laws of Nature.[11] This sounds like Malebranche's position (that we see all things in God), but Berkeley is at pains to stress that the resemblance is only superficial.[12] The most important difference is that, in Malebranche's system, the physical things which God comprehends and exhibits to our view are external to him, as they are to us, while in Berkeley's system, they exist in God's mind, as the internal objects of his conception.

If God ensures that our sensory ideas accurately represent physical things, as he conceives them, then in one weak sense we are assured of physical knowledge. We have, that is, a reliable way of reaching the truth about the physical world by following the evidence of our senses. But, clearly, this does not settle the real epistemological issue. For what really matters is whether, on Berkeley's theory, we can have good reason for believing that our senses are reliable in this way. Do we have good grounds for believing that there is a world in God's mind and that God reveals it to us, in piecemeal and partial fashion, through the control of our sensory ideas?

On this point, Berkeley's own reasoning is woefully inadequate:

It is evident that the things I perceive are my own ideas, and that no idea can exist unless it be in a mind. Nor is it less plain that these ideas or things by me perceived, either themselves or their archetypes, exist independently of my mind, since I know myself not to be their author, it being out of my power to determine at pleasure, what particular ideas I shall be affected with upon opening my eyes or ears. They must therefore exist in some other mind, whose will it is they should be exhibited to me.[13]

This argument is clearly fallacious. The fact that our sensory ideas are not within our own volitional control does not, as such, establish that they or their archetypes (and it could only be their archetypes) exist in some other mind. Indeed, the whole argument seems to be based on a confusion of two senses in which the things we perceive may be independent of us: (1) the sense in which they are independent if we are not causally responsible for them, and (2) the sense in which they are independent if they do not exist in our minds. In effect, Berkeley reaches his conclusion by appealing to the first kind of independence and then reinterpreting it as the second.

Although Berkeley's argument is, as it stands, fallacious, it might

[11] *Dialogues*, 231.
[12] *Dialogues*, 214. Malebranche elaborates his position in his *De la Recherche de la Vérité*.
[13] *Dialogues*, 214–15.

still be possible to transform it into something sound and effective by inserting, between the premises and the conclusion, certain further steps of reasoning. We could make a start in this direction by invoking another argument which Berkeley supplies, though to a weaker conclusion, and which we examined in our earlier discussion. I am thinking of his argument for God's volitional role—the argument that because our sense-experiences are not the product of our own volition and their orderly character is not of our own making, we should take them to be directly caused by God and their orderly character to be the reflection of God's volitional policies. If this argument is sound—and given Berkeley's basic assumptions, it seems very reasonable—what we need, to complete the whole argument, is some way of inferring God's perceptive role from his volitional role. It is the possibility of such an inference which we must now consider.

One thing which suggests that such an inference might be available is that God's volitional strategy already includes a conception of a certain kind of physical world. As we have seen, what renders our experiences orderly is that they are conspicuously amenable to physical interpretation, and God's overall strategy, in selecting the types of experience to cause, is to make them orderly in that way. In effect, God has to start with a conception of the kind of physical world whose existence he wants us to accept and then ordain that our experiences are to be such as to accord with, and invite our acceptance of, the hypothesis that such a world obtains. If we now equate the actual physical world with the internal object of this conception—with the complex sensible idea by which God identifies the kind of world in terms of which he frames his volitional strategy— it seems that the epistemological problems are solved: we are entitled, by means of an explanatory inference, to move from the sensory order we observe to the postulation of God's volitional strategy; and from the postulated strategy we can then deduce the existence and character of the physical world. In short, it seems that the physical world becomes epistemologically accessible to us, because God's perceptive (i.e. conceptive) role is implicit in his volitional role: we have good reason for believing that the physical world exists and that our sensory ideas accurately represent it, since the divine conception, by which it exists, forms an indispensable part of the divine strategy, which the sensory order reveals. Berkeley himself may be making this point when he remarks in his *Notebooks* (*PC*, 812):

The propertys of all things are in God i.e. there is in the Diety Understanding as well as Will. He is no Blind agent & in truth a blind Agent is a Contradiction.

This looks promising. And I think it is the best argument that we can construct on Berkeley's behalf. Nevertheless, I think that it can be shown to fail. For while we may be justified in explaining the sensory order in terms of God's volitional strategy and also justified in taking this strategy to involve a conception of a certain kind of physical world, we are not, I think, justified in supposing that this conception has an internal object of the appropriate sort. In fact, there are two problems here, as we shall now see.

Let us assume for the moment, in line with Berkeley's requirements, that the kind of world in terms of which God frames his volitional strategy is purely sensible, i.e. is a spatio-temporal arrangement of sensible qualities. Let us also assume, again in line with Berkeley's requirements, that it is possible for God to conceive of the arrangement by framing an image, or quasi-image, which instantiates it, thus providing an actual sensible particular, of the appropriate world-type, as the internal object of the conception. Even so, it is not clear what entitles us to suppose that it is this kind of conception which features in the volitional strategy. All that God's adoption of the strategy entails is that he, in some way or another, knows the character of the hypothetical world with which he intentionally makes our experiences accord. To suppose, in addition, that this knowledge is derived from some quasi-imagist conception, with an internal object which exemplifies the character in question, seems to be pure speculation. And without this supposition, there is no valid step of inference from God's adoption of the strategy to the existence of an actual physical world in his mind.

This point alone may well be decisive. But even if it is not, there is a second point which undermines the proposed argument at a more fundamental level. The only reason why we are even tempted to suppose that the conception within the volitional strategy is of a quasi-imagist kind is that we are assuming the kind of world in terms of which the strategy is framed to be purely sensible. And in making this assumption, we are implicitly assuming that the physical theory by reference to which the sensory order is defined is some version of naïve realism: we are assuming, in effect, that what renders our experiences orderly is their accordance with the hypothesis that we are located in a certain kind of sensible world (some concrete spatio-temporal arrangement of sensible qualities) and that our sense-experiences present to us portions of this world in the perspective of our current viewpoint. Now when it is contrasted with the claim that the sensory order can be specified in purely phenomenal terms, this assumption seems perfectly acceptable. It is, indeed, a move in the right direction, since vastly more of the sensory order can be captured at the level of this naïve physical interpretation than at the level of phenomenal regularities. However, our physical theorizing does not stop at naïve realism. It develops into the scientific theorizing of chemistry and physics, which postulate objects and properties of a non-sensible kind and, indeed, take these objects and properties to be the fundamental ingredients of the physical reality. Now the crucial point is that it is only by reference to the scientific theory that the sensory order can be fully and exactly specified. The order revealed by naïve realism considerably surpasses anything discernible at the phenomenal level, but it is crude and incomplete in relation to the order revealed by science. This does not mean merely that science postulates simpler laws. It means that the ways in which experience is orderly in relation to the physical world of science (or strictly, the physical world plus certain psychophysical laws) subsume and transcend the ways in which it is orderly in relation to the world of naïve realism. Certain aspects of the sensory order simply cannot be specified at all in the naïve realist's theoretical framework.

Since what calls for explanation is the whole sensory order, not just those aspects of it which are captured by naïve realism, we must suppose that the kind of physical world in terms of which God frames his volitional strategy is the kind of world which would be postulated by a hypothetically perfected science with access to all the actual and possible sensory evidence. It follows that, in framing this strategy, God has no need to form any conception of a *sensible* world. Indeed, if he confines himself to the perspective of science, his conception of the relevant kind of world—the kind which informs his strategy—will be 'topic-neutral': it will be a conception which specifies the structure and laws of the world without specifying its intrinsic content.[14] Clearly, such a conception would not have an internal object of the appropriate sort—one which instantiates the structural and nomological properties thus conceived. It would not, indeed, have an internal object at all in the relevant sense.

[14] On this notion of topic-neutrality, see my *The Case for Idealism*, chs. 4–5.

V

In his *Principles of Human Knowledge*, which was published a few years before the *Dialogues*, Berkeley does not equate the physical world with the internal object of God's perception (conception). There are, admittedly, passages which seem to point in this direction. Thus in section 6, having claimed that 'all those bodies which compose the mighty frame of the world, have not any subsistence without a mind' and that 'their being is to be perceived or known', he adds:

. . . consequently so long as they are not actually perceived by me, or do not exist in my mind or that of any other created spirit, they must either have no existence at all, or else subsist in the mind of some eternal spirit . . .

And he seems to pick up this point in section 48, when dealing with the problem of what happens to physical objects 'during the intervals between our perceptions of them'. But these passages fall short of the *Dialogues* theory in three crucial respects. First, the perceptive role of God is left as something merely hypothetical. The claim is not that God *does* perceive physical objects at times when we do not, but only that he *may* do so. Secondly, as well as being merely hypothetical, God's perception is only invoked as a supplement to human perception. The possibility which seems to matter to Berkeley is not that God perceives the whole physical world, but that he perceives those portions of it which we fail to perceive. Thirdly, and most crucially, however extensive God's perception, the physical world is thought of as something to which *we* also have direct perceptual access. Perhaps God keeps my desk in existence at times when I do not perceive it. But while I am perceiving it, my sensory ideas are genuine elements of that physical desk. They are not merely representations of some desk-like idea which exists in God's mind and which only God can directly perceive. Indeed, even the suggestion that God's perceptions may serve as a blueprint for his volitional procedures is one which, it seems, Berkeley finds 'too extravagant to deserve a confutation'.[15]

Not only do the claims in sections 6 and 48 fall short of the *Dialogues* position, but they are also out of line with the theory which predominates in the *Principles*. Right at the outset, Berkeley explicitly allows for the possibility of unperceived physical objects. For in section 3 he says of his table: 'if I were out of my study I should

[15] *Principles*, 71.

say it existed, meaning thereby that if I was in my study I might
perceive it, or that some other spirit actually does perceive it.' The
clear implication is that even if no one is actually perceiving the table,
it can still continue to exist solely in virtue of being, in principle,
perceptible. Now this implication, of course, is not compatible with
the Simple View, which equates the existence of a physical object with
its being actually perceived. And, on the face of it, it is the Simple
View which Berkeley is defending in the next few sections. This might
lead one to dismiss the concession in section 3 as a momentary
aberration. But this would be a mistake. For the same point occurs in
section 58, with more elaboration and with the full awareness that the
Simple View is being denied. The point is prompted by a hypothetical
objector, who claims that Berkeley cannot accommodate the finding
of astronomy that the earth moves, since 'the motion of the earth is
not perceived by sense'. Berkeley's reply is that the motion of the
earth reduces to the fact that we *would* perceive it, if we were
transported to a suitable viewpoint. Moreover, he claims that this
reply is in agreement with the principles he has advanced.

In making this claim, Berkeley has more in mind than his brief
remarks about the table in section 3. What he has primarily in mind
are sections 29–36, in which he tries to show how his position
preserves the existence of an objective physical world. In these
sections, he does two things. First, he draws attention to the fact that
our sensory ideas are not the product of our own volition, and that
they collectively exhibit a 'steadiness, order and coherence' which is
not of our making. From this he infers that they are the result of
God's volition, and that their orderly character is a reflection of
God's fixed volitional policies, which constitute, from our standpoint, the 'laws of nature'. (All this we have already examined.)
Secondly, he appeals to the first point to rebut the objection that 'by
the foregoing principles, all that is real and substantial in Nature is
banished out of the world: and instead thereof a chimerical scheme of
ideas takes place', in which 'houses, rivers, mountains, trees, stones'
are 'but so many chimeras and illusions on the fancy' (section 34).
Berkeley's answer is that there *is* an objective world, and one which
our perceptions directly reveal, simply in virtue of the orderly and
thematic way in which human experience is divinely controlled. Our
sensory ideas exist only in our minds; but they are not just 'illusions
on our fancy', since they feature in an objective and independent
sensory order sustained by God's volitional policies. They are, as it

were, *subjective* in their existence, but *objective* in their organization. And it is the presence of this organization, divinely imposed, which allows us to speak of a physical world.

Taken to their logical conclusion, these points would yield a form of reductive phenomenalism, in which the physical world is excluded from the ultimate reality, but admitted as something whose existence is logically sustained by God's volitional strategy. In effect, a certain kind of physical world is held to be *non*-ultimately realized in virtue of the fact that our experiences are organized as if it were *ultimately* realized. This, of course, as well as according the physical world the requisite objectivity, unity, and publicity, allows for the existence of unperceived physical objects and of perceived physical objects with unperceived aspects. And, in the sorts of case which Berkeley considers, the organizational factors on which the existence of these unperceived items depends involve (though they are not exhausted by) our potential to have the appropriately perceptive experiences in suitable circumstances.

Berkeley himself, it must be admitted, does not seem to think of his position as fully reductive in this way. Indeed, in sections 29–36, he seems to think that our sensory ideas are, quite literally, elements of the physical world, although it is their organization which makes them that, by determining their spatio-temporal arrangement. In effect, this would involve giving a reductive account of physical *facts*, while retaining certain physical *entities* in the ultimate ontology. Of course, the account would have to be ontologically reductive with respect to *unperceived* objects. And this should have led Berkeley to adopt the reductive account quite generally. For it would be absurd to suppose that the physical desk (or its perceptible surface) is constantly varying in its ontological status according to whether it is currently perceived. Clearly, whether he realizes it or not, Berkeley's phenomenalistic approach commits him to adopting the fully reductive position, which excludes both physical facts and physical entities from the ultimate reality and takes them to be the logical product of the organization of human experience. And, for the purposes of our discussion, we may take this to be, in the *Principles*, Berkeley's true position.

Although this position is incompatible with the Simple View, it comes closer than the *Dialogues* theory to that version of the view which Berkeley initially favoured. For by making the existence of the physical world depend solely on God's organization of human experience, it comes closer to the claim that physical objects are things which we directly perceive. Strictly speaking, of course, this claim is rejected, since the immediate objects of perception are ideas and ideas are not to be taken as literal constituents of the physical world. But since the physical world is nothing over and above the organization of our experience and since this organization is reflected in the sensory order whose elements we directly detect, there is a sense in which the position preserves the spirit of the claim. Certainly it does so when contrasted with representative theories of perception, like that of Locke and like that of Berkeley himself in the subsequent *Dialogues*.

In preserving the spirit of this claim, it also, of course, avoids those problems for the *Dialogues* theory which we discussed in the previous section. Where the phenomenalist account itself seems vulnerable is in coming perilously close to physical nihilism. For there seems to be only a fine dividing line between saying that there is a physical world, but one which is wholly created by the organization of human experience, and saying that there is no physical world, but our experiences are organized as if there were. Indeed, on the face of it, the first formulation seems to be only a euphemism for the second. Berkeley might reply that what substantiates the claim that there really is a physical world is that the sensory organization is imposed by God with the intention of creating a world-for-us. But, in this respect, there seems to be only a difference in name and motivation between Berkeley's benevolent God and Descartes's malevolent demon. Why should we say that, by imposing the organization, God succeeds in creating a physical world rather than that he creates the illusion of such a world? Looked at objectively, is not the latter the more natural conclusion?

Modern phenomenalists have sometimes tried to avoid this problem by claiming that statements about the physical world can be analysed into statements about sense-experience, so that the existence of a certain kind of physical world can be logically deduced from a description of an appropriate sensory organization. It would then be incoherent to say that there is no physical world, but our experiences are organized as if there were, since in conceding the sensory facts, one would be implicitly acknowledging the physical facts as well. However, though Berkeley himself shows some leanings towards it (e.g. in the passage from section 3 quoted above), this analytical version of phenomenalism is clearly untenable. Even if the existence of the physical world is wholly sustained by the sensory organization, there is no denying that our physical language, with its distinctive ontological perspective, enjoys a certain conceptual autonomy—an autonomy which prevents any replacement of physical statements by sensory statements without some radical change in meaning. Maybe the ultimate reality is as Berkeley describes it. But the commitment of physical statements to an external and mind-independent world cannot be simply eliminated by semantic analysis. The suspicion remains, then, that, in denying the ultimacy of the physical world, Berkeley has, in effect, denied its existence altogether.

I think that Berkeley's best response to this problem would be to appeal to the distinction, which I have drawn in another context,[16] between *prospective* and *retrospective* sustainment. If *A* is a set of facts and *B* some fact which *A* logically sustains, the sustainment is said to be *pro*spective if and only if someone who knew *A* could, on that basis alone, establish its sustainment of *B*; and the sustainment is said to be *retro*spective if and only if it could only be established by someone who, in addition to knowing *A*, had independent knowledge of *B*. The relevance of this distinction to the present issue is that while the conceptual autonomy of the physical language undermines the claim that the existence of the physical world is prospectively sustained by the sensory organization, it does not undermine the claim of retrospective sustainment. It excludes the possibility of establishing the existence of a physical world on the sole basis of the sensory organization. But it leaves open the possibility of arguing that, given the existence of the physical world, it is by this organization that its existence is ultimately sustained.

We can illustrate this point by developing an analogy within the framework of physical realism. Let us suppose, from this realist standpoint, that science has shown the physical world to be ultimately composed of just space and time (or space-time), a stock of minute, insensible particles (characterized, say, as point-sources of causal influence), and certain laws controlling the spatio-temporal arrangement of these particles. It has also shown, let us suppose, that there are certain psychophysical laws, assigning experiential effects to certain 'neural' configurations of particles, and that these laws, together with the physical laws and facts about particle-arrangement, account for the sensible appearance of things to us. The question now arises as to what status we should accord to the sensible world of

[16] In *The Case for Idealism*, ch. 14.

ordinary perception (the world of extended, coloured, and tangible objects) in the light of these scientific findings. Clearly, if we distance ourselves from the perspective of ordinary perception and just focus on the physical world and psychophysical laws as science specifies them, we cannot legitimately infer the existence of a sensible world of the kind we ordinarily accept. All we can infer is that the subjects whose experiences are controlled by the physical processes and psychophysical laws would find it useful and natural to think of themselves as the inhabitants of such a world. On the other hand (though leaving aside any independent sceptical arguments), it seems possible to start from the epistemological perspective of our ordinary beliefs and consider how the sensible world, whose existence we are now taking for granted, is metaphysically related to the underlying world which science reveals. And, proceeding in this fashion, the legitimate conclusion is that the existence of the sensible world is wholly sustained by the scientific world and the psychophysical laws. It might be objected that the scientific findings, if correct, would show the ordinary perspective to be illusory, so that our ordinary beliefs and the scientific account cannot be coherently combined. But this, I think, is not so. The scientific findings on their own fail to validate the ordinary perspective. But this does not mean that someone who enjoys the perspective has to repudiate it before he can accept the findings. Nor does there seem to be anything else which obliges him to do this. Indeed, if there were, the supposed findings would themselves be discredited. For, since we cannot adopt a God's eye view, it is only by theorizing with respect to the evidence available in this perspective that we can acquire knowledge of the scientific facts.

In an analogous way (though the analogy is not perfect) there are two distinct perspectives in which we can evaluate the claim that the sensory organization sustains the existence of a physical world. If we just consider in the abstract an ultimate reality composed of only God and a group of finite minds whose experiences he controls in the appropriate (world-suggestive) way, we can find no basis for accepting the existence of a physical world. At most, we are entitled to conclude that the postulation of such a world would, from both a descriptive and an explanatory standpoint, be useful and natural for the minds whose sensory organization we are contemplating. But this does not prevent us starting from the assumption that there is a physical world and then employing anti-realist arguments to establish its phenomenalistic status—so that the sensory organization is then viewed as the reality which underlies and wholly sustains this physical world, whose existence is taken to be independently secure. And if we can find such arguments and if, apart from these arguments, our acceptance of the physical world is well-founded, then this seems to be the correct procedure. The only objection might be that, since it is an essential part of our conception of a physical world that it be something external to, and logically independent of, human minds, the phenomenalist view is already excluded by the ontological perspective of our physical beliefs. But this can be met, I think, by distinguishing the two theoretical frameworks in which the question of the world's externality can be raised. Within the framework of the *physical* theory it is a conceptual truth that the world is external to human consciousness and (apart from its sensible appearance) independent of how human experience is organized. It is this, indeed, which gives the physical language its conceptual autonomy and prevents its analysis in sensory terms. But within the framework of the *philosophical* theory, which is concerned with the metaphysical status of the external world which the physical theory describes, it is a conceptual truth that the existence of this world is ultimately sustained by the sensory organization. I can see no incoherence here.[17]

Of course, if Berkeley were to follow the line I am suggesting, he could not employ his phenomenalism as a way of defeating a radical scepticism about the physical world—a scepticism which called all our physical beliefs in question and demanded their justification in terms of something else. For if the phenomenalistic sustainment is only retrospective, we have to accept the existence of the physical world before we can establish the sustainment. As it turns out, however, Berkeley would not be sacrificing anything here. For since we need to rely on our physical knowledge to obtain most of our information about the sensory organization (this is obvious in the case of our information about other minds, but also holds, to a large extent, in the case of a subject's information about himself[18]), phenomenalism (even with prospective sustainment) would not defeat the sceptic anyway. Whether anything would defeat him is a further question and one which I shall not pursue here.

No doubt it was because Berkeley *thought* his phenomenalist account was in danger of collapsing into nihilism that he came later to

---

[17] See *The Case for Idealism*, ch. 15.
[18] See *The Case for Idealism*, p. 228.

adopt his realist position. It must be stressed, however, that his revised account does not repudiate phenomenalism entirely. For although the physical world gets identified with a complex idea in God's mind, this idea only achieves its physical status by serving as the blueprint for God's volitional procedures. This is why, in discussing the Mosaic account of creation, Berkeley speaks of a 'two-fold state of things', the one 'archetypal and eternal' (the world as it exists in God's mind) and the other 'ectypal or natural' (the world as God volitionally creates it for us).[19] Berkeley is not here acknowledging two physical worlds, one to be construed realistically and the other to be construed reductively. But he is acknowledging that the thing which exists eternally in God's mind only qualifies as *our world*, and thereby as a *physical* world, because God empirically manifests it to us through the organization of experience. To this extent, even his revised account remains phenomenalistic. Perhaps this goes some way towards explaining how, at the end of the *Dialogues*, he manages to misinterpret his own position, in supposing that, despite its location in God's mind, our perceptual access to the physical world is still direct.

[19] *Dialogues*, 250–6.

CHAPTER 6

IDEALISM: KANT AND BERKELEY

R. C. S. WALKER

KANT has often been compared to Berkeley.[1] His description of his own position as a kind of idealism inevitably suggests that he had much in common with Berkeley, but he repudiates this very firmly, and dismisses Berkeley as 'degrading bodies to mere illusion' (B 71).[2] Many writers on Kant have held that this dismissal shows how little he understood what Berkeley was saying; had he done so, in their view, he would have seen how similar Berkeley's idealism was to his own. But others, especially in recent years, have argued that he understood Berkeley quite well, and had an effective argument against him. If so, the argument is obscurely stated, and requires reconstruction.

The matter is worth examination, because it is not immediately clear exactly what either kind of idealism involves; by seeing how they relate to one another one can come to understand each of them better. In particular one can find in Kant's approach certain outstanding strengths, and also a fatal weakness. For Kant does have a point to make against Berkeley. But it is a point he cannot press home without destroying his own system entirely.

On the whole, I shall argue, Kant understood Berkeley's theory correctly, and did not misrepresent it (as has been suggested[3]) in order

---

[1] The discussion there has been in recent years starts from C. M. Turbayne, 'Kant's Refutation of Dogmatic Idealism', *Philosophical Quarterly* 1955 (reprinted as 'Kant's Relation to Berkeley' in L. W. Beck, ed., *Kant Studies Today*, La Salle, Open Court, 1969). Turbayne considers Kant to have been arguing in bad faith against Berkeley, since his own position is so similar. The articles I have found most useful are H. E. Allison, 'Kant's Critique of Berkeley', *Journal of the History of Philosophy* 1973; G. J. Matthey, 'Kant's Conception of Berkeley's Idealism', *Kant-Studien* 1983; and G. D. Justin, 'Re-relating Kant and Berkeley', *Kant-Studien* 1977. My debt to these, and particularly to the last, will be clear from what follows. I am also indebted to Lesley Brown, Hugh Rice, John Kenyon, and the editors of this volume for valuable comments in discussion.

[2] References to the *Critique of Pure Reason* are given in the text in the customary fashion, 'A' referring to the first edition and 'B' to the second.

[3] Notably by C. M. Turbayne, op. cit. note 1 above.

to exaggerate its differences from his own. But we must notice at the outset that his first attempt to distinguish the two views does entirely mislocate the issue. This comes towards the end of the third note to section 13 of the *Prolegomena*, where he says that Berkeley's 'mystical and visionary' idealism is an idealism concerning the existence of things, whereas his own transcendental idealism is not. By 'things' here he means things in themselves, for he goes on to say that on his own view space, time, and appearances (*Erscheinungen*) in general are not 'things', but only 'the sensible representations of things'. So (Kant is claiming) Berkeley denies the existence of things in themselves, while he himself affirms it; and therein lies the difference.

This cannot be right (as has often been observed). If Berkeley had claimed there was nothing in the world but ideas Kant might reasonably have described him as denying things in themselves, but he is very far from claiming that: he is confident of the reality of a multitude of finite active spirits, and also of God, who causes our perceptions. Where he differs from Kant is not in denying a reality independent of and prior to the phenomenal world that we construct, but in asserting that we can know what that reality is like. Kant thinks it unknowable, because beyond the limits of possible experience. Berkeley, on the other hand, thinks that it consists of spirits, and that these spirits can be known by us: not, certainly, by way of ideas (for there can be no idea of an active thing), but by way of the notions we have of them. In *De Motu* and *Siris*, where his views on notions are most fully worked out, it appears that our knowledge of spirits and particularly of God is a kind of intuitive apprehension that cannot properly be called empirical.

But although here Kant mislocates the contrast between himself and Berkeley, he does better when he returns to the subject in the Appendix to the *Prolegomena*, which he wrote in reply to Garve's review of the *Critique*. What he says there is more complex. It is that Berkeley 'regarded space as a mere empirical representation', whereas both space and time are actually a priori forms of intuition; and that in consequence of this 'experience with Berkeley can have no criteria of truth', while on Kant's own view space and time 'prescribe their law a priori to all possible experience', which makes it possible to distinguish, within experience, truth from illusion.[4] There are thus

---

[4] *Prolegomena*, in the edition of *Kant's gesammelte Schriften* by the Preussische Akademie der Wissenschaften (Berlin, 1902– ; henceforth abbreviated 'Ak'.), iv. 374 f.; in the translation by P. G. Lucas (Manchester University Press, 1953), pp. 145 f.

two points here, one about the empirical character of space and the other about the criteria of truth, and the second is supposed to follow from the first.

Space for Berkeley is certainly an 'empirical representation', in the sense that we learn about space as we learn about colours, by observing features of our ideas and their relations. (The same applies to time, though since he does not mention time in the works Kant is likely to have read Kant was not aware of this.[5]) For Kant it is in this fashion that we learn how particular things and events are spatially and temporally related, but space and time themselves are imposed by the mind upon its experiences and not learnt about empirically. The contrast sounds clear enough. But it is not quite so clear what it comes to. Berkeley would no doubt agree with Kant that our ideas of spatial relationships depend in part on the nature of our own minds, as indeed he would hold also in the case of our ideas of colour. These ideas of ours may be caused in us by God, but they cannot altogether resemble their archetypes in the divine intellect, since in God 'there is no sense nor sensory'.[6] There must therefore be something in them which is due to our natures and the character of our senses. Berkeley does not speak of this something as a priori, or describe space as an a priori form of intuition, but could he not have done so if he had sought to express himself in Kantian terminology?

The answer is that he could not properly have done so, because Kant does not really regard the fact that space is in some sense contributed to experience by our minds as sufficient to make it a priori—although he does not always make this clear. The difference between Kant and Berkeley at this point is not so much over what the mind can be said to contribute, as over what the consequences are of its being thus involved in determining the character of experience. Kant's contention is that *because* space (and time) are contributed by us, 'space (and likewise time . . .) with all its determinations can be known by us a priori'.[7] It is this alleged consequence that is quite foreign to Berkeley, whatever he may think about the mind's own nature helping to determine what its sensory experience is like. This gives us a second significant difference between Kant and Berkeley.

---

[5] He says that 'Berkeley paid no attention to time' (ibid). He is likely to have read the *Dialogues, De Motu,* and *Siris*; cf. the articles by Turbayne, Allison, and Matthey referred to in note 1 above.

[6] *Siris*, 289; cf. *Dialogues*, 241.

[7] *Prolegomena*, loc. cit. note 4 above.

Kant thinks that synthetic a priori knowledge about space (and time) is possible, and Berkeley does not.

Kant goes on to say that it is because Berkeley does not that he is unable to distinguish empirical reality from illusion. The accusation that Berkeley is unable to distinguish reality from illusion has been made often enough, and Berkeley himself attempts a reply to it. Kant considers this reply to be ineffective, and for a fundamental reason: his failure to admit the Kantian synthetic a priori. 'For us space and time (in conjunction with the pure concepts of the understanding) prescribe their law a priori to all possible experience, and this yields at the same time the sure criterion for distinguishing truth in it from illusion.'[8]

What Berkeley does is to draw the distinction in two different, but complementary, ways. One appeals to an empirically discernible difference between veridical and non-veridical ideas. Veridical ideas are 'vivid and clear', and 'have not a like dependence on our will' with non-veridical ones.[9] Moreover (and perhaps more importantly) they are 'connected, and of a piece with the preceding and subsequent transactions of our lives'; when one mistakes an illusion for reality, one's mistake lies in inferring from the present perception that a certain pattern of others may be expected in future, or would be experienced under other conditions.[10] Veridical ideas, in other words, are ideas that belong to collections of an appropriately coherent sort, and such collections are what we commonly call objects. 'A *cherry*, I say, is nothing but a congeries of sensible impressions, or ideas perceived by various senses: which ideas are united into one thing (or have one name given them) by the mind; because they are observed to attend each other.'[11]

The other way of drawing the distinction draws it non-empirically, by reference to God. God is aware of all that there is, and he is the cause of our perceptions; veridical ideas are those that God produces in us to correspond to the appropriate archetypes in the divine intellect. 'The ideas imprinted on the senses by the Author of Nature are called *real things*.'[12] For Berkeley these two ways of seeing the matter go together naturally, since the 'steadiness, order, and

---

[8] Ibid.
[9] *Dialogues*, 235; cf. *Principles*, 29 ff.
[10] *Dialogues*, 235 and 238.
[11] *Dialogues*, 249.
[12] *Principles*, 33.

coherence' of our veridical ideas reflects and testifies to 'the wisdom and benevolence of its Author'.[13]

Kant has objections to both ways of drawing the distinction. His objection to the second we have already met: it takes us beyond the limits of possible experience, and therefore beyond the limits of possible knowledge. Neither God, nor the archetypes in the divine intellect, can be discovered by empirical means; in his later works Berkeley claims we can know them by some sort of intellectual apprehension,[14] but this is not a legitimate kind of knowing for Kant. In his preliminary notes for the *Prolegomena* he explicitly objects to Berkeley on this ground: 'Berkeley found nothing permanent, nor could he find anything that the understanding grasped in accordance with a priori principles; therefore he had to look for another [kind of] intuition, namely the mystical intuition of the divine ideas.'[15]

His objection to Berkeley's first way of distinguishing between veridical and non-veridical ideas is quite general, and does not depend on the particular suggestions that Berkeley makes, for it is an objection against any way of founding the distinction on straightforwardly empirical considerations—i.e. without the assistance of synthetic a priori principles. 'As truth rests on universal and necessary laws as its criteria, experience with Berkeley can have no criteria of truth because nothing was laid (by him) a priori at the ground of appearances in it, from which it then followed that it is nothing but illusion.'[16] But why does Kant think that something must be 'laid a priori at the ground of appearances' in order for the distinction to be possible?

Berkeley actually cites two different sorts of empirical test for determining whether ideas are veridical. On the one hand there is the comparison in terms of the internal qualities of the ideas themselves: how vivid they are, or how clear. On the other hand there is a more complex kind of comparison, that depends upon some form of inference (commonly inductive) that takes us beyond the internal qualities of the ideas presently before us. If someone is to make a judgement 'concerning the ideas that, from what he perceives at present, he imagines would be perceived in other circumstances',[17] he is making such an inference. So is he if he claims that certain of his

[13] *Principles*, 30.
[14] Particularly in *Siris*, 264, 294–5, 337, etc.; but also in *De Motu*, e.g. 71–2.
[15] Ak. xxiii. 58.
[16] *Prolegomena*, Ak. iv. 375, Lucas p. 146.
[17] *Dialogues*, 238.

present ideas belong to a pattern which has 'a steadiness, order, and coherence', and that they 'are not excited at random, as those which are the effects of human wills often are, but in a regular train or series'.[18] Kant's objection to Berkeley is that it is only those criteria which depend upon inference that are worth taking seriously, and that the principles of inference on which they rest must necessarily be synthetic and a priori—and hence not properly available to an empiricist like Berkeley. Or at least this is the first instalment of his objection.

He is right to claim that it is only the criteria which depend upon inference that are worth taking seriously. Vividness, clarity, and the like may serve us (in the right conditions) as evidence that our perceptions are veridical, but it cannot be in qualities such as these that their veridicality *consists*. More generally, no plausible analysis of the concept of objective reality could lead to the conclusion that this reality *consisted* in nothing more than some inspectable feature of particular perceptions, taken in isolation from their relationship to other perceptions at other times or circumstances. For whatever else the concept of objective reality involves, it must at least require that the existence of what is objectively real should not wholly depend on my present perception.

Is Kant then right to say that the inference beyond one's immediately present ideas must rely upon synthetic a priori principles? This again seems to be correct, though no doubt its correctness was less evident before Hume. If the inference is to be justifiable, it must be justifiable by reference to principles of inference, the validity of which cannot be simply given in present experience; and if they are to be more than just logical principles they must be (by definition) synthetic. No principle could ever be justified solely by appeal to the content of one's present experience, for a principle is in its nature general and one's present experience is ineluctably particular. Nor could the content of one's present experience, together with purely logical principles, warrant any conclusions about experiences at other times, or by other persons, or indeed any inferences beyond itself. It is true, of course, that an experience can be correctly described in such terms as 'the most memorable experience I had the day before I saw the great fire', and that from my having this experience, so described, it follows by logic alone that I saw the fire on the following day; but that is because this description does not give

[18] *Principles*, 30.

the content of the experience. Ascriptions of content are always intentional. It may no doubt be part of the content of an experience that the subject believes himself justified in inferring that he will see a fire tomorrow, or that God exists, and feels much confidence about these things; but such beliefs and such feelings are intentional states, and nothing about tomorrow's experiences or about God's existence is entailed by the subject's being in these states now. This, indeed, is why one's present experience is ineluctably particular. Even if the experience involves the belief that one intuits the truth of some universal proposition, the experience itself is a particular event, and its occurrence constitutes no justification for the universal proposition (save with the aid of some extra principle to the effect that such intuitions are warranted).

Thus if Berkeley is to give an account of reality which requires that certain inferences from one's present ideas to other (actual or possible) ideas be justifiable, these inferences must rest on principles which are non-logical and non-empirical; in Kantian terms, synthetic and a priori. He could avoid relying on such principles only by making a very radical move. This would be to claim that although our distinction between veridical and non-veridical ideas depends upon inferences these inferences are not justifiable: nothing more can be said about them than that we make them. All idea of justification would be abandoned, at least in this context, and we should be left— as Hume suggests and Quine at times proposes—with only the descriptive task of saying how human minds react and what inferences they tend to draw under what conditions.[19] One could observe that under such-and-such circumstances people do infer that their perceptions have the coherence, or connectedness, or whatever, that is considered appropriate for objectivity, and that under such-and-such others they do not; one would no longer seek to claim that they were ever justified in this, or even in the most elementary of inductive inferences.

If Berkeley had taken this line, as of course he never did, there can be no doubt that Kant would have regarded him as playing into his hands. He accused Berkeley of failing to provide criteria of truth: on the present suggestion there are no criteria of truth to provide. No criteria, that is, in the sense of means whereby we may justifiably determine how things are in the objective world. The present

---

[19] Quine, 'Epistemology Naturalized', in his *Ontological Relativity and Other Essays* (Columbia University Press, New York and London, 1969).

suggestion does not deny that there is an objective world, and that the things we say about it may be true, but it does deny that there is any way to justify our claims about it. In Kantian terms, this is to deny the possibility of knowledge about it, since for Kant one cannot be said to know in matters where justification is lacking. The objective world becomes as unknowable as the Kantian world of things in themselves, concerning which Kant himself thinks that people have certain natural beliefs, but which he thinks remains unknowable none the less, because there is no way in which these beliefs could be justified. Indeed, it can be equated with that world; which is tantamount to saying that empirical knowledge as Kant understands it, the empirical knowledge of an objective world, is on this view impossible.

To say this is not to reject the suggestion of Hume and Quine; it is only to say why Kant rejected it. It cannot be dismissed out of hand, and it properly requires an extended discussion. Such a discussion, however, would divert us from our present purpose, and would be more appropriate in an examination of Kant's relationship with Hume than in a comparison of his position with Berkeley's. It may be observed in any case that it is a counsel of despair. We normally seek to justify our inferences and the knowledge claims that depend upon them, and to distinguish those that can be justified from others that are foolish, irrational, the products of confusion or unthinking prejudice. If the suggested approach is correct this distinction is ill-founded, and the views we call rational are only those that accord with the habits of thought of a certain section of the population. This is a conclusion to which one might eventually be driven, but not one to be embraced while there is still a hope of making headway with epistemology as it has traditionally been conceived.

Berkeley, at any rate, has no wish to embrace it, and is therefore bound to rely upon principles of inference that Kant would call synthetic and a priori. He prefers, certainly, to make as modest a use of such principles as he can. The criterion he offers in terms of coherence or connectedness seems designed to make use of little more than induction: the expectation that a certain pattern of ideas will be continued, or 'would be perceived in other circumstances'[20] or by other spirits, being an inductive one. But the principle of induction is still a principle of inference, and one that (notoriously) lacks empirical justification; it therefore lacks any justification that is available to Berkeley, and hence (Kant concludes) Berkeley can be

[20] *Dialogues*, 238.

not unreasonably described as committed to the view that the objects of experience are 'nothing but illusion'.

There is some temptation to feel that this criticism is unfair, because empiricists should at least be allowed induction. Empiricists commonly do rely on inductive inference, and this creates the impression that they have a right to. Kant's point—or the first part of it—is that all such principles require defence, since their validity is not given to us in experience itself; this is one of the major messages of the *Critique*. He himself can provide such a defence, though it is one which places the principle of induction alongside a number of other synthetic a priori principles which are equally important and equally justifiable. And the second part of his point is that some of these other principles, left aside by Berkeley (as by other like-minded empiricists), are just as important as induction in distinguishing reality from illusion.

According to Kant synthetic a priori principles may be justified, despite their non-empirical character, if they can be justified 'transcendentally'. They can be justified transcendentally if it can be shown that they are required for the possibility of experience itself, or at any rate of experience of such a kind as ours is.[21] But it is important to notice that Kant recognizes two different ways in which a principle may be required for experience to be possible, and that he therefore admits two different kinds of transcendental justification, or (as he calls it) transcendental deduction.

In the first place, it may be a condition of the possibility of experience that the principle in question should actually be *true* (of the world as we know it, the world of appearances). The principles that have this status are those Kant calls the principles of pure understanding, like 'Every event has a cause', together with such subordinate truths as can be derived from them. It is on these that Kant concentrates in the first half of the *Critique*. Such principles are said to be constitutive of experience, because it is them that the mind uses in constructing the phenomenal world: they are guaranteed to be true of the phenomenal world just because that world has been constructed in that way.[22]

[21] A 92 ff./B 124 ff.; A 154 ff./B 193 ff.; and see further my *Kant* (Routledge and Kegan Paul, London, 1978), ch. 2.

[22] 'Phenomenal world' and 'world of appearances' I take to be equivalent; 'phenomenal' is not, of course, meant to suggest that any kind of phenomenalistic analysis is appropriate. Similarly I take 'noumenon' to be synonymous with 'thing in itself'.

The principle of induction is not amongst them. Unlike the principles of pure understanding, the principle of induction (in any plausible version) gives us no *assurance* that experience, or the world experienced, will take such-and-such a form. The principle of induction does not (in any plausible version) deny it is possible that the course of nature will change quite arbitrarily tomorrow; it says only that this is an *unreasonable* thing to expect. Roughly, it says something like this: 'Given a long run of A's that have been B's, and given that we have no other relevant information as to whether the next A will be a B or not, it is reasonable to expect that it will be.' A priori principles of this kind Kant calls regulative, rather than constitutive. We do not ensure their truth by reading them into the world of appearances, but we must nevertheless rely on them in the attempt to understand the world about us, for they provide us with a way of unifying things comprehensibly, and without that we should get nowhere. Kant argues that there is no alternative to seeking such comprehensible unity if we are to attain an understanding of things, and maintains also that the nature of reason—a faculty essential for any experience—leaves us no alternative to the search for as complete an understanding as possible. In this way he claims to provide a transcendental justification for the regulative principles as well; or in his own terminology, a transcendental deduction of the ideas of pure reason (A 669 ff./B 697 ff.).

Berkeley differs from Kant not only in having no way of justifying the synthetic a priori principles on which he needs to rely, but also in making no use of constitutive principles; only of regulative ones, and indeed rather few of those. Besides induction he makes use of a principle licensing inference to the simplest explanation, but that is also regulative, since it says that such inference is reasonable but not that it necessarily yields the truth. Because of this his attempted account of reality is a great deal simpler than Kant's, and a great deal too simple in Kant's opinion to be at all satisfactory. Just as Hume's empiricist account of causality was bound to fail because the concept of causality is a constitutive a priori concept, so on Kant's view Berkeley's account of empirical reality is bound to fail as well because it leaves out the constitutive a priori elements that are essential to the distinction between that reality and mere illusion.

Berkeley frequently says that an object *is* an idea. His position can be better expressed by saying that what we normally call an object is a collection of ideas, a collection which will typically include ideas in various finite minds and ideas in the mind of God.²³ (At one stage in his career he certainly thought it should include potential and non-actual ideas as well: whether this reflects his mature position is a matter for dispute.²⁴) Membership in such a collection is determined by the criteria which distinguish veridical from illusory ideas: an idea of mine belongs to such a collection just in case it has the appropriate kind of coherence or connectedness with other ideas, and is produced in me by God to correspond to an archetype in the divine intellect. The coherence or connectedness in question can obtain without my being aware of it, but I can find out about it by relying on induction.

Kant's account is so totally different that it is very strange he has sometimes been said to be a phenomenalist along very much the lines just sketched—or at any rate to favour a phenomenalist account of the world of appearances. One way to show that this ascription is ill-founded is to go over the text, looking on the one hand at those passages which most seem to support a phenomenalistic view, and on the other at those which seem to offer an alternative. As this has been done elsewhere by various people, including myself,²⁵ I shall only observe here that those passages in which he speaks of objects as 'representations' or as 'totalities of representations' establish very little because the words are so vague, 'representation' (*Vorstellung*) in particular having all the unclarities and ambiguities of Locke's 'idea'. Moreover the references to the transcendental object in the first-edition Deduction suggest (if not perhaps in the perfect context) a much more sophisticated alternative view, whereby the non-empirical notion of an object serves as a kind of focus for uniting together the perceptions that Berkeley just concatenates.

Whether or not what is said in these passages reflects the detail of Kant's final view of the matter it does bring out the crucial element of difference. Details of text apart, Kant's whole theory of space, time, the categories, and their role in the construction of experience precludes him from giving a phenomenalistic account of objects in the way Berkeley or J. S. Mill did. In supplying the categories, as schematized in space and time, the mind supplies to its experience certain a priori concepts, like the concept of cause, in such a way as to

²³ He sometimes expresses it in this way himself, e.g. in the passage about the cherry quoted above from the *Dialogues*, 249.

²⁴ On this see G. Pitcher, *Berkeley* (Routledge and Kegan Paul, London, 1977), ch. 10.

²⁵ Cf. G. Bird, *Kant's Theory of Knowledge* (Routledge and Kegan Paul, London, 1962), ch. 1; and my *Kant*, ch. 8.

make true corresponding principles of an equally a priori character about the way in which those concepts are instantiated—principles like 'Every event has a cause'. These principles are constitutive of experience: we are assured (by transcendental arguments) not just that they are sensible to adopt in practice but that they are actually true of the world of appearances, true because our minds so construct that world that these principles are built into it and constitute its structure. The a priori concepts must include the concept of an object: necessarily so, because objects, no less than causes, are among the structural features of the phenomenal world. The corresponding principle is the principle 'That there exist objects in space outside me' (cf. B 275); and although the narrowness of Kant's architectonic prevents him from listing it in its proper place alongside the other principles of pure understanding, there is no room to doubt that it is as much a constitutive synthetic a priori principle as they are. The concept of an object does not appear on Kant's list of categories, but the concept of substance does, and a substance is a sort of super-object: ordinary objects exist independently of people's perceptions, but because substances are permanent they exist independently of all alterations there may be. The concept of an object is presumably to be derived from that of substance, in Kant's view. Such derived a priori concepts he calls predicables.[26]

Thus according to Kant the synthesis involved in putting together various of my perceptions as perceptions of a single object involves an a priori concept, the concept of an object. It is not simply a matter of collecting perceptions together into a set, as it was for Berkeley. Just as the concept of a cause is not to be analysed (or analysed away) along Humean lines, so the concept of an object is not simply the concept of a collection of perceptions; there would be nothing a priori about that over and above the (logical) notion of a set. Like Berkeley, Kant requires induction in order to decide in the *particular* case which perceptions go with which and what object, if any, they represent; presumably nearly everyone will agree with Berkeley that we *discover* which of our perceptions represent objective reality by seeing which of them will satisfy the appropriate inductive tests. (If, for instance, my present perception of a cup is veridical, induction leads me to expect like perceptions in other observers, at other angles, and at other times; the failure of these expectations is a reason for thinking there is no cup there.) Where Kant and Berkeley differ is over what

[26] A 81 f./B 107 f. On this see further my *Kant*, pp. 107–8.

the concept of an object involves. For Kant it is an a priori concept, instances of which are to be recognized empirically in the fashion just described, just as the concept of cause is an a priori concept the instances of which are to be recognized through constant conjunction. For Berkeley it is the concept of a collection of ideas, and there is nothing specifically a priori about it: Berkeley no more allows an a priori concept of an object than Hume allows an a priori concept of a cause.

There is an important sense in which Kant's world of physical objects is a construction and Berkeley's not. Berkeley's objects are nothing over and above ideas;[27] by introducing talk of objects we introduce a new and compendious way of talking about ideas, and that is all. For Kant objects are something additional, entities of a different kind from perceptions or collections of perceptions, whether the perceptions be actual or possible, human or of some other variety. And that additional something is genuinely there in the world of appearances, there because it has been put there by our minds in constructing that world. *How* our minds achieve such a feat is no doubt a problematic matter, and Kant's position is not without its difficulties here, but he clearly thinks they do achieve it.

And the distinction goes deeper. Berkeley's ideas are simply given: it is a fact that we have the ideas we do, though no doubt it is a fact which is partly determined by the nature of human sensibility. Kant on the other hand regards even the most elementary sense-data as constructions that our minds effect in accordance with space, time, and the categories.[28] Since the constructing is not undertaken voluntarily the question arose earlier—in connection with space— whether this amounts to more than a picturesque way of putting the Berkeleian point that the character of our ideas is in part a function of our human sensibility, but the answer was that it does, because it renders possible a priori knowledge about the world through our knowledge of what features our minds must contribute. Our minds so determine the material given in intuition as to make certain a priori concepts to apply, and certain a priori truths to hold, in the world as we experience it: in other words they create a coherent picture of the way the world is, a picture which we can treat (except for metaphysical purposes) not as a mere picture but as *constituting* the

---

[27] Realism about sets would be deeply foreign to him, of course.

[28] Otherwise there would be no place for a synthesis of apprehension. A 98 ff.; B 129 ff.; B 160 f.

objective reality we are concerned with every day. We can treat it in this way because the transcendental arguments which establish what our minds must contribute assure us that we must all construct similar pictures of the world, and must continue to do so as long as we have experience.

Kant's criticism of Berkeley in the Appendix to the *Prolegomena* was that he could not distinguish reality from illusion because he did not see that space (and time) were a priori respresentations and thus laid 'nothing . . . a priori at the ground of appearances'. It is slightly misleading of Kant to single out space and time in this way, for it is the categories quite as much as the forms of intuition which in his own system provide the necessary grounding, and yield the criterion of reality. He does so because he regards the a priori status of space and time as being particularly fundamental: it is *because* space and time are a priori that the categories can be applied a priori to intuition, and that experience can be constructed in accordance with the principles of pure understanding. 'For thus I can understand how I can judge a priori and with apodeictic certainty about objects of the senses.'[29]

In fact he has another reason as well for emphasizing that their difference over the status of space is central to the disagreement between Berkeley and himself. This is brought out in what he says about Berkeley at the start of the Refutation of Idealism, in the second edition of the *Critique*. His remarks here are very brief and have sometimes been found puzzling, but they fit in neatly with what has been said above. Berkeley is called a dogmatic idealist, who 'maintains that space, with all the things of which it is the inseparable condition, is something which is in itself (*an sich selbst*) impossible', and who 'therefore regards the things in space as merely imaginary entities' (B 274). Kant goes on to assert that 'Dogmatic idealism is unavoidable, if space be interpreted as a property that must belong to things in themselves. For in that case space, and everything to which it serves as condition, is a non-entity. The ground on which this idealism rests has already been undermined by us in the Transcendental Aesthetic' (ibid.). It needs, he clearly thinks, no further refutation, and the rest of what he says is devoted to the quite different 'problematic idealism' which holds the existence of objects in space to be doubtful but not impossible (and which he ascribes to Descartes).

The passage indicates, not that Kant was ignorant of Berkeley's views, but that he knew them well. Berkeley leaves us in no doubt that

[29] Ak. xxiii. 58.

he takes corporeal things to be essentially extended in space, and frequently uses this in arguing for his own position. On the view which he opposes, corporeal substance is independent of anyone's perceptions, and therefore space must be independent likewise. But that is contradictory, according to Berkeley, for extendedness and spatiality are features of our ideas, and cannot therefore belong to this alleged corporeal substance; so that space, with 'everything to which it serves as condition', must be ideal. So far Kant just reflects what Berkeley says himself. What is not obvious, if one reads only the passage in the *Critique*, is why Kant should think that by making them *ideal* Berkeley makes them *non-entities*. After all, he considers them ideal himself, and quite shares Berkeley's view that space is impossible *an sich selbst*, i.e. as something wholly independent of our cognitive faculties. But the *Prolegomena* has shown us what his reasons are: Berkeley lacks the criterion of truth, of reality within the world of appearances, which Kant is able to provide. It is unfortunate, but not uncharacteristic, that he should omit to explain this here. Perhaps, as G. J. Matthey has recently suggested, he sees no particular need to spell the matter out because Berkeley himself downgrades the reality of bodies in a work Kant may have known better than most philosophers do nowadays, namely *Siris*.[30]

Despite the emphasis on space, though, the basis of Kant's objection to Berkeley is (as we might have expected) an objection to his empiricism. Berkeley has his non-empirical moods, it is true— especially in *Siris*; in these moods he casts discretion aside and talks of an intuitive apprehension of God and of the ideas in the divine intellect. This 'mystical intuition' Kant dismisses as a gratuitous claim to insight into that unknowable realm which lies beyond the limits of possible experience. But the empiricist line of thought, very much the dominant one in Berkeley's earlier writings, is incapable of sustaining any distinction between illusion and objective reality. For if objective reality is to be discoverable, principles of inference are required in order to identify it, and these principles must be a priori;

---

[30] *Siris*, 266; Matthey, 'Kant's Conception of Berkeley's Idealism'. It is surprising that some have thought Kant did not read *Siris*; his summary of Berkeleian idealism in the *Prolegomena*—'All knowledge through the senses and through experience is nothing but illusion, and only in the ideas of pure understanding and reason is truth' (Ak. iv. 374, Lucas p. 145)—fits badly with the *Principles* and *Dialogues*, but is remarkably close to *Siris* 264. Matthey also points out that in Eschenbach's 1756 translation of the *Dialogues* into German, Berkeley is rendered as denying the reality of bodies.

even if reality were to be reductively handled along phenomenalist lines, induction at least would be required to find out about it, and the principle of induction cannot be empirical. If on the other hand objective reality is *not* discoverable, it must be consigned once more to the realm of the noumenal, leaving *us* with nothing better than illusion and with no criteria of truth.

As we have seen, the principle of induction is in Kant's terminology a regulative a priori principle. He differs from Berkeley not only in insisting on its a priori status but in admitting constitutive a priori principles as well, and a priori concepts whose application in experience is assured by the fact that experience is so constructed as to guarantee it. The concept of an object, and the principle that corresponds to it, are constitutive in this way, and the concept of an object is therefore not to be analysed in any phenomenalistic fashion. Since it is the constructive aspect of Kant's transcendental idealism that many people seem to find distasteful it is natural to ask how Kant would have replied to a Berkeley who so far modified his empiricism as to accept the regulative a priori, while rejecting the constitutive.

The answer is that he would have replied in two ways. First there is the objection that such a theory is too weak to accommodate our concepts of cause, object, and the like. The principle of induction in its regulative form may tell us what it is reasonable to expect, but it does not give us the concept of causation. In the same way, the concept of an object is not to be equated with that of a set of actual and possible perceptions; and against the phenomenalist who claims that it is, Kant can employ all the standard arguments against phenomenalism. In particular he can observe that the phenomenalist's proposed analysis cannot be carried through, because the conditionals required in specifying the relevant non-actual perceptions would be bound to make use in their antecedents of the concept of an object, the very concept which is supposed to be under analysis. For the possible perceptions that are relevant are not those that just anyone might have, however insane or deluded; they are the perceptions that would be experienced in the appropriate circumstances by someone who *perceived what was there*, and was not suffering from any kind of hallucination.[31] Objections of this kind to

---

[31] To be effective this would require more elaboration, of course. Cf. R. M. Chisholm, *Perceiving* (Cornell University Press, Ithaca, 1957), Appendix, and my *Kant*, pp. 107 f.

phenomenalism do not tell against Kant's own position, because for him the concept of an object is a priori and unanalysable.

The second reply, which goes deeper, is that one is not entitled to modify one's empiricism little by little, and choose what kinds of a priori principle to accept and what kinds to reject. One is not entitled to help oneself to the a priori at all without some defence, for otherwise there would be no answering those who adopted the strangest metaphysical positions, and no resolving the antinomies to which their differences lead. Since the defence cannot be empirical, Kant considers it can only be transcendental; the alternative Cartesian strategy of accepting as true whatever one very clearly and distinctly perceives being untenable, first because people take themselves clearly and distinctly to perceive different and conflicting things, and secondly because there can be no reason (short of divine benevolence) why a great confidence in some matter—even a great confidence shared by all the species—should ensure that matter's truth, when it lies beyond anyone's experience.[32] The principle of induction, therefore, must be justified transcendentally. We saw that he thinks it can be justified in that way; along with such other regulative principles as reason requires in its search for unity and completeness in the understanding of the world around us. But he also thinks (and devotes much of the central part of the *Critique* to arguing) that a like transcendental justification can be given for constitutive a priori principles, and for the application of the categories (and therefore the predicables) to the world of appearances. Thus his objection to the modified Berkeleian position, which admits the regulative a priori but not the constitutive, is that by admitting even the regulative it must concede the legitimacy of transcendental arguments, while arguments of just the same kind compel the acceptance of the constitutive too. It has moved away from the purest empiricism by accepting a priori principles that can be transcendentally justified, but fails to recognize that constitutive as well as regulative principles can be justified in that way.

Of course, this reply of Kant's will be effective only if the transcendental arguments that he claims to work actually do. Whether they do or not, or whether others can be found which will achieve the same objectives, is a large question and well beyond the scope of the present paper; but it has often been felt that most of the

---

[32] Cf. Kant's letter to Herz of 21 February 1772 (Ak. x. 123 ff.), or B 166 ff.

arguments Kant gives are less than adequate.[33] There is a possible answer to Kant here, then, for someone seeking to defend the modified Berkeleian position. It is conceivable that a defence may be available for the regulative a priori, but none for the constitutive. Conceivable; but (it must be admitted) very far from obvious.

But there is also another line of attack, which the Berkeleian can mount against Kant even if all Kant's transcendental arguments work. It turns on the fact that the principle of induction is not the only regulative a priori principle which Kant thinks he can justify, or on which Berkeley tacitly relies. The transcendental deduction of the ideas of pure reason gives us a general warrant for adopting such principles as enable us to see the world as a systematically unified totality, not by giving us any assurance that it really is such a totality, but by making clear that they provide the only way to satisfy a demand inevitably set before us by the nature of reason. Among these principles clearly belongs the one which licenses inference from given facts to the best explanation of those facts. It is a principle that Berkeley makes use of, as also—in a way that is rather crucial to his system—does Kant himself.

It is crucial to Kant's system because upon it rests his belief in things in themselves. Without it he can establish claims only about the world of appearances, and the standard neo-Kantian criticism, that he has no right to assert the existence of the noumenal world, becomes unavoidable. It is true that his account of how the mind acts in its construction of the phenomenal world gives him an alternative argument (of the transcendental kind) to the real existence of the 'I' that thinks, not as part of the phenomenal world but as the subject of it—a point sufficiently illustrated by the untenability of Fichte's early doctrine that the knowing self posits itself as well as the world that it knows; but Kant is firm in his insistence that there must also be things in themselves lying behind the objects of knowledge, as 'the ground of the sensible world and therefore also of its laws', since 'otherwise we should be landed in the absurd conclusion that there can be appearance without anything that appears' (B xxvi).[34] This as we saw was the basis of his first objection to Berkeley in the *Prolegomena*, where he accuses him of denying things in themselves and claims never to have doubted them. But his only reason for asserting their

---

[33] A considerable range of objections have been made against them. I have put some of them forward, and considered others, in my book *Kant*.

[34] See my *Kant*, pp. 131 ff.

existence is that otherwise there could be no source for the given, outside my own mind; no explanation for the shared *content* of experience between different percipients (for though his transcendental arguments may show that their minds must *structure* experience similarly, through the same forms of intuition and the same category-governed synthesis, they do nothing to ensure a similarity of empirical content). This is his only reason—but by his own standards it is a quite good enough reason, in view of the transcendental deduction of the ideas. It is as good a reason as we ever have for any explanation of a phenomenon, for although the Second Analogy guarantees that every event has a cause Kant is very clear that it does not determine a priori what causes what; this is to be found by examining the content of experience and employing regulative principles.[35]

Berkeley also makes great use of inference to the best explanation, for he depends on it to establish the existence of God. We find that many of our ideas of sense are not under our own control; 'there is therefore some other spirit that causes them, since it is repugnant that they should subsist by themselves'; the order, beauty, and harmony that they exhibit shows that this spirit must be God.[36] Berkeley is *not* inferring to the best explanation when he says that if they are caused they must be caused by some spirit, for he thinks he has arguments which show any other alternative to be impossible. But he is making use of such a principle when he infers from the orderliness that the spirit must be God, and also when he initially rejects as 'repugnant' the suggestion that the ideas should simply exist without a cause. In fact this argument of Berkeley's is very close to Kant's argument for things in themselves. To explain the regularities and similarities we find among perceptions both of them postulate a cause which cannot be more directly known; Kant insists that no more can be said of it than that it produces these effects, Berkeley argues that it is a unique, eternal, and omnipresent spirit, namely God.

[35] Kant often connects adopting a regulative principle with proceeding *as if* something were the case; it is therefore important to notice that regulative principles do enable us to make specific claims quite categorically (e.g. the claim that *this* causes *that*). These claims are not proved conclusively, but it is reasonable to believe them true; and this is not just a matter of treating them as if they were true. Kant's point is only that to regard e.g. the inductive principle as valid is tantamount to looking on the world *as if* it were created by a God who operates systematically (A 672 ff./B 700 ff.). We do not actually have to believe in such a God, though the natural dialectic of human reason pushes us in that direction.

[36] *Principles*, 146.

Kant's objection to this further move of Berkeley's was that it goes beyond the limits of possible experience. But this is a bad objection; bad in its own right, and bad from the point of view of Kant's system. To take it seriously would be to reject his ground for believing in things in themselves, for things in themselves lie equally beyond the limits of possible experience. And his ground is a perfectly good ground, for the rationality of that belief is assured by an a priori regulative principle which we rely on all the time, and which he regards as justifiable in the same transcendental fashion as the other synthetic a priori principles on which we depend. If he had objected only that Berkeley has no right to think God must be the cause of our perceptions, because the evidence leaves other explanations equally possible, that would have been another matter and an eminently discussable issue. But he is wrong to suppose that the regulative principle which makes reasonable a belief in things in themselves cannot also justify conclusions about what things in themselves are like. One cannot rule out in advance the idea that the best explanation will assign to them one character rather than another (a point which in a way he tacitly accepts when rejecting the thought that the only thing in itself is my knowing mind).

The trouble, of course, is that Kant never appreciated that his own methods do make it possible for knowledge to outrun the limits of possible experience; and not just in one way but in two. There is no reason in principle why transcendental arguments should not reach conclusions about what the world must be like in itself, as well as conclusions about what we must build into the world of appearances. It may be possible, in other words, to find arguments to the effect that the noumenally real world must be thus and so if experience is to be possible at all.[37] (Indeed Kant himself uses such arguments, without being explicit about it, when he infers that there must be an 'I' that thinks and that it must be active in synthesis.) And there is also no reason in principle why regulative principles, themselves justifiable transcendentally, should not entitle us to put forward claims about the noumenally real world by inference from what we can observe: claims we cannot be wholly sure of, any more than we can be wholly sure of a scientific explanation or of any conclusion which rests upon ordinary induction, but claims which can be perfectly reasonable and proper none the less. A sound transcendental idealism should make

---

[37] See my *Kant*, pp. 11, 131 ff.—developing a point of Stroud's in his paper 'Transcendental Arguments', *Journal of Philosophy* lxv (1968) pp. 252 f.

no such allegations as Kant is prone to, about the impossibility of justifying assertions about things in themselves. To take the alternative line and confine even regulative principles to a use wholly within the world of appearances would be a move for which Kant has no shadow of a justification to offer; and by depriving him of his own ground for believing in things in themselves it would render him liable to the accusation he once made against Berkeley, of holding a 'visionary idealism' which denies the ultimate reality of things and thus leaves us with 'the absurd conclusion that there can be appearance without anything that appears'.

CHAPTER 7

BERKELEY AND THE ESSENCES OF THE CORPUSCULARIANS

MARGARET D. WILSON

I

IN the *Principles* and the *Dialogues* Berkeley repeatedly connects his defence of the unproblematic reality of things as we sensibly experience them with the denial that we are ignorant of 'the internal constitution, the true and real nature' of physical objects. The issue is raised insistently in the *Third Dialogue*, particularly towards the beginning. Hylas keeps asserting that the restriction of our knowledge to the sensible appearances of things means that it is not possible for us ever to know the real nature of any thing in the universe, 'what it is in itself' (*Dialogues*, 227). As he further explains to Philonous:

> You may indeed know that fire appears hot, and water fluid: but this is no more than knowing what sensations are produced in your own mind, upon the application of fire and water to your organs of sense. Their internal constitution, their true and real nature, you are utterly in the dark as to *that*.

Philonous, in return, stigmatizes these pessimistic views as 'wild and extravagant' contending that Hylas is led into them by the belief in material substance:

> This makes you dream of those unknown natures in every thing. It is this occasions your distinguishing between the reality and sensible appearances of things. It is to this you are indebted for being ignorant of what every body else knows perfectly well. (*Dialogues*, 229.)

The same point is expressed more colourfully in a later exchange;

HYLAS. . . . . you may pretend what you please; but it is certain, you leave us nothing but the empty forms of things, the outside only which strikes the senses.

PHILONOUS.What you call the empty forms and outside of things, seems to me the very things themselves. Nor are they empty or incomplete otherwise, than upon your supposition, that matter is an essential part of all corporeal things. (*Dialogues*, 244.)

In the *Principles* Berkeley explicitly describes the doctrine of hidden inner natures as a primary source of scepticism, and maintains that his philosophy removes this ground for challenging the adequacy of human knowledge. He goes so far as to indicate that his position allows us to claim 'perfect comprehension' of physical things.

. . . all that stock of arguments [the sceptics] produce to depreciate our faculties, and make mankind appear ignorant and low, are drawn principally from this head, to wit, that we are under an invincible blindness as to the *true* and *real* nature of things. . . . We are miserably bantered, say they, by our senses, and amused only with the outside and shew of things. The real essence, the internal qualities, and constitution of every the meanest object, is hid from our view; something there is in every drop of water, every grain of sand, which it is beyond the power of human understanding to fathom or comprehend. But it is evident from what has been shewn, that all this complaint is groundless, and that we are influenced by false principles to that degree as to mistrust our senses, and think we know nothing of those things which we perfectly comprehend. (*Principles*, 101.)

These passages appear to develop a theme already sounded in the *Philosophical Commentaries*: 'My Doctrine affects the Essences of the Corpuscularians.'[1]

Daniel Garber has recently focused on Berkeley's remark about hidden natures in an original and interesting paper, 'Locke, Berkeley and Corpuscular Skepticism'.[2] Garber plausibly relates Berkeley's statements to Locke's contention that the real essences of things are unknowable to us because of the limitations of our faculties.[3] As Garber notes, Locke connects his conception of inaccessible real essences with the corpuscularian theory of matter: our inability to know real essences is linked by Locke to the view that we are unable to perceive the inner corpuscular structure of things, because of the grossness of our senses.[4] (Locke acknowledges that corpuscularianism may not provide the ultimate truth about the nature of physical

---

[1] *PC*, 234.

[2] *Berkeley: Critical and Interpretive Essays*, ed. Colin Turbayne (Minneapolis, 1982), pp. 174–93.

[3] It would be incorrect, however, to suppose that Berkeley had Locke in mind exclusively. Cf. *Dialogues*, 214, where he ascribes the doctrine of unknown real natures to Malebranche.

[4] Garber, pp. 174 ff.

things; however, he evidently thinks it is the best theory we will ever have. And if real essences are not, in fact, corpuscular structures, they consist in something 'still more remote from our comprehension'.[5] Garber stresses that this 'corpuscular skepticism' 'infects' Locke's *Essay*. He observes that it is an issue of more persistent and systematic interest to Locke than the 'veil of perception skepticism' engendered by the view that we do not immediately perceive material things, but only the 'ideas' they supposedly cause in us. Part of the purpose of Garber's paper is to insist on the distinction between corpuscular and veil-of-perception scepticism, and to call attention to the fact that commentators have tended to ignore Berkeley's repudiation of the former, while dwelling on his concern with subverting the latter.[6]

Garber's discussion indicates, however, that Berkeley's position on corpuscular scepticism is considerably more complex than his position on absolutely existing matter. Berkeley, we know, is able to reject this 'matter' as a useless hypothesis: not only is it unperceivable (as the wholly 'external' cause of our perceptions); it also lacks any prospect of explanatory value, since the materialists themselves admit that they are unable to explain how it is *possible* or *conceivable* that matter should produce ideas of sense. (See, for instance, *Principles*, 50.) But, Garber holds, Berkeley does not categorically take such a position with respect to the corpuscular theory of inner structures. In *Principles* 60–6, in particular, Berkeley seems to assume the existence of inner mechanisms, and to ascribe genuine explanatory power to this conception. Garber goes on to argue that (1) Berkeley accepted the reality of corpuscles insensible to us; (2) Berkeley had at hand the theoretical resources for satisfactorily reconciling this position with his idealistic immaterialism (though he did not explicitly utilize them in this connection); and (3) Berkeley's explicit rejection of scepticism relating to our ignorance of inner natures is also reconcilable with his manner of embracing corpuscularianism.

---

[5] *Essay Concerning Human Understanding*, ed. Peter H. Nidditch (Oxford, 1975), IV. iii, 11, p. 544.

[6] As Garber recognizes, the distinction between corpuscular and veil-of-perception scepticism is by no means sharp in the texts. At the beginning of the *Third Dialogue*, for example, the scepticism about the existence of physical things that arises from materialist principles is presented as a sort of intensification of the problem about knowing natures: 'we are not only ignorant of the true and real nature of things, but even of their existence.' (*Dialogues*, 228.)

I wish to dispute—with varying degrees of opposition—Garber's conclusions on each of these points. First I will try to show that Garber overreads *Principles* 60–6 in taking these sections to imply endorsement of an 'immaterialist corpuscularianism'. (He says that these sections provide 'the most convincing evidence' (in the early works) that Berkeley accepted a form of corpuscularianism.[7]) Second, I will challenge his claim that Berkeley could successfully reconcile immaterialist corpuscularianism with the fundamental principles of his philosophy in the way that Garber proposes, while also exploring some further complexities in the problem of insensible entities. Third, I will examine Garber's reasons for holding that Berkeley's reconception of the doctrine of inner structures enables him to retain such a doctrine while avoiding the 'corpuscular scepticism' of his opponents. Although I think that part of what Garber says in support of this view is interestingly correct, I will suggest that his conclusion is still overly optimistic. I will also try to show that the interest of this latter issue does not wholly depend upon whether Garber is warranted in ascribing 'immaterialist corpuscularianism' to Berkeley. For it is at least clear that Berkeley accepts in some form the view that microscopic science is capable of vastly extending our comprehension of nature, presumably in an open-ended, non-terminating way. And it is at least prima facie doubtful whether the acceptance of such a view can be reconciled with his rejection of inner qualities and constitutions, or his affirmations that we 'perfectly comprehend' physical things.

II

In *Principles* 60–6 Berkeley is attempting to answer a quite specific objection to his position. On Berkeley's view ideas are 'inert' or causally inefficacious, and physical things are only ideas of sense or collection of such ideas. All causal efficacy with respect to the production of ideas of sense is ascribed to God, who causes these ideas in our minds directly, or without material intermediary. According to the objection that Berkeley wants to meet, his theory

---

[7] Garber, p. 182. Like Garber (see his note 8, p. 193) I will ignore here the complex question of Berkeley's attitude toward corpuscularianism in works later than the *Dialogues*. For an interesting discussion of aspects of this question, see I. C. Tipton, 'The "Philosopher by Fire" in Berkeley's Alciphron', in Turbayne, pp. 159–73, especially section III. Tipton also touches on the issue of corpuscles in the early works.

about God's direct causation of ideas renders *unaccountable* 'that curious organization of plants, and the admirable mechanism in the parts of animals'—or for that matter the relevance of inner springs and wheels to the observed movement of the hands of a watch.

... might not vegetables grow, and shoot forth leaves and blossoms, and animals perform all their motions, as well without as with all that variety of internal parts so elegantly contrived and put together, which being ideas have nothing powerful or operative in them, nor have any necessary connexion with the effects ascribed to them? If it be a spirit that immediately produces every effect by a *fiat*, or act of his will, we must think all that is fine and artificial in the works, whether of man or Nature, to be made in vain. (*Principles*, 60.)

If it is 'an intelligence' that directs the hand of a watch, why may he not do it without the artisan going to the trouble to construct the inner movements; 'Why does not an empty case serve as well as another?' Berkeley concludes the objection:

The like may be said of all the clockwork of Nature, great part whereof is so wonderfully fine and subtle, as scarce to be discerned by the best microscope. In short, it will be asked, how upon our principles any tolerable account can be given, or any final cause assigned of an innumerable multitude of bodies and machines framed with the most exquisite art, which in the common philosophy have very apposite uses assigned them, and serve to explain abundance of phenomena. (60.)

In 64 the objection is restated in this way:

... ideas are not any how and at random produced, there being a certain order and connexion between them, like that of cause and effect: there are also several combinations of them, made in a very regular and artificial manner, which seem like so many instruments in the hand of Nature, that being hid as it were behind the scenes, have a secret operation in producing those appearances which are seen on the theatre of the world, being themselves discernible only to the curious eye of the philosopher. But since one idea cannot be the cause of another, to what purpose is that connexion? And since those instruments, being barely *inefficacious perceptions* in the mind [according to Berkeley's philosophy], are not subservient to the production of natural effects; it is demanded why they are made, or, in other words, what reason can be assigned why God should make us, upon a close inspection into his works, behold so great variety of ideas, so artfully laid together, and so much according to rule ...?

Berkeley's response to this objection includes two basic claims.

First, the 'ideas' we observe on 'close inspection' of God's works are indeed no more causally efficacious than any other ideas, but are rather to be understood as *signs*. Secondly, the fact that there are such ideas, beheld on close inspection, is necessary for *regularity* in nature; it accounts for our ability to systematize and make more predictable, 'what we are to expect from such and such actions, and what methods are proper to be taken for the exciting such and such ideas' (*Principles*, 65).

Garber acknowledges that 'Berkeley does not explicitly use the *word* "corpuscle" in these passages'.[8] Nevertheless, he interprets *Principles* 60–6 as supporting the attribution to Berkeley of an 'immaterialist corpuscularianism'. In defending this reading Garber first notes, correctly, that 'never once in the course of his lengthy response does [Berkeley] suggest that the objects in question do not really have internal parts'.[9] Secondly, in portraying 'mechanisms' as necessary to the order and regularity of natural phenomena, 'Berkeley does *not* say that God set things up in such a way that we can always *actually discover* the mechanism behind the manifest properties of things.'[10] Further, Berkeley does not in any way imply an *instrumentalist* conception of the inner constituents of things (as he does, for example, in the case of gravitational attraction).

But even if all this is granted, why should we suppose that Berkeley 'meant to include the hidden corpuscular substructure of things'[11] when he argues, in these passages, that his conception of the causation of phenomena does not actually render explanatorily nugatory the inner mechanisms of organic bodies or human machines? Garber offers the following reasons for supposing that Berkeley had 'insensible corpuscles' in mind.[12] First, corpuscles are after all needed to explain magnetic and chemical and physical phenomena just as wheels and springs are needed to explain the movement of a watch hand. Second, although Berkeley doesn't mention corpuscles by name, 'his language is virtually identical with the language that Locke uses when talking about corpuscles'. For example, like Locke, Berkeley speaks of the 'size, figure, motion, and disposition of *parts*'.[13] (Garber also cites other examples.) Finally,

---

[8] Garber, p. 184.
[9] Ibid., p. 182.
[10] Ibid., p. 183.
[11] Ibid., p. 184.
[12] Ibid.
[13] Ibid., Garber's emphasis.

'Berkeley makes use of the most characteristic metaphor of the corpuscularians when he compares the mechanisms of nature to the workings of a clock'.[14]

I do not find these arguments convincing. In these sections Berkeley is confronting an opponent who simply argues that on his principles the organization of nature as we know it makes no sense. Berkeley contends that this organization does have a point, though not a causal role. It is true that the passage shows that Berkeley shares an important component of the corpuscularians' conception of nature: the notion of natural mechanisms. This is no evidence, however, that he shared the specifically corpuscularian component: the notion of *imperceptible* mechanisms. The fact that the language Berkeley uses in this passage (or puts into the mouth of his objector) resembles Locke's language when he talks about corpuscles need reflect no more than the fact that Locke, like other corpuscularians, models corpuscularian theory on observable mechanistic structures (like clockworks). It need not be taken to imply that Berkeley himself accepts this extension.

Of course the discussion in this passage may legitimately raise the question *whether* Berkeley has in mind 'imperceptible' as well as observable mechanisms. But in considering this question I think one must note that throughout these sections Berkeley persistently phrases both objection and response in terms of mechanisms that are at least minimally perceivable by us: that are, in fact among our 'ideas'.

The like may be said of all the clockwork of Nature, great part whereof is so wonderfully fine and subtle, as scarce to be discerned by the best microscope. . . . (*Principles*, 60) . . . *ideas* are not any how and at random produced, there being a certain order and connexion *between them* . . . there are also several combinations *of them* . . . which *seem* like so many instruments in the hand of Nature, . . . *being themselves discernible only to the curious eye of the philosopher.* (*Principles*, 64; emphasis added.)

Berkeley's account of the order of nature in terms of the relationship, among ideas, of sign to thing signified seems especially to imply that he is conceiving the problem in terms of observables.

. . . the reason why ideas are formed into machines, that is, artificial and regular combinations, is the same with that for combining letters into words. That a few original ideas may be made to signify a great number of effects and

[14] Ibid.

actions, it is necessary they be variously combined together: and to the end their use be permanent and universal, these combinations must be made by *rule*, and with *wise contrivance*. By this means abundance of information is conveyed unto us, concerning what we are to expect from such and such actions, and what methods are proper to be taken, for the exciting such and such ideas: which in effect is all that I conceive to be distinctly meant, when it is said that *by discerning* the figure, texture, and mechanism of the inward parts of bodies, whether natural or artificial, we may attain to know the several uses and properties depending thereon, or the nature of the thing. (*Principles*, 65; last emphasis added.)

According to this picture mechanisms are conceived in terms of 'original ideas' that function as signs *to us*. Similarly, Berkeley does not merely fail to mention imperceptible corpuscles: he couches his whole account in terms of figures, textures, and mechanisms that we discern.[15]

I would claim, then, that nothing in these sections strongly indicates that Berkeley is trying to establish the consistency of his principles with any doctrine of imperceptible corpuscles—materialist or 'immaterialist'—and a good deal indicates that he is not. Still, the first point raised by Garber remains significant: aren't insensible entities *needed* for a comprehensive predictive science of nature? Indeed, this is a crucial reason for concern about Berkeley's position on insensible corpuscles: it certainly seems that a science recognizing only correlations on the level of sensible appearances must be explanatorily deficient in comparison to one that admits 'theoretical entities'. Despite the importance of the question, however, it seems to me wishful to think that Berkeley implicitly addresses it in *Principles* 60–6.[16]

Further, there is an additional important point that must be kept in mind. To the extent that Berkeley's opponent is conceived as a Lockean 'corpuscular skeptic', he is not being conceived as someone in a position to claim much explanatory superiority over Berkeley in this area. Such a sceptic (as personified by Hylas) holds that we are altogether ignorant of the specific natures of things (not just that our knowledge of them is imperfect or partly conjectural). We are not likely to find *this* figure opposing Berkeley by arguing that a realism about insensible entities is needed to provide ontological grounding for elegant explanations of why gold is fusible and wood not!

[15] Cf. R. J. Brook, *Berkeley's Philosophy of Science* (The Hague, 1973), pp. 100–1.
[16] Tipton also indicates that *Principles* 60–1 are concerned just with sensible mechanisms: op. cit. note 7 above, p. 168.

III

After ascribing a version of corpuscularian doctrine to Berkeley, Garber goes on to raise the question how Berkeley can 'recognize the existence of insensible corpuscles if external objects are to be clusters of *ideas*'.[17] He notes that Berkeley doesn't address this question directly, but he believes that a satisfactory answer can be proposed on Berkeley's behalf. In effect, Berkeley's appeal to ideas in God's mind to provide for the existence of ordinary sensible objects, when they are not being perceived by finite minds, may be extended to 'insensible corpuscles' as well.

This proposal, while resourceful, runs into several weighty problems. I will first summarize the details of Garber's explanation, then sketch some objections to his strategy.

Garber expresses Berkeley's position concerning 'the real existence of external objects when no one is sensing them' in the following terms: 'sensible things, when not being perceived by finite minds, exist as ideas in God's mind, ideas that He would produce in us if we were in appropriate circumstances'.[18] Garber argues that Locke did not regard corpuscles as *in principle* unobservable: that is, we *would* be able to observe them if we had more acute senses or more powerful instruments. But Berkeley too refers to microscopes, and the possibility of more acute sense organs than we in fact have. So he too may be supposed to distinguish between things that are in fact observable, and things only observable in principle. Thus,

> Given that it is not in principle impossible to observe the corpuscles, one can give an account of their real existence that is exactly parallel to Berkeley's account of the real existence of the hidden wheels of the watch. The insensible corpuscles may be said to exist as ideas in God's mind, which we would have if we were in appropriate circumstances. Of course, the specification of appropriate circumstances involves more than just opening the watch case; it involves positing appropriately strong microscopes or appropriately penetrating sense organs. But this makes no difference with regard to the question of their real existence.[19]

It is true that in the *Dialogues* Berkeley holds that sensible things 'depend not on my thought, and have an existence distinct from being

---

[17] Garber, p. 185.
[18] Ibid.
[19] Ibid. Both Garber and Tipton point out that if Berkeley is to conceive corpuscles as perceivable in principle, they must be ascribed more than just primary qualities. Cf. Garber, p. 193, n. 17, and Tipton, 173, n. 33.

perceived by me . . .' (*Dialogues*, 212). He regards this claim, together with the fundamental doctrine that sensible things cannot exist otherwise than in a mind or spirit, as showing that there must be some other mind in which they exist: 'As sure therefore as the sensible world really exists, so sure is there an infinite omnipresent spirit who contains and supports it.' (*Dialogues*, 212.) Unfortunately, this and other related passages invite many questions about just what conception of existence in God's mind Berkeley means to advance, and how it relates to other tenets of his philosophy.

Aspects of these questions have been explored by other writers.[20] Here I need only indicate a few central points. First, although Berkeley does sometimes talk of God's 'perceiving' things, he cannot really mean that God has sensuous awareness like ours. For he definitely tells us that God, a wholly active being, 'perceives nothing by sense as we do', 'can suffer nothing, nor be affected with any painful sensation, or indeed any sensations at all'. God, he says, 'knows or hath ideas; but His ideas are not convey'd to Him by sense, as ours are' (*Dialogues*, 241). The divine ideas, it later emerges, may be considered 'archetypes' to which our various ideas of sense are 'referred' (*Dialogues*, 248; cf. 254).

These moves, if taken seriously, render it very unclear what, after all, the existence of sensible objects consists in for Berkeley (not entirely, it would seem, in being *perceived*); or indeed what they *are* (not, it would seem, just congeries of sensations). Certainly, the remarks render very problematic Garber's claim that 'insensible corpuscles may be said to exist as ideas in God's mind, which we would have if we were in appropriate circumstances.'[21] Assuming it is of the nature of an idea of sense to be 'conveyed by sense' the infinite all active spirit can hardly be said straightforwardly to *'have' such ideas*—though I suppose he might be ascribed some intellectual comprehension of *what it is to have* such ideas. Further, Berkeley's statements leave unilluminated the question of what existence in God's mind might consist in, if not in 'being perceived'. In being understood? But then, it seems either Berkeley must subscribe to the unpopular Spinozistic view that everything in God's understanding is

---

[20] See, for instance, R. A. Lascola, 'Ideas and Archetypes: Appearance and Reality in Berkeley's Philosophy', *Personalist* 54 (1973), pp. 42–59; George Thomas, 'Berkeley's God Does Not Perceive', *Journal of the History of Philosophy* 14 (1976), pp. 163–8; and, especially, George Pitcher, *Berkeley* (London, 1977), Ch. X.

[21] Garber, p. 185.

actual,[22] or he must provide some way of conceptualizing the distinction between *mere* existence in God's understanding, and the way that *actual* things exist in God's understanding.[23]

I conclude, therefore, that the allusions to existence in God do not provide us with a way of establishing that Berkeley can coherently maintain the existence of insensible corpuscles. For the statements about existence in God are themselves both exceedingly unclear, and very hard to reconcile with other fundamental Berkeleian doctrines.

Of course not all attempts to explain 'unsensed existence' in Berkeleian terms rely directly on appeal to existence in God's mind. But is there any other way than the one chosen by Garber that will help reconcile the postulation of insensible corpuscles with the basic tenets of Berkeley's position?[24] Consideration of this issue will at least serve to show the need for greater precision in the statement of the problem.

Consider first George Pitcher's explication, within Berkeleian constraints, of the notion that ordinary sensible objects continue to exist when no one is in fact perceiving them. Sensible objects are, for Berkeley, collections of ideas of sense. But, Pitcher asserts, the ideas belonging to the 'collection' that is the physical object are by no means all actual ideas.

. . . for Berkeley, what we ordinarily call a (single) physical object—e.g., a fig tree—is actually a huge metaphysically grounded family of ideas of sense.

---

[22] In fact this is an oversimplification even with respect to Spinoza. See M. D. Wilson, 'Infinite Understanding, *Scientia Intuitiva*, and *Ethics* I, 16', in *Midwest Studies in Philosophy* VIII, ed. P. A. French, T. E. Uehling, Jr., and H. K. Wettstein (Minneapolis, 1983), pp. 184–5.

[23] See Pitcher, pp. 171–2. Pitcher holds that Berkeley *should* have given an account of unperceived existence in terms of God's will or intentions (sc. to cause appropriate ideas, belonging to a given object, in us in appropriate circumstances). Pitcher's account is well-motivated (by glaring defects in the likely alternatives), but it is not very precisely formulated. For instance, sometimes Pitcher phrases his analysis in terms of 'a dispositional state of God's will' (p. 179): but *can* an all-active being have 'dispositions'? Sometimes he formulates it in terms of intentions, leading to grammatical incoherence: 'there is a readiness, indeed a positive intention, on God's part, to create whatever members of the family would have been required if various circumstances had existed.' (p. 165.) Despite these flaws, his treatment of the problems is very illuminating.

[24] A nice text that seems to count for Garber's view that Berkeley in some sense countenances corpuscles is the following statement in *Dialogues* 213: 'Let any one of these abettors of impiety but look into his own thoughts, and then try if he can conceive how so much as a rock, a desert, a chaos, or *confused jumble of atoms*; how anything at all, either sensible or imaginable, can exist independent of a mind . . .' (emphasis added). But of course this doesn't tell us that Berkeley thinks corpuscles are *real*.

Some of these are actual ideas of sense, but most of them are non-actual, possible ideas of sense. The series of *actual* ideas of sense that belong to the family that constitutes any given object is almost certain not to be temporally dense—that is, there will be moments at which none of them occurs. These are the moments when the object is unobserved. But Berkeley's system by no means entails that the object lapses into non-existence at such moments.[25]

(Pitcher explains 'possible sense ideas' in terms of God's intentions or dispositions; see note 24 above.) A key statement in this passage is the remark, 'some of these are actual ideas of sense'. As Pitcher elsewhere expresses the point, possible ideas of sense 'give an *extra degree* of reality to any object'.[26] The explicit wording of this analysis restricts its relevance to objects that are in fact, actually, sometimes perceived, or in other words can be considered as families of the ideas that include some actual ones. It may be extended to 'insensible corpuscles' just in case such entities are only, so to speak, temporarily or partially unsensed—just in case, that is, they are actually sensed at some (future) time by us.[27]

A good deal depends, therefore, on exactly how we understand Garber's phrase 'sensible in principle', as it allegedly applies to corpuscles. If we take it to imply that corpuscles, while insensible in respect of not being among our present objects of observation, will come to be sensed, then the case of corpuscles does collapse to that of Pitcher's fig tree.[28] Suppose, on the contrary (as Garber seems to suppose)[29] that Berkeley regarded corpuscles as 'sensible in principle' in some sense that does not assume that they will ever be sensed by us. Then there are two options to consider. The phrase could mean only that corpuscle-perceptions are a logical possibility: that their imperceptibility to us has to do with the system of regularities that God has ordained in our world—in simple terms, with the laws of physics and physiology. Various complications would then ensue. For example, we could not simply say 'God stands ready to cause sensible ideas of corpuscles—to make them [the ideas] actual—in case any finite mind should be in a position to perceive them.'[30] We should have further to

[25] Pitcher, p. 166.

[26] Ibid., p. 164; emphasis added.

[27] Garber seems to hint that corpuscles could be counted among the unperceived *properties* of objects, some ideas of which are actual (p. 182, middle). I cannot make good sense of this passage; perhaps I have misunderstood it completely.

[28] It is another question whether Berkeley could be *justified in claiming* that they exist.

[29] Garber, p. 190 (quoted below).

[30] Cf. Pitcher, p. 165.

tie the possible perception of corpuscles to God's willingness to suspend the laws of regular association that he has ordained. The notion of 'being in a position to perceive them' would be tied to the possibility of a miracle. We might even wonder whether, on this understanding, the 'perceivability in principle' of corpuscles is sufficient to ground their actuality, or *only* their possibility. (In some possible world, different from the actual one, human beings perceive corpuscles, which therefore exist in that world.')

Perhaps on these assumptions the case of corpuscles would be similar to that of *other* kinds of entities that we want to postulate even though it is, or *seems*, physically impossible that human beings should ever perceive them, such as extremely distant stars, or the primal soup. It is at least worth considering, though, whether the case with respect to corpuscles would not be even worse. For one thing, at least many of the physical things that we want to say exist though we will never be able to perceive them, are of the same sort as things that we do perceive, for example, stars. They have, so to speak, a generic perceivability. We may therefore say, 'Stars exist, though some are too far away to be perceivable', anchoring this generic actuality statement in actual star perceptions. No similar claim can be made about corpuscles, on the present assumptions.[31]

Suppose, finally, that when we say that corpuscles are perceivable in principle we mean not that they *are* perceived (at some future time, though not yet), nor, on the other hand, that they are merely possible perceptions in the sense that there exist in God's mind possible worlds, with different 'laws' than ours, in which corpuscles are perceived. Suppose we mean that there is no 'physical impossibility' in perceiving corpuscles, but that corpuscle perceptions are absent

---

[31] I mention this notion simply because it seems somewhat intuitive. I do not know whether it is consistent with Berkeley's nominalism.

Tipton suggests that, 'for Berkeley in *Siris*, there is nothing corporeal that is "insensible," except in the sense that, because it is "inconceivably small" (sect. 261), it lies, and may always lie, beyond the range of our most powerful microscopes.' (p. 168.) This suggestion is indeterminate between the second and third of the interpretations of 'sensible in principle' that I sketch—or perhaps among all three. Tipton adds parenthetically, 'One would expect Berkeley to hold that if no human will ever perceive the aether [postulated in *Siris*], other spirits can or could.' The significance of the disjunction of modalities at the end of this sentence is not clear; it seems simply to leave us with a regress of the problem of interpreting 'sensible in principle'. Berkeley is not above invoking 'other created intelligences' (besides men) to help adjust his doctrine to ordinary conceptions of what exists (or did exist). Cf. *Dialogues*, 252. It is not clear in Berkeley's own text whether he is invoking them as a possibility or an actuality—or, for that matter, whether he is invoking them as *perceivers*, or quasi-divine understanders.

from our world because (say) no one gets around to constructing a powerful enough microscope. (Whether we could be entitled to claim that corpuscles are forever unperceived *only* for such reasons is of course a separate problem.) In this case corpuscles would be more problematic, in Berkeley's system, than the unobserved fig tree in the quad; but arguably they would be very near in status to the tree that grows and perishes in an unexplored forest. (Though here again the issue of generic perception might need to be considered.)

I do not claim, then, to have shown that the hypothesis of insensible corpuscles, on every natural understanding of that hypothesis, raises problems within Berkeley's system different from every problem that may be raised about ordinary physical things. I only claim that the hypothesis raises considerably more difficulties than Garber recognizes. These have to do mainly with the general significance of 'existence in God', but partly also with special problems that arise with respect to 'insensible' entities. The problems are not avoided by claiming that corpuscles are 'perceptible in principle'; and weaker interpretations of the latter phrase—such as Garber seems to intend—make them more difficult than the stronger ones I have also sketched.

It might seem in any case, that the supposition that corpuscular structures exist as mysterious archetypes in God's mind—*at least* presently inaccessible to us because of the grossness of our faculties— runs Berkeley dangerously near to the assumption of unknowable inner natures that he was so bent on denying. Garber evidently believes, however, that Berkeley can accept immaterialist corpuscles, while avoiding corpuscular scepticism. In the last section I will evaluate this claim.

IV

Garber assumes that Berkeley will grant that the corpuscular substructure of things is 'unknown and for all practical purposes unknowable'.[32] He believes, however, that this position does not entail corpuscular scepticism, because it does not entail ignorance of real natures. Corpuscular substructures are only collections of ideas, albeit ideas that we can or will never have. As such they are causally inefficacious: in particular, they do not satisfy the Lockean concep-

---

[32] Garber, p. 190.

tion of a real nature as the productive source of the appearances a thing presents to us. Garber observes:

... this removes the principal motivation for considering the corpuscular substructure to constitute the real nature of body. Since the corpuscular substructure is not the productive cause of the manifest properties of bodies, it has no claim to represent the real nature of bodies.[33]

In a sense Berkeley's philosophy does not reduce the scope of our ignorance, in comparison to Locke's, but it does transform that ignorance 'from a matter of great importance' to 'ignorance of a much more benign sort'.[34] We need no longer think of ourselves as ignorant of the '*true* and *real* nature of things', but only of 'empirical facts about the interconnection of ideas'—an inevitable and non-demeaning consequence of the fact that our minds are finite.[35]

At first sight this victory over 'corpuscular skepticism' may well seem far too cheap. It does not seem clear why the denial of genuine causal efficacy in nature should be in itself sufficient to resolve the problem of unknown 'real natures'.[36] After all, even if corpuscular ideas do not strictly cause anything, they must evidently be ascribed the same systematizing and predictive—even 'explanatory'—role as what we ordinarily *treat* as causes (when we say, for example, that the watch hand's movement is caused by inner wheels and springs). Why shouldn't 'corpuscular substructures' still be regarded as inner natures of things, when they are reinterpreted as fundamental 'original' elements of the divine system of ideas?

There is, however, another consideration that lends support to Garber's distinction between 'ignorance of corpuscular structures' and 'corpuscular skepticism' of the non-benign sort. Locke's real essences, it seems, do not merely stand in the relation of efficacious cause to sensible properties; they also stand in the relation of transcendental reality (what a thing 'is in itself', as Berkeley puts it) to *mere* subjective ideas in our minds. The immaterialist corpuscularianism that Garber ascribes to Berkeley would enable him to retain

[33] Ibid.
[34] Ibid.
[35] Ibid.
[36] Garber himself observes that 'Berkeley's answer to the corpuscular skeptic, as I have interpreted it, may look like a mere linguistic move.' He goes on to claim that 'this is not entirely fair to Berkeley', because Berkeley, in denying that ignorance of corpuscular substructures is ignorance of real natures, renders the ignorance relatively innocuous. Garber, however, does not consider the line of reply to this claim that I sketch in the text.

corpuscular theory, while denying both that corpuscular structures stand as unknown causes to the effects we observe, and that they stand as transcendental realities in contrast to the mere sensible appearances with which we are amused. Although Garber emphasizes the first point, the second may actually be more persuasive.

The second point is persuasive, that is, *provided* that the status of corpuscles as divine archetypes, different from our ideas of sense and (perhaps) wholly inaccessible to us, does not itself generate a reality-appearance distinction closely analogous to the materialists'. This concern is very similar to one expressed by Samuel Johnson, to which Berkeley disappointingly failed to reply. As Johnson implies, the more archetypes are divorced from our ideas of sense, the more they threaten to play the role of matter all too well.[37] From this point of view, too, reliance on existence in God's mind seems a problematic and potentially self-destructive device within Berkeley's empiricist system.

Finally I would like to mention two problems connected with this discussion that arise whether or not one follows Garber in ascribing immaterialist corpuscularianism to Berkeley. The first is rather obvious. It seems that Berkeley's acknowledgement, in *Principles* 60–6, of the scientific extension of our knowledge of nature, cuts directly against his ebullient claim that we 'perfectly comprehend' physical things, his dismissal of the view that there is something that exceeds our comprehension in every drop of water or grain of sand. Of course these claims fare even worse if one agrees with Garber that Berkeley means to affirm the reality of corpuscular substructures that are 'unknown and for all practical purposes unknowable'.[38] But they remain quite baffling even if one merely assumes that the divine language of nature, however accessible to us, is also inexhaustible.[39]

Another problem is this. Part of what Berkeley means when he says that we perfectly comprehend sensible objects is, presumably, that things should not be supposed to be systematically *different* in reality from how they appear to the senses. For instance, they do not in reality lack the colours that we perceive 'in' them. A theory of 'inner structures', whether sensible or insensible, may not at first seem to

---

[37] See his letters in Berkeley's *Works*, ii. 274–6; 285–6. Berkeley did reply to most of Johnson's other objections.

[38] Garber cites these remarks at an earlier phase of his discussion (p. 179), but does not return to them.

[39] See Tipton, p. 173, n. 29, for a relevant quotation from *Siris*.

cause any trouble for *this* position. Just as a thing can look different from the front and the back, so it can look different (to us, or so to speak, to God) from the outside and the inside. Different aspects or ideas may to this extent non-competitively constitute a thing. Berkeley attempts to extend this analysis to the distinction between the ordinary appearance of something and the way it appears under a microscope. Thus, Hylas introduces the example of the microscope to challenge Philonous' defence of the common-sense image of reality:

HYLAS. You say you believe your senses; and seem to applaud your self that in this you agree with the vulgar. According to you therefore, the true nature of a thing is discovered by the senses. If so . . . why should we use a microscope, the better to discover the true nature of a body, if it were discoverable to the naked eye? (*Dialogues*, 245.)

Philonous replies that microscopes just give us new ideas to add to our collections of appearances of things. They do not get us any closer to 'the nature of the thing'. Hylas' assumption that there is an 'inconsistency' among our ideas of sense—with those derived from microscopic examination to be regarded as the more accurate—is just one more noxious outcome of his 'preconceived notion of (I know not what) one single, unchanged, unperceivable, real nature' (*Dialogues*, 245). But in fact the example Hylas has adduced raises a problem that is not at all closely tied to either 'corpuscular' or 'veil of perception' scepticism. One may reject nearly every aspect of the doctrine of unperceivable real natures, and remain convinced that the ordinary sensory experience of things is not to be 'trusted'. Berkeley's position that microscopic examination merely adds to our ordinary sensible ideas of things, without correcting them, may well be a consistent one; the problem is just that it is so very hard to believe. Similarly, it is equally hard to believe that things are *on the surface* just as we ordinarily experience them—smooth, homogeneous, etc. In other words, the issue whether ordinary sense experience is challenged or corrected by microscopic examination is not at all the same as the question whether things have 'true natures'—imperceptible, transcendentally real, causally potent material essences—that are inaccessible to us. From this perspective the problem for Berkeley's vindication of the reality of ordinary sensible appearances lies less in the fact that we are ignorant of some inaccessible inner natures, than in the fact that we know too much.

CHAPTER 8

BERKELEY'S PHILOSOPHY OF SCIENCE

W. H. NEWTON-SMITH

BERKELEY's philosophy of science appears to betoken a failure to appreciate the significance of the developments of the relatively novel style of post-Galilean science. At first glance it appears to be a mere regression back to the instrumentalism of Osiander and Cardinal Bellarmine rather than a recognition of the achievements of his own day. He shares with them his language, his central argument and his concern for the negative effects on religious belief of the realist construal of science. And he can appear like them as one in the grip of a theory (perhaps more philosophical and less theological in Berkeley's case) whose views on science are simply expounded as consequences of that general theory without independent reference to the actual practice of science. It will be argued that this impression is quite misleading. Berkeley's central argument is independent of his general philosophical position. His argument rests on a speculative idea, that of the under-determination of theory by data. This idea, of crucial importance in the debates at the time of Galileo, animates Berkeley's philosophy of science and its considerable contemporary interest is illustrated by the crucial role it has played in the writings on science of Duhem and Quine. In this paper I note pressures that lead Berkeley to look backwards and examine the insight which makes his preferred philosophy of science of continuing interest.

Berkeley's preferred philosophy of science is, it will be argued, a form of *instrumentalism*. For the instrumentalist the aim of the scientific enterprise is merely the production of theories that are empirically adequate in the sense that they give successful observational predictions. The question of the truth of the theoretical postulates of science simply does not arise. The only proper concern of the scientist is that those postulates give rise to correct predictions. This was the prevalent pre-Galilean view of astronomy. Osiander, writing in the preface to Copernicus' *The Revolutions of the Heavenly Spheres* said of astronomical hypotheses that they 'need not be true nor even probable; if they provide a calculus consistent with the observations that alone is sufficient'.[1] All forms of instrumentalism presuppose a dichotomy between observation sentences and theoretical sentences. The observation sentences (sentences reporting particular observations) are true or false, as the case may be, in virtue of how the world is. It is assumed that the truth-value of any observation sentence can in principle be ascertained. On one form of instrumentalism, to be called *semantical instrumentalism*, the theoretical sentences are held not to have been provided with the kind of meaning that gives them truth-values. Theoretical sentences are not hypotheses which are either true or false. Their role is not to express facts about the world but to facilitate the business of making correct observational predictions. A theory is just a tool which can be used to derive observational predictions about the state of a system at one time from statements giving its observational state at another time. On another form of instrumentalism, to be called *epistemological instrumentalism*, the theoretical sentences are thought of as having a truth-value. However, that fact plays no role in understanding scientific practice. The scientist is represented as merely being interested in empirical adequacy. Whether the theoretical sentences are true or false is not something he can ascertain nor should he be interested in trying to do so.

This differentiation between these two forms of instrumentalism represents a latter day refinement in characterization not recognized by the pre-Galileans. For the moment this difference is not of importance since both versions of instrumentalism stand in opposition to the sort of realist theory of science that Berkeley wishes to resist. Realism as a doctrine in the philosophy of science involves a number of ingredients. First, the sentences of a theory both observational and theoretical are regarded as being true or false independently of us in virtue of how the world is. This will be called the *ontological ingredient* in realism. It was Galileo's insistence on this element which lead Cardinal Bellarmine to warn that:

To say that by assuming the earth in motion and the sun immobile one saves all the appearances better than the eccentrics and epicycles ever could is to speak well indeed. This holds no danger and it suffices for the mathematician. But to want to affirm that the sun really remains at rest at the world's center,

---

[1] Rosen, E. (ed.), *Three Copernican Treatises* (Dover, New York, 1959), pp. 24–5.

that it turns only on itself without running from East to West, . . . that is a very dangerous thing.[2]

The success of the new science led to the presumption that it was possible to determine whether the theoretical sentences were in fact true or not and to the assumption that truths (or approximate truths) were to some extent accumulating. This will be called the *epistemological ingredient* in realism. The third ingredient to be called the *explanatory ingredient* is the two-fold assumption that the aim of science is the discovery of truths which can be used to explain observations and that this explanatory end is to be achieved in physics by postulating theoretical items. By Berkeley's time these items had come to include entities such as corpuscles, magnitudes such as mass and gravitational attraction, and *sui generis* items like absolute space.[3]

The style of the new science was to select for allegiance the theory which provided the best available explanation of the observable phenomena, presuming that its providing the best available explanation meant that it was the best bet as to where the truth lay. Though Newton himself had qualms about this style he provides some of the finest uses of it. Consider, for example, his arguments for the existence of absolute space. Not infrequently Newton is represented as believing in the existence of absolute space for theological reasons. While he did advance such reasons he also argued more convincingly that space should be assumed to be absolute in order to explain the observations resulting from rotating a bucket of water. The structure of that particular argument can be more easily characterized through his thought experiment of a world consisting of nothing but two spheres connected by a cord.[4]

We are to imagine a world consisting of nothing but two homogeneous spheres connected by a cord. We can fruitfully elaborate Newton's thought by imagining that we inhabit one of the globes and that we have found that Newtonian mechanics best 'saves the phenomena' on the surfaces of our sphere. Having discovered a tension in the cord joining the spheres we seek its cause. Given

---

[2] Bellarmine writing to Foscarini, quoted in P. Duhem's *To Save the Phenomena* (Chicago University Press, Chicago, 1969) p. 107, trans. E. Doland and C. Maschler.

[3] For further elaboration of the characterization given of realism and instrumentalism see my *The Rationality of Science* (Routledge and Kegan Paul, London, 1981).

[4] See the Scholium to Definition VIII of Newton's *Principia*, reprinted in *Newton's Philosophy of Nature* (Hafner, New York, 1953), ed. H. S. Thayer.

Newtonian mechanics, if the spheres were in fact rotating that rotation would give rise to a centrifugal force *causing* a tension in the cord. What better explanation could there be in the circumstances? As there is no rotation of one body relative to another, and as motion must be relative to something it must be motion relative to space itself. Against the warranted background belief in the laws of Newtonian mechanics we would be justified in positing the existence of absolute space on the grounds that it provided the best available explanation of an observable phenomenon: the tension in the string.

Bellarmine resisted the realist move in astronomy because once the astronomical hypotheses were regarded as candidates for being true there was the risk of conflict with the Scriptures. Instrumentalism (in either form) appeared theologically safer. For if theories were only devices for 'saving the phenomena'—for obtaining correct observations—and not hypotheses about how things (apart from observations) were, theories could not come in conflict with the Scriptures. Clearly Berkeley too has to resist the realist strategy. For example, to accept the Newtonian arguments for absolute space is straight away to admit to the legitimacy of items to which Berkeleian ideas do not correspond. Furthermore it proceeds by introducing items to provide causal accounts where Berkeley wants the only cause of ideas to be spirits. But Berkeley is appropriately appreciative of the achievements of science. His strategy is therefore not to deprecate science but to reconstrue its contents so that he can preserve most (but not all) of its fruits. At least two strategies have been deployed by those wishing to resist by reconstrual the deliverances of the new realistically construed science: one is reductionism and the other is instrumentalism. Both are to be found in Berkeley.

It would be natural for Berkeley to attempt to extend his reductionist treatment of the houses, mountains, and rivers in terms of ideas to, say, corpuscles and gravitational force. Reductionism in this context amounts to the claim that all talk about the former sort of item can be transformed in a meaning-preserving way into talk about the having of ideas (actually and potentially). And similarly on one of Berkeley's philosophies of science, one can reduce all theoretical notions to observation notions which in turn are reduced to ideas. Berkeley tells us that 'force' and 'gravitation' are 'supposed to mean something different from moving, moved, motion, and rest, but, in point of fact, the supposed difference in meaning amounts to nothing at all' (*De Motu*, 11). Such terms have been invented by common habit to abbreviate speech, and in part they have been thought out by philosophers for instructional purposes, not that they are adapted to the natures of things which are in fact singulars and concrete, but they come in useful for handing on received opinions by making the notions or at least the propositions universal. (*De Motu*, 7.)

And the corpuscularian theory, we are told, accounts for things in terms of 'figure, motion, and other qualities, which are in truth no more than mere ideas' (*Principles*, 50).

In order to focus specifically on Berkeley's view of science let us assume for the moment that he has made good his reductionist programme as applied to the objects of everyday life. We can then ask whether it is at all plausible to suppose that scientific discourse involving theoretical terms can be reduced to the level of talk about the relatively mundane objects of everyday life. The reduction would have the effect of defining the theoretical term exclusively in terms of the observations which we would naïvely think of as caused by the presence of an item denoted by the theoretical term. For example, to take a contemporary example, the sentence 'An electron is present' would come to a complex disjunction 'There is a scintillation in the cathode ray tube or . . .' in which the disjuncts cover the other observable phenomena associated with the presence of an electron. Without exploring the details of such a programme we can see that it is not at all plausible. For the point of introducing the notion of an electron was to provide a causal explanation of the scintillations in the cathode ray tube. But if part of what is meant by saying there is an electron present is that there is a scintillation in the cathode ray tube we do not have an explanation. Instead of a further description of the situation with explanatory power we simply have the same description expressed more tersely.

To object that since science uses theoretical items to explain observations reductionism must be false, on the ground that this precludes the possibility of having any explanations, would not be recognized by Berkeley as a legitimate objection. For on Berkeley's account of the matter science cannot provide explanations in any event. It can only discover which things are the signs of which other things. But there is an obvious difficulty with the reductionist programme that Berkeley has to acknowledge even on his own terms. For the onus is on one who thinks that the theoretical terms of science really are abbreviations for concatenations of observational terms and who also stresses the importance of being clear about meanings to specify the meanings of some theoretical terms in observational vocabulary. And in this regard Berkeley simply does not deliver the goods. Of course it is commonplace to object that neither he nor anyone else has ever effected the translation of talk about mountains into talk about ideas. But in the case of theoretical terms of science there are problems over and above these. If we think of 'reducing' talk of the desk at which I work to ideas we think we have some idea of how to begin. We think of how it looks and feels to us. Perhaps even with corpuscles we think we have some idea as to how to develop such an account by reference to potential as well as actual experiences (what corpuscles would feel like if only our hands were small enough, what they would look like if only our eyes were sharp enough). But for many terms in science we are bound to be at a complete loss. For they are not supposed to be terms for items which are at all analogous to items given in experience. The term 'electron' was introduced, for example, to refer to some constituent of matter which causes a particular observable phenomenon (scintillations in cathode ray tubes). The term functioned simply as the designator of the cause while investigation led to the ascription of further properties to the cause. It is hard to see how Berkeley with his strictures against causal explanation can admit the legitimacy of a term introduced in this way. There is no reason to assume that a term introduced in this way could ever be replaced by an observation term however complex. To the extent that it is correct to represent the meaning of a theoretical term, *Tx*, in science by a schema of the form *Tx if and only if x is such and such a kind of cause of observable phenomena P*, no viable theory of science can be built up using only observation vocabulary and eschewing any strong notion of causation. Since for a wide class of terms such a scheme is arguably correct Berkeley's reductionist programme cannot succeed.

Berkeley himself was aware of the fact that certain notions used in physics such as absolute space cannot be treated reductionistically. For that notion allows for the possibility of motion in cases where there is no observable motion. Berkeley's response is courageously to deny the legitimacy of the notion. 'Courageous' is the operative word. For it might well have turned out that Newtonian mechanics was the best theory of the physical world and that the observable phenomena were best explained on the basis of the postulation of absolute space. Indeed, it could have been that there was not even any serious rival theory. In which case it would take courage to maintain a philosophy of science which had to deny the legitimacy of notions which were an integral part of the only explanatorily successful theory of the world. Happily, as will be seen, Berkeley has another and preferred philosophy of science which does not have this embarrassing consequence.

Reductionism, then, fails. The requisite translations have not been forthcoming and its avowedly anti-metaphysical inspiration is sustained only by a metaphysical conviction that there must be some such translation to be found. Happily for someone like Berkeley who does not see the aim of the scientific enterprise as the production of explanations there is a move which avoids this objection to reductionism. This is what was called semantical instrumentalism. That Berkeley held this view in at least an embryonic form is indicated in the following passages:

Force, gravity, attraction, and terms of this sort are useful for reasonings and reckonings about motion and bodies in motion, but not for understanding the simple nature of motion itself or for indicating so many distinct qualities. As for attraction, it was certainly introduced by Newton, not as a true, physical quality, but only as a mathematical hypothesis. (*De Motu,* 17.)

The imperfect understanding of this situation has caused some to make the mistake of rejecting the mathematical principles of physics on the ground that they do not assign the efficient causes of things. It is not, however, in fact the business of physics or mechanics to establish efficient causes, but only the rules of impulsions or attractions, and, in a word, the laws of motions, and from the established laws to assign the solution, not the efficient cause, of particular phenomena. (*De Motu,* 35.)

Instrumentalism avoids the translation objection. Theoretical sentences are not translatable even in principle into observational sentences. They function as 'mathematical hypotheses', as devices for facilitating the calculations, not as hypotheses intended to be true.

Berkeley's argument to support his instrumentalism might seem to rest simply on the claim that since only spirit can cause ideas, realism, which assumes the legitimacy of causal explanations of physical phenomena in physical terms, must be rejected. Instrumentalism then would gain credibility through being an alternative to realism that avoids the problems of reductionism. If this were his position, resting on this engaging but utterly implausible doctrine concerning spirits and causation, it would be of little interest. However, Berkeley has another argument, an argument which rests on a major premiss which has seemed and still seems to many philosophers of science to be true or at least plausible. This is the underdetermination of theory by data.

The thesis of the underdetermination of theory by data (hereafter cited as *UTD*) is the claim that for any subject matter there will be a pair of evidentially equivalent theories which are logically incompatible. To be evidentially equivalent theories must first be empirically equivalent. Empirical equivalence means that the theories make exactly the same predictions so that no possible observation or test will confirm (disconfirm) one without confirming (disconfirming) the other. Secondly, the theories fare equally well on any principle of theory choice which is of epistemic value. For instance, if simplicity is a guide to the truth, two empirically equivalent theories will be evidentially equivalent only if they are equally simple.[5]

If *UTD* holds for some subject matter it is not possible to maintain realism as characterized above. For if one maintains that the sentences of the theory are true or false, one has to abandon the claim that it is possible to find out which it is. Thus even though truth is at stake, the fact that it is cannot matter as nothing can count in favour of one theory over an underdetermined rival theory. Making this move in the face of underdetermination is what I have called elsewhere the *ignorance* move for it amounts to saying that there is some matter of fact at stake (which theory is true), a matter of fact about which we will be for ever ignorant.

A philosopher of science who starts with a realist orientation but comes to believe in *UTD* and makes the *ignorance* move will adopt what has been called *epistemological instrumentalism*: theoretical sentences are true or false but, in cases where *UTD* holds, that fact cannot influence our choice of theories, so any understanding of theory choice must be based on factors other than conjectures as to the truth or approximate truth. This is the position advocated recently by van Fraassen and by Laudan.[6]

Alternatively one might withdraw the assumption that the theoretical sentences which give rise to underdetermination are true or false; that is, one might move towards the kind of instrumentalism I

---

[5] For further discussion of *UTD* see my 'Trans-theoretical Truth without Transcendent Truth?' in *Kant oder Hegel* (Klett-Cotta, Stuttgart, 1983), ed. D. Henrich, pp. 466–78.

[6] See B. van Fraassen *The Scientific Image* (Oxford University Press, Oxford, 1980) and L. Laudan *Progress and Its Problems* (University of California Press, Berkeley, 1973).

ascribed to Berkeley which was called *semantical instrumentalism*. This move as a response to *UTD* is problematic relative to the particular characterization given of *UTD*. For it was said that it involved cases of logically incompatible theories. But if we adopt semantical instrumentalism and hold that the theoretical sentences responsible for the underdetermination lack truth-values this restricts at least the understanding we can give of the notion of incompatibility in the context. Assuming we do not want to render this notion in a purely syntactical fashion we have to say something like: the theories would be incompatible if construed realistically. Since they are empirically equivalent they are to be construed instrumentally. And, so construed, we need not say they are inconsistent.

As the following passage indicates, Berkeley rests his case on an argument from *UTD*:

It is clear, moreover, that force is not a thing certain and determinate, from the fact that great men advance very different opinions, even contrary opinions, about it, and yet in their results attain the truth. For Newton says that impressed force consists in action alone, and is the action exerted on the body to change its state, and does not remain after the action. Torricelli contends that a certain heap or aggregate of forces impressed by percussion is received into the mobile body, and there remains and constitutes impetus. Borelli and others say much the same. But although Newton and Torricelli seem to be disagreeing with one another, they each advance consistent views, and the thing is sufficiently well explained by both. For all forces attributed to bodies are mathematical hypotheses just as are attractive forces in planets and sun. But mathematical entities have no stable essence in the nature of things; and they depend on the notion of the definer. Whence the same thing can be explained in different ways. (*De Motu*, 67.)

Forces are not determinate since Newton and Torricelli tell different stories about them. Both 'attain the truth', both 'explain' things equally well. Given Berkeley's strictures about both explanation and truth, which are repeated both before and after this passage, the reference to truth is to be construed as being the truth about observations, and 'explanation' as meaning merely subsuming under the 'mathematical hypotheses'. Physical 'explanation' is said not to be assignment of a true cause but of showing the connection between what is explained and the mechanical principles via establishing 'the rules for the communication of motions' (ibid., 69). One who has made the move to semantical instrumentalism and takes Newton and

Torricelli as a case of *UTD* can describe the theories, as Berkeley does, as consistent. For, as noted above, once we withdraw the realist assumption the theories are in a sense consistent simply because neither is construed as having a truth-value.

But why should we believe with Berkeley that for every situation for which some Newton has a theory some Torricelli has an empirically equivalent rival theory? That this situation ever arises is controversial. Some have argued that any case of apparent *UTD* can be treated as a case of *notational variance*; that is, as a case where we have two formulations of the same theory, formulations that merely look incompatible owing to variation in the notation used to express the theory. And even if one concedes that there are some cases of *UTD* this is not at all adequate for Berkeley. For if there are areas of physics not subject to *UTD* the realist will be able to cite these in vindicating realism. No one has produced an argument to show a priori that for any theory there is an underdetermined rival theory. Even Quine, for whom *UTD* is the cornerstone of a philosophical system, regards it as something he believes, not as something for which he has an argument.[7] Perhaps one might obtain some support for *UTD* by showing for a wide range of sample theories that one can with ingenuity generate an underdetermined rival. For example, in the context of Newton's thought experiment considered above one might develop some theory to the effect that the spheres were repelling one another in order to explain the tension. But such a theory would only be convincing if it is given in a form as precise and as detailed as the Newtonian theory. It would have in addition to share the explanatory virtues of Newton's theory. Unless the inhabitants of the spheres have such a theory which worked equally well with the objects on the spheres, the reasonable move for them to make is the realist one of assuming the truth or approximate truth of the only theory they have available.

While Berkeley gives us no reason to assume that the world is radically underdetermined, he is certainly right to hold that if it is so the realist position will not do. He has, then, an argument in favour of instrumentalism which does not simply rest on the thesis that only spirits can be causes. In this way Berkeley's philosophy of science has the virtue of resting on claims about the actual practice of science. His instrumentalist account derives from the claim that for any Newton

---

[7] See his 'On Empirically Equivalent Theories of the World' *Erkenntnis* 9 (1975), pp. 313–28.

there is a Torricelli; that is, that science displays underdetermination. That claim of underdetermination was crucial to the case of Osiander and Bellarmine and it appeared more plausible in their time than in Berkeley's. For it was not obvious that Copernicus was superior to Ptolemy at 'saving the phenomena'. In that context arguing for a realist treatment of the theories in question was therefore not as persuasive as it was for Berkeley's contemporaries. For Newtonian mechanics lacked any serious worked-out rival theory, let alone an empirically equivalent rival. Its great success, therefore, seemed best explained on the assumption that it had latched on to important theoretical truths about the world. In this way then Berkeley's instrumentalism was, when propounded, dated. For it looked back to a feature (the presence of apparently empirically equivalent rival theories) which characterized pre-Galilean but not Newtonian science.

To this juncture the argument would not support instrumentalism of one sort over the other. It has been suggested that Berkeley in fact holds an embryonic form of semantical rather than epistemological instrumentalism. And clearly this form fits better with his general philosophical position. For in the face of *UTD* the epistemological instrumentalist makes what was called the ignorance move and is committed thereby to the existence of utterly unknowable states of affairs, states of affairs about which we could have no 'ideas'. Such a position would be anathema to Berkeley whereas semantical instrumentalism gives a much more congenial position. In the face of *UTD* one makes the move of denying that there are any matters of fact at stake in regard to the theoretical hypotheses which give rise to underdetermination. We have mere 'mathematical hypotheses' and no utterly, unknowable states of affairs.

Berkeley's semantical instrumentalism rests then on an entirely speculative conjecture of *UTD*. While there is no good reason to think the conjecture is true, his philosophy of science would be appropriate should it be true. And while the science of his day did not render the conjecture plausible, the arguments of Duhem and Quine have generated sufficient interest in *UTD* to give Berkeley's philosophy of science contemporary significance. This instrumentalism which I have suggested is his preferred philosophy of science does, however, engender uncomfortable tensions in his overall philosophical position. First, his decided preference when talking of houses, mountains, and streams is for a form of reductionism. The houses, mountains, and streams are nothing but ideas. And hypotheses about them will be true or false in virtue of what ideas are had (and, perhaps, 'could be had') by what spirits. If Berkeley had an equally decided preference for reductionism in the case of the theoretical terms of science he could avoid the particular question of what licenses a difference in treatment between everyday items and theoretical items. But to the extent that his preference in physics is for instrumentalism and not reductionism we have to inquire what it is about the 'mathematical hypotheses' that means that truth is not at stake with regard to them. I have suggested that his answer is that these hypotheses suffer from underdetermination.

If underdetermination arises at the theoretical level in science how can we be confident that it does not arise at the level of hypotheses of the most mundane kind about the macroscopic features of the medium-sized dry goods of the world? Perhaps I could come to formulate entirely different beliefs about such objects which would fit equally well with any experiences I might have. Should I not therefore treat the mundane hypotheses in an instrumentalist fashion? However, if reductionism is appropriate for such objects this situation does not arise. Any mundane hypothesis translates into a hypothesis about actual and possible experience and therefore has a fixed truth-value which can in principle be determined. All talk of houses, mountains, and streams is an abbreviation for talk about my ideas and hence there is no room for two different stories each of which would accord equally with my stock of ideas.

The picture then is that for a range of items, such as houses, streams, and mountains, reductionism is rendered plausible in part by the fact that we have some idea of how to start the reduction. There is also a range of terms which we use non-reductionistically which are used to formulate 'mathematical hypotheses' suffering from underdetermination. But how do we know that there is no gap between these two realms? Why should a term for which no reductionist analysis is possible be one which gives rise to underdetermination? There is no reduction of the notion of absolute space. Why should underdetermination take over so conveniently just at this point giving us other theories of mechanics not invoking absolute space? Unless Berkeley can show there is no such gap his position is threatened by the realist. For through this gap the realist will drive his theoretical entities. If 'absolute space' cannot be parsed away and if there is no rival theory to account for what it accounts for, the realist will argue that the explanatory success of the theory counts for its truth and hence for the existence of what Berkeley cannot countenance. Berkeley then needs not only to have *UTD*; he has to have it ready to come into play at just the moment that reductionism fails. The central problem then arises from the fact that Berkeley needs reductionism at the mundane level and instrumentalism at the theoretical level. He has no reason for thinking that the *UTD* which sustains his instrumentalism comes in precisely at the point at which reductionism is no longer plausible. Berkeley does not have a solution to this problem. Indeed his characterization of his own position is not sufficiently sharp for this particular problem to emerge. And in fairness to Berkeley it should be noted that contemporary instrumentalists have failed either to see or answer a similar problem. For instance, van Fraassen's epistemological instrumentalism depends crucially on the assumption of underdetermination. But no proof is given that any departure from the observational realm will bring with it underdetermination. And if there is any departure from observation which does not give rise to underdetermination the realist can argue that the best construal of that bit of theory is the realist one. That that bit of theory gives rise to correct predictions is best explained on the assumption that it is true or at least approximately true.

In the long run Cardinal Bellarmine and Osiander lost out to the style of the new science through not being able to produce evidentially equivalent rivals to the Copernican programme. To have produced a case for his instrumentalism Berkeley would have had to have provided an evidentially equivalent rival to Newtonian mechanics. Manifest as his achievements were this was not one of them. None the less his embryonic philosophy of science would, arguably, be the most plausible move to make should the speculative idea that all theories are underdetermined by the data be vindicated.

CHAPTER 9

THE GENERAL FORM OF THE ARGUMENT FOR BERKELEIAN IDEALISM

HOWARD ROBINSON

My objective in this essay is to outline the argument required to establish Berkeleian idealism. At some points I shall sketch the argument briefly, at others I shall argue in greater depth. My aim in presenting a survey containing hard argument at some crucial places is to show that the overall endeavour of defending idealism is more plausible than it is generally believed to be.

I THE PROBLEM

A defender of Berkeleian idealism must justify two propositions. He must prove (1) that the ordered nature of our experience both requires and is susceptible to explanation by reference to something other than experience itself. He has to show (2) that the postulation of a non-human spiritual agent or agents provides a better account of the structure of experience than the postulation of a mind-independent physical world.

These propositions can be further broken down. There are various grounds for claiming that experience requires explanation. The simplest, and Berkeley's own, is that the very existence of ideas of sense requires explaining 'since it is repugnant that they should subsist by themselves'.[1] As we do not produce our own sensations, there must be an external cause. Hume notoriously denied that nothing could come into existence without a cause, and I can see no way to disprove this.[2] If one accepts that Hume is not demonstrably wrong, then it is necessary to point to some particular feature of

---

[1] *Principles*, 146.

[2] *A Treatise of Human Nature*, ed. J. Selby-Bigge (Clarendon Press, Oxford, 1888), Bk I Pt. iii, Sect. 3, 78–82.

experience other than its mere existence which puts it in need of explanation. The natural feature to select is its orderedness—the fact that our sensations are so regular in their contents that we can interpret them as being of a stable physical environment.

Furthermore, arguing that experience *requires* explanation is not the same as showing that it is susceptible to it, for it could be the case either that (i) experience called for an explanation, but that nothing would count as an explanation of it, so that its nature was necessarily mysterious and improbable or that (ii) the nature of experience did not require an explanation—there was no reason not to treat it as a brute fact—yet it might have an explanation (i.e. a cause) in fact. I know of no philosopher who adopts the former view, but it is a prima-facie conceivable position. Someone who held both that the order of experience was a priori improbable but that there could not be such a thing as causal power or necessity might hold that experience both called for, and could not receive, a causal explanation. Someone who disagreed with Hume about a priori probabilities but agreed with him on causation might think himself to be in this position. (ii) is the position of someone who holds, with Hume, that there are no a priori probabilities and hence that the ordering of experience does not stand in need of an explanation, and, hence, that a sceptical phenomenalism is all that reason justifies; but believes also that there might in fact be an external cause of experience. Whether one chose to believe in such a cause would be a matter of taste or instinct—perhaps determined by 'natural belief'. Someone in this position who chose to explain experience by the direct action of God would be a sort of Berkeleian idealist, but would not be holding that his theistic idealism was positively supported by reason. A more likely position under (ii) is that of a naturalistic Humean who would allow instinct to lead him to believe in an external physical world, though reason in no way supports the conclusion. A hard-line Humean position would be that experience neither requires nor is susceptible to explanation and that any object of instinctual belief located beyond experience could not figure as an explanation or cause of experience: if it be present there, it is an epiphenomenon with regard to the physical world and its postulation serves only to satisfy our impulse to believe. An orthodox Berkeleian, on the other hand, must hold both that experience requires and that it is susceptible to explanation.

The argument for (2) involves both discrediting the postulation of a mind-independent physical world and giving credibility to the belief that some non-human mind or minds are responsible for our experience. Typically, most of the argument is devoted to the former task, and, this done, it is usually assumed to be enough to argue that a will could be efficacious in bringing about the phenomena. Like most other writers I, too, shall concentrate on how to discredit the postulation of a mind-independent physical world.

Although (2) is, logically, the second task, usually one aspect of it is given priority over (1). My account of what a Berkeleian has to do would probably have seemed more familiar if I had broken it down into three stages. The first would have been the refutation of the naïve realist theory of perception, followed by (1) and (2) as given above. This is wrong for two reasons. First, if the order in experience requires no explanation then we would have no reason to believe that the objects of our experience or anything lying behind them existed when we were not perceiving them. (Which means, in the case of things lying behind experience—i.e. of any represented, but not directly perceived reality—we would have no reason to believe in its existence at all.) Thus, even if naïve realism were true and the immediate objects of sense were physical, we would have no reason to believe they existed when not perceived unless there were something inherently improbable in those objects existing only at the times we perceived them. Rationally, it would be mere speculation to suggest that they existed otherwise. Secondly, the refutation of naïve realism is really part of the process of discrediting belief in the physical world and hence belongs with (2). From an idealist standpoint, the significance of refuting naïve realism is not only that it generates epistemological difficulties for belief in a mind-independent physical world, but that it is the first stage in an argument which is meant to prove that we can form no positive conception of the fundamental properties of the matter of such a world. Its purpose is to show that the sensible qualities of which we are aware are mind-dependent and hence to put difficulties in the way of attributing them to anything independent of mind. By contrast, if naïve realism were possible then it would seem that there was no difficulty attributing a sufficiency of properties to matter, for we could attribute the primary and secondary qualities of sense to it.

If I am right in describing the Berkeleian's task as that of proving (1) and (2), it follows that his opponents are, first, the sceptic and, second, the devotee of mind-independent matter. The arguments against the sceptic are sometimes passed over briefly, because the idealist's dialectical opponent is usually, nowadays, a physical realist and so both parties have an interest in playing down the sceptical arguments. An idealist, however, has less right than most to dismiss counter-intuitive positions. I shall try, therefore, to take seriously the sceptical opinion that the organized structure of our experience is something which requires no explanation.

II   SCEPTICISM CONCERNING A PRIORI PROBABILITIES

Our experience is sufficiently highly structured for us to be able to interpret it as experience of a fairly stable physical world. The phenomena are pretty highly and reliably ordered. Our natural response to this is to assume that experience has a cause: it doesn't just happen in this ordered way by accident. Berkeley himself takes it for granted that, given that we do not cause our own sensations, some other agent must be responsible, but this assumption is rationally justified only if it is rational to accept the principle that it is objectively improbable that such order would occur by accident— that is, without something explaining (presumably by causing) it. I shall call this the principle that Order Requires Explanation. In applying this principle to our experience we are presuming that it is an a priori principle; we do not learn a posteriori that the order in the phenomena has a cause, for we have reason to believe that experience has a cause only if we take its orderedness as being evidence for such an hypothesis. The Humean tradition rejects the application of a priori probabilities to empirical questions. On the other hand, belief in such an application is as difficult to doubt as it has been to justify. Common sense argues that if there are no causal constraints on a succession of events then those events should not exhibit clear and distinctive regularities. We assume that, in the absence of causal influence, all possibilities are equally likely and that no striking regularities should emerge. The sceptical rebuttal of this common sense assumption is well known.[3] The sceptic argues that a highly ordered sequence is, a priori, no less probable than any other. Taking the example of throws of a die, a succession of ten throws of six is no more improbable than a succession of any other numbers, including apparently random ones; e.g. 2, 4, 1, 4, 6, 3, 3, 2, 5, 1. This is because at each throw each number has a chance of one in six, so a sequence of

[3] See, for example, A. J. Ayer, *Probability and Evidence* (Macmillan, London, 1972), 27–53.

sixes and the random series each have a probability of $\frac{1}{6} \times \frac{1}{6} \times \frac{1}{6} \ldots$ for each throw; that is, of $1^{10}/6^{10}$. It follows from this that an apparently random sequence of experiences would have just the same improbability as an ordered sequence. A priori probabilities merely state how many possibilities there are and assign a probability to each of one over the total.

Although this argument often fails to carry conviction, it has proved difficult to refute. Indeed most non-sceptical philosophers, especially ones not expert in probability theory—are tempted to follow the strategy of the Scottish minister preaching on the problem of evil ('Brethren, this is a very difficult problem, which we must look squarely in the face, and pass on'). Their intuition that order requires explanation remains undimmed, though they abandon the task of justifying it. I, too, am tempted by such involuntary modesty and what I have to say is extremely tentative.

Perhaps one can solve the problem by switching attention from the probability of particular series to the probability of types of series. What we are interested in is the probability of a series which is *so structured that a conscious subject is able to discern manageable recurrent regularities*. There are obviously many more series of logically possible experiences that do not fit this requirement than ones that do. What we are interested in is the probability of a series *qua* member of such a class. As there are many more series which do not fit this requirement than ones that do, a priori it is improbable that one fitting the requirement would occur by chance. A standard reply to this is that we can always invent a class for any given series which makes it improbable in this way. Thus supposing the series 2, 4, 1, 4 etc. actually occurred, we could say that it belonged to the class containing it alone, or a class containing it and another equally undistinguished series, and argue that it was a priori improbable that a member of such a class should occur. It is essential to my suggested approach that it be true and important that such classes do not pick out a genuine kind of series, but are only classes connected by enumeration. Assuming (as I shall) that there is a difference between genuine kinds, whose members are really similar, and artificial classes, then classes of the arbitrary sort are just irrelevant to questions concerning whether a particular *kind* of series is probable or not. It is natural to suspect that the introduction of kinds of series in preference to individual series as bearers of probability is jerrymandering. Why aren't the probabilities of individual series relevant too? I think the answer to this might lie in the fact that probabilities are comparative and an improbability is only salient if it shows an event to be improbable relative to the other options. All series taken as individuals are equiprobable, so the outcome would not have been less improbable if a different series had occurred. From the perspective of genuine kinds of series this is not so, and on this basis series can be differentiated.

I leave this issue with no confidence that I have advanced it. Even if I have not, this is no comfort to the realist, and the Berkeleian can still fall back on the strong intuition that there must be *some* explanation of order, though the intuition is not yet justified. Popper rejects solipsism on the grounds that he is sure that he could not have produced the music of Bach; to establish the principle that manifest order is not self-explanatory we need only add to Popper's modesty a conviction that the music of Bach did not write itself.[4]

III   BERKELEY'S CREDIBILITY GAP

Given that it can be shown that it is rational to believe that the order in experience requires an explanation, we have to decide what is the best explanation. The most obvious hypothesis is that it is explained by the activity of a mind-independent physical world. This is the most obvious explanation because it spontaneously seems to us that it is an independent physical world we experience. Notice that I do not say that it spontaneously seems to us that it is such a world which *explains* our experience, but that it spontaneously seems to us that we experience a mind-independent physical world. No doubt it follows from the latter that the physical world does explain our experience and no doubt only a moment's reflection is needed to see this, but it is important that what we believe spontaneously is not some explanatory theory which could be common to both direct and representative realism, but is direct realism itself. This is directly relevant to how one should weigh the relative merits of the arguments for idealism and for physical realism.

When it comes to evaluating Berkeley's idealism, even rational thinkers are often openly not disposed to proportion their belief to the evidence or the force of the arguments. Boswell's remarks are typical: 'to me it is not conceivable how Berkeley can be answered

[4] Karl Popper, *Realism and the Aims of Science*, ed. W. W. Bartley III (Hutchinson, London, 1983), 83.

from pure reasonings'; 'though we are satisfied his doctrine is not true, it is impossible to refute it'.[5] Berkeley's audience, philosophers or intelligent laymen, have their consciences tried because they are conscious both of the power of the argument and of their unwillingness to accept the conclusion however powerful the argument may seem. The question is whether this common refusal to follow the argument where it appears to lead is a genuinely disreputable stubbornness, or a manly determination to stand four-square on common sense. I shall argue that it is the former and my principle ally in so arguing is Hume. Hume correctly diagnosed the source of the resistance to Berkeley and showed it to be unreasonable. Not all Berkeley's opponents accept his arguments whilst rejecting his conclusions. Many reject the arguments too. The danger of bad faith comes principally at the point where the arguments purporting to refute naïve realism are accepted, but the idealist response to this situation is ruled out of court. That is, the prejudice against Berkeley shows itself in those who, following the refutation of naïve realism, are determined to hang on to a representative realism, however obscure, rather than adopt idealism, because they believe a priori that any form of physical realism is more plausible than idealism. Hume sees through this prejudice and argues that '[representative realism] has no primary recommendation either to reason or the imagination, but acquires all its influence on the imagination from the former [i.e. naïve realism]'.[6]

In other words, the seemingly overwhelming intuitive priority of realism entirely draws its force from our feeling that the immediate objects of our awareness are mind-independent physical objects. This is the sole origin of the psychological power of realism. Once one is persuaded that these immediate objects are not mind-independent, then the intuitive priority we give to realism has entirely lost its rationale. It is bad faith to pretend that representative realism answers to the intuitions which make realism psychologically compelling, because to get to the representative level we have already discounted as false the substance of that intuition, which was that the immediate objects of awareness are mind-independent. This is surely one matter on which Hume's sceptical argument rings true. Once naïve realism is refuted, the explanation of the nature of the physical

---

[5] *Life of Johnson* (Oxford University Press, London, 1953), 333.
[6] *A Treatise of Human Nature*, 211.

world is entirely open and no one type of account starts with any greater legitimate claims on our credence than any other.

Against this it might be argued that a theory which makes out the origin of our experience to be rather like the world which naïve realism posits is inherently more plausible than a theory which makes the origin of our experience very different from what we had supposed. Now such a theory is likely to go some way towards satisfying our psychological urge towards realism, but that does not mean that it answers to the intuitive ground or rationale of that urge. To see this, suppose that all our experience seemed to have subjective immediate objects, so that we were no more naturally inclined to think of our visual, tactile, or auditory sense-data as external than we are to think it of our pains. Suppose, further, that we were nevertheless still prone to look for an explanation of our experience and of why it fitted into such useful patterns. In these circumstances a representative physical realist explanation would not commend itself intuitively any more than the alternatives. Indeed, we would probably be inclined to doubt whether the notion of something rather like these phenomena yet outside the mind really made sense, just as we think it obvious that nothing outside the mind could resemble pains or other bodily sensations. It is surely not plausible to claim that representative realism is made genuinely more plausible by its fitting a *mistaken* understanding of our experience (namely our inclination to take the immediate objects of our experience as independent of mind) when, if we were not prone to make that mistake, it would seem especially implausible amongst the accounts of the origin of experience.

IV　THE REFUTATION OF NAÏVE REALISM

In the *Third Dialogue* Philonous says,

I do not pretend to be a setter-up of *new notions*. My endeavours tend only to unite and place in a clearer light that truth, which was before shared between the vulgar and the philosophers: the former being of opinion, that *those things they immediately perceive are the real things*; and the latter, that *the things immediately perceived, are ideas which exist only in the mind.* Which two notions put together, do in effect constitute the substance of what I advance.[7]

In the present section I am concerned with Berkeley's defence of

---

[7] *Dialogues*, 262.

the philosophic refutation of that naïve realism which takes the immediate objects of sense to be extra-mental. In section V I shall defend the vulgar view that the realm of immediate experience is the physical world.

As well as his a priori arguments against all forms of extra-mentality, Berkeley has some conceptual arguments specifically against naïve realism. They roughly follow the line of thought that what we perceive are ideas, and such ideas are sensations and that it is 'plainly repugnant' that sensations should exist independently of sense.[8] But in addition to these rather dubious arguments he also employs both the argument from illusion and the causal argument.[9] Although he employs this last argument only in the First Dialogue, I wish to take it up because it is the best prospect for refuting naïve realism. Pitcher states Berkeley's version of the causal argument as follows:

Let us suppose for the moment that there really are, surrounding us, physical objects that exist independently of my mind, and that have colors, emit sounds, and so on. The question then arises: how can anyone perceive the supposed properties of these supposed distant objects? The answer must be that the properties start, or anyway contribute to, a causal chain of events that includes the stimulation of the perceiver's relevant sense organs and, later, of his brain. The brain stimulation, finally, produces in the perceiver's soul sensations of red, C-sharp, or whatever—i.e., ideas of sense. The properties that a person directly perceives, then—i.e., what we have called perceptual properties—are, in every case, nothing but ideas of sense.[10]

At first sight it might seem odd for Berkeley to use such an argument. Tipton claims that it is not available to an idealist because it depends on the physical realism of the scientists.

Locke could take for granted the scientific explanation of perception because he believed that neurophysiological processes played a causal role in the production of data. Not so with Berkeley. Berkeley is quite clear on the point that any physiological apparatus which we suppose plays a causal role in the production of ideas will itself consist of ideas and thus be incapable of playing the causal role.[11]

This criticism is mistaken. Russell said that naïve realism led to

---

[8] *Principles*, 4.
[9] For use of both, see *Dialogues*, 178–91.
[10] G. Pitcher, *Berkeley* (Routledge, London, 1977), 106–7.
[11] I. C. Tipton, *Berkeley: the Philosophy of Immaterialism* (Methuen, London, 1974), 253.

science and that science refutes naïve realism.[12] *If sound*, the causal argument shows that the discoveries of science are inconsistent with naïve realism, and I doubt whether any naïve realist would wish to be committed to denying the accounts of the causal mechanisms of perception which science discovers. Hence the argument is a legitimate *reductio*. Berkeley's idealist reinterpretation of what it is for there to be a mechanism of perception is on the same footing as his reinterpretation of any other micro-physical explanation. It simply reinterprets the view that the neural process caused the experience, saying instead that in those circumstances under which someone observing S's brain would have certain experiences, which we treat as perceptions of, for example, the visual cortex, S himself will invariably be having visual experience.

Pitcher's objection to the causal argument is a familiar one, namely that it confuses the false claim that the stimulation of the brain produces an object of awareness with the correct claim that it produces a state or act of awareness of something.[13] This objection will be unsound if it is the case that a state or act of awareness must invariably possess an internal object, for then production of the state or act carries with it the production of an object. I shall argue that this is the case.

First, it is a necessary truth that without an object in some sense there cannot be an experience, for any experience must be *of* something. Second, in the case of pure hallucination the object of the experience must be something generated internally by the brain, and not an external thing, for there is no appropriate external thing involved. So if we can show that what is true of hallucinations must also be true of normal perception the causal argument is vindicated. What we require to achieve this generalization is the truth of the following two propositions.

(1) It is theoretically possible by activating some brain process which is involved in a particular type of perception to cause a hallucination which exactly resembles that perception in its subjective character.

(2) It is necessary to give the same account of both hallucinating and perceptual experiences *when they have the same neural cause*. Thus, it is not, for example, plausible to say that the hallucinatory experience

    [12] B. Russell, *An Inquiry into Meaning and Truth* (George Allen and Unwin, London, 1940), 13.
    [13] *Berkeley*, 108.

involves a mental image or sense-datum, but that the perception does not, if the two experiences have the same proximate—i.e. neural—cause.

Together they entail that perceptual processes in the brain produce some subjective experiential content—that is some object of awareness which cannot be identified with any feature of the external world. This is contrary to any form of naïve or direct realism, which requires that, in ordinary perception, features of the external world constitute the only objects or contents of experience. It is irrelevant for present purposes whether the subjective experiential content be construed as sense-data, qualia, intentional objects, or modes of sensing (though I think the first two options represent the most plausible accounts). What matters is that there is some sort of 'veil of perception' dividing us from the mind-independent world.

Of these two propositions, the second is the more controversial. Indeed, (1) seems to be generally accepted and for present purposes I shall assume that it is uncontroversial and concentrate on (2).

A perceptual realist will probably decide to concede (1), accepting that the appropriate brain process is sufficient to produce a given subjective type of experience however it itself is brought about; whether, that is, it is activated in the course of perception, or artificially. To prevent the refutation of naïve realism he therefore denies proposition (2). He denies that the brain process produces more than a bare act of awareness in the case of normal perception, whilst allowing that the same process produces an internal object when artificial stimulation produces a hallucination. 'I agree', he might say, 'that being in a certain brain state is a sufficient internal causal condition for having an experience of a certain subjective type, but I believe that we must give a separate account of hallucinatory or artificial experiences from that which we give of normal experiences. When the brain process is induced artificially, the subject has a hallucination, and he "sees" or "has" images of physical objects, but when the objects are the causes of the brain state in the normal way, then he sees them themselves directly.' Someone who argues in this way is adopting what Hinton calls *the disjunctive analysis* of experience: that is, he is claiming that two radically different states constitute subjectively similar experiential states, as between perception and hallucination. There would, of course, be nothing strange in such a theory, if we had not stipulated that both experiences have the same immediate neural cause. This is what makes it seem strange to say that the experiences which result from this one type of cause can be of intrinsically different types.

The disjunctive theory has achieved something of a vogue, but its two most recent exponents, Snowdon and McDowell, ignore the difficulties posed for the theory by allowing that perception and hallucination might have the same immediate cause.[14] Pitcher and Hinton, however, take note of the case where hallucination and perception operate through precisely the same brain state and see the need to defend the view that nevertheless the products of that brain state are essentially different in the two cases.[15]

The general principle lying behind (2) could be put in the form of the slogan 'Same proximate cause, same immediate effect'. Call this slogan 'S'. Pitcher accepts S, but in a form which would not sustain (2). He says, 'this principle S although it may be true for every cause-and-effect pair, is not true for them *under every description*.'[16]

The idea is that though the immediate effects of a certain brain state may always involve 'seeming to see something red', and thus in that respect always be of the same type, they may also be of different types in that sometimes the immediate effect will fall under the description 'hallucinating something red' and sometimes under the description 'seeing something red'. The general principle that immediate effects of the same type of proximate cause need not be of identical type under all descriptions is quite sound. For example, if someone strikes identical nails into identical walls with identical hammers with identical force the effect in one might be describable as 'the picture's being hung' and in the other as 'the gas pipe's being severed', each description applying to only one of the effects. The description common to both effects will concern a nail moving a certain distance into a wall. However, it is plainly not arbitrary what the common description is. If it were sufficient for the satisfaction of S simply that there be *some* common description then it would become vacuous. Suppose that, despite the qualitative identity of hammers, nails, walls, and force of blow, in one case the nail penetrated one inch, in the other two inches. This would involve an infringement of S, for the

[14] P. Snowdon, 'Perception, vision and causation', *P.A.S.* LXXXI (1980–1), 176–92. J. McDowell, 'Criteria, defeasibility and knowledge', *Proc. Brit. Acad.* 1982 (Oxford University Press, London, 1983), 455–79.
[15] G. Pitcher, *A Theory of Perception* (Princeton U. P., New Jersey, 1971), 54–7. J. Hinton, *Experiences* (Clarendon Press, Oxford, 1973), 75–93.
[16] *A Theory of Perception*, 56–7.

same cause would have had relevantly different effects, but nevertheless the effects are identical under some descriptions; e.g. the description 'a nail's penetrating a wall'. It is often said that any two things are similar in some respect: if this is true, then any effects of some one type of cause will be identical under some description or other. To save S from vacuity it is therefore essential to say something about the descriptions under which the events must be similar: some restrictions must be imposed. Intuitively, it is not difficult to do this. The different descriptions which applied to the nail applied in virtue of features of the situation more remote from the causal event—the hammer blow—than was its immediate effect, the nail's movement. They relate either to context—e.g. the presence of the picture—or to further effects—e.g. the nail's piercing the pipe. Intuitively, S applies to the most specific and immediate characterization of the effect. Thus the communality of a generic description such as 'entering the wall' will not satisfy S if one nail entered by one inch, the other by two: nor will it do that both hammerings had the remote or mediate effect of hanging a picture if each did so by moving the nail a different distance. The former situation parallels what Pitcher says about the mental state caused by the brain process. He says that the same brain state will always cause a 'seeming to see something red' but that sometimes it will do this by causing a genuine seeing and sometimes by causing a hallucination, where these two states are quite different. We do not in fact have a genuine case of S where the effects brought under the same description are analysed as having relevantly different structures or component elements. A sense-datum theorist, for example, has no problem with this, for he says that the same brain state causes something—a having of a sense-datum—by which it causes either seeing or hallucinating and which common element is a part of both larger effects, each depending also on further circumstances. But on the disjunctive analysis seeing and hallucinating are not to be analysed into a shared element plus differing extra features.

It seems, then, that when one realizes the need to apply S to certain sorts of effect, Pitcher's argument will not work. Hinton does what is required and simply denies S. He says that it rests on 'dubious and arbitrary general and metaphysical beliefs . . . about effects of causes'.[17] He presents an explicitly disjunctive analysis of such generic concepts as 'experience' or 'seeming to see'. Such expressions are taken as referring not to something common to both perception and

[17] *Experiences*, 75.

hallucination but generically to a disjunction of them both. Thus he deals with the final outcome of the causal process as follows:

The impulse reaches certain specified structures, and then what? My continuation was, '—and then one perceives a flash of light or has the illusion of doing so, as the case may be, according to the nature of the initial stimulus'.[18]

He is quite aware of the motives that gave rise to belief in S.

But it is natural to make some such retort as this, that what then happens cannot depend on the initial stimulus; what happens next must be the same, whether the initial stimulus was light striking the retina, or an electric current passing through the retina, or whatever it was.[19]

But he rejects this 'natural retort' on the grounds cited above, namely that it rests on arbitrary and dubious metaphysical beliefs. Hinton holds that S is a sound principle when applied to causal laws that relate physical or public events, but that it is mere prejudice to extend it to psychophysical connections (or, for that matter, to mental-mental ones). His argument is that we know that S applies to physical laws because we can in these cases identify the effect independently of identifying the cause—this is part of the publicity of physical events— and have thereby been able to establish empirically the truth of S in these contexts. But we cannot do this for mental effects; for example, it follows *ex hypothesi* that one cannot tell the type of hallucination that we are considering from a perception without knowing the causal ancestry of the experience: the experience itself does not reveal which it is. Therefore we are not compelled to apply S in the mental case, for we have not identified the nature of the effect independently of the causal context and verified that S applies.[20] However, this is an adequate argument only if there are no general considerations in favour of S—only if, that is, S relies upon empirical proof in each type of context.

First, we can concede that one is under no compulsion to accept S, if by compulsion one means logical necessity. Second, we can concede that S is more incontrovertibly established in purely physical contexts. However, it seems that there are good reasons for extending it to psychophysical contexts and indeed for adopting it as a perfectly general principle. The reason for applying it in psychophysical contexts is that if one does not do so one is saddled with two bizarre mysteries. First, there would be the problem of trying to understand how a brain process could alter its causal properties in response to its own remote causes. It would be as if the brain knew that when it was being activated artificially it needed to provide subjective content for the experience, whereas when activated normally it knew that the external world would perform that task for it! Second and consequently, there is another problem, namely that unless S applies to psychophysical connections the existence of hallucinations becomes a mystery. Given that Hinton is conceding that hallucinations could be produced by stimulating just those brain states involved in perception (i.e. he concedes (1)) how are we to make sense of why this should be so if it is not by thinking of these as cases in which the state is activated and performs its normal function—i.e. has its normal upshot—in an abnormal context? Otherwise the production of hallucinations in this sort of way would seem to cast the brain state in a role something like that of a Cartesian demon, producing an effect specialized solely to the context of deception. This would be a strange expedient to adopt in an attempt to save direct realism. In order to make sense of why it should be possible to produce hallucinations in the way specified in (1) we have to be able to make sense of the notion of 'what the brain state does in both cases'—that is of a common element not itself analysable into Hinton's disjunction. Thus we face a choice between accepting the radical unintelligibility of why there should be hallucinations in these contexts or of accepting that S is applicable here.

It seems, therefore, that S is sound (*contra* Hinton) and sound in a strict enough sense (*contra* Pitcher) to justify (2), for the production of an internal object of experience is part of the brain state's immediate effect and failure to characterize it as 'internal' would be to fail to describe it specifically. Hence Berkeley is right to believe that the causal argument refutes naïve realism.

V   THE REFUTATION OF REPRESENTATIVE REALISM

Once naïve realism is refuted the idealist can see his objective in sight. Naïve, common-sense realism can no longer be transformed into a philosophical position, and physical realism has lost any legitimate hold on our intuition.

At this point the modern idealist's argument must diverge from

Berkeley's own in one important respect. Berkeley's argument against representative realism rests fundamentally on the impossibility of conceiving of unperceived objects. His arguments for this have a stronger and a weaker form. In the strong form he argues that the very notion of unperceived existence is unintelligible: the weaker version is specifically directed against Locke's theory and maintains that the existence of primary without secondary qualities is inconceivable.[21] The emphasis on what we can conceive is associated with an imagist theory of thought and together they generate a very restricted and nominalist theory of meaning. If such a theory is defensible at all, I know of no way of defending it. Nevertheless, the spirit of Berkeley's attack on representative realism can be disconnected from these doubtful arguments. Two genuinely Berkeleian thoughts can be used to generate arguments against a transcendental material realm beyond the veil of perception. First there is the thought that we can give no adequate content to our conception of such matter. Second is the conviction that our conception of the physical world is so tied to the manifest and discoverable structure of the world as we experience it that nothing transcendental and possibly remote from that structure could qualify as our world. We shall see that these lines of thought are mutually supporting. I shall begin by pursuing the first.

Apart from undermining the intuitive legitimacy of realism, the main significance of the refutation of naïve realism is that it makes it implausible to impute non-dispositional secondary qualities to matter itself. The arguments for this are too well known to need rehearsing here. This leaves us with the problem of trying to decide what properties matter is supposed to possess. Notoriously, the Cartesian idea that it is purely geometrical will not do for it leaves no distinction between matter and empty volumes: a filler for these volumes is required. Notoriously too, Locke's filler, solidity, will not do the job, for that quality collapses on examination into a composite of the dispositional-cum-relational property of impenetrability, and the secondary quality, hardness. What the physical realist requires is clearly put by Harré:

Solidity is the alleged quality, the possession of which is responsible for the fact that two material things cannot occupy the same place at the same time and is logically connected with impenetrability, the power to resist penetra-

²¹ Stronger version, *Principles*, 22–4; weaker version, *Principles*, 9–10.

tion, in that the possession of the former is supposed to account for the manifestation of the latter.[22]

Mackie appears to believe that this is possible. He says that our conception of solidity is 'only the indirect and relative notion of it as the supposed or inferred ground of a power which is itself learned from its manifestation'.[23]

We can presume here that Mackie intends 'ground' to signify something stronger than contingent connection, otherwise the grounding of impenetrability would no more explain impenetrability than would colour if all impenetrable objects were coloured. I take it that Mackie is after something of the sort Harré describes. But how can there be a necessary connection between a dispositional and a categorical property? Such a connection can be made trivially by use of a 'bridge concept'. A puncture is by definition a double event consisting first of the breaching of a surface, then of the escape of a contained gas or liquid, but the existence of this concept does not explain the connection of the first event with the second. Similarly, calling something 'solid' if it possessed quality Q in association with impenetrability, would not explain how the former grounded the latter. Mackie seems to be confused about what would constitute the prescribed sort of necessary connection. He says: 'Modern physics will not use [solidity]; but electric charge is one feature which has come into physical theory to play a corresponding part, and mass (rest mass) is perhaps another.'[24]

Electric charge is akin to concepts such as energy or field and is a dispositional or power concept. Mass, too, is either defined in, for our purposes, a question-begging way as a 'quantity of matter' or simply records how objects behave in their interactions. Now some philosophers have claimed that the physical world consists essentially of relational properties—generally of active powers or fields. Hume's objection to conceiving bodies as volumes of impenetrability is still essentially the objection to such conceptions, namely that they are vacuous.[25] An object cannot simply be a spatially extended capacity to effect other spatially extended capacities to effect . . . An ontology of mutual influences is not an ontology at all unless the possessors of the influence possess more substantial features.

[22] R. Harré, *Principles of Scientific Thinking* (Macmillan, London, 1970), 305.
[23] J. L. Mackie, *Problems from Locke* (Clarendon Press, Oxford, 1976), 25.
[24] Ibid.
[25] *Treatise* I. iv. 4, 228–30.

It might be objected that the claim that there could not be a categorical property which was logically connected with a power is an a priori prejudice, probably inspired by atomistic and empiricist assumptions: we cannot legislate a priori about what types of property there may be. But the objection to this sort of property is not based upon such an appeal to intuition.

It is trivially true that there is no property P the possession of which analytically entails the possession of a power Q, P not itself being explicitly a power. As the connection would not be nominal or analytic, it would have to be *de re* a posteriori. In fact two sorts of such connection are sometimes considered. The first is not properly a posteriori, but rather lives in the shadow cast by the 'paradox of analysis'. There are some truths which are not analytic in the sense of being trivially obvious or merely verbal, but which are still knowable a priori by conceptual analysis. Those physicalists who seek to prepare the way for identifying mental with physical properties by giving the former a topic neutral analysis see truths about mentality in this way. One way in which a necessary connection might be discovered between some non-power property and a power would be if a philosophical analysis uncovered an unobvious connection between them. I do not see how this method could lead to a solution in the present case, because I do not see how, once the non-power concept was fully analysed, if it revealed a power-entailing element, that could be other than contingently associated with its non-power aspect. Anyway, I know of no such analysis. The second and properly a posteriori necessary connection which is nowadays discerned between concepts would be some form of *de re* necessity. It is often said, for example, that a *de re* necessity links the property of being hot and that of possessing a high mean kinetic energy of its constitutive molecules. Such necessities, however, seem to be more a matter of verbal definition than is generally allowed. Even if we decide to annex the term 'heat' to phenomena associated with mean kinetic energy and 'mean kinetic energy' to behaviour which includes the normal phenomena of heat, it does not follow that there could not be phenomena in all other respects just like either of them yet lacking this connection. (Indeed, if Kripke is correct in his explanation of how such identities can be a posteriori, there must be such possibilities.[26]) Heat and mean kinetic energy, therefore, seem to be only 'bridge concepts', like 'puncture' and do not non-trivially

[26] S. Kripke, *Naming and Necessity* (Blackwell, Oxford, 1980), 132 f.

explain the connection between the two sets of phenomena which belong paradigmatically to each. The same would apply to any attempt to explain impenetrability in terms of any underlying quality or structure.

The situation is, therefore, that the following three negative propositions concerning the nature of matter can be proved beyond reasonable doubt: (i) that matter does not possess non-dispositional secondary qualities; (ii) that matter does not possess any sort of primary quality which could logically ground its basic powers—e.g. its impenetrability; (iii) that matter cannot consist solely of spatially arranged powers or dispositions. As far as I can see this leaves only one possible conception, namely (iv) that matter possesses some unknown quality or qualities, conceived on analogy with a sensible quality such as colour. As we have shown that there cannot be an internal or necessary connection between an intrinsic quality of this sort and causal properties, the causal properties of matter must be dictated by laws or powers which are only contingently connected with the matter: that is, there is nothing about the intrinsic nature of the matter which determines what laws govern its conduct, nor to prevent its being governed by different laws at different times.

We have done all we can to develop the first Berkeleian thought, which was that we can give no adequate content to our concept of matter, and have forced the realist to (iv) in his defence. Against that we now bring to bear our second Berkeleian thought, which was that a transcendental world beyond the veil of perception would not be the physical world that we inhabit.

The picture of the physical-cum-empirical world which the present conception of matter, when combined with the refutation of naïve realism, requires might be called a 'two-world' picture. There is the world of transcendental physical reality, which consists of objects possessing the unknown qualitative nature, and there is the common, collective, or intersubjective phenomenal 'world', which is the world-as-experienced. The latter world is usually thought of as *representing* the former by *resembling* it, at least in structural or abstract ways. One thing which is meant by saying that the phenomenal world represents or resembles the transcendental physical world is that the scientific laws devised to apply to the former, if correct, also apply (at least approximately) to the latter. Physical science, though developed through our acquaintance with the world-as-experienced, aspires to describe the formal features of the world-in-itself. On the present theory of matter, however, there is no need for there to be such a match between the laws discovered by empirical science and those which govern the world in itself. The world-in-itself consists of the qualitative core contingently governed by certain laws. Amongst these laws are those which determine how the world will appear. In this way the transcendental physical world gives rise to the empirical world. But it is logically possible that there might be many different exclusive sets of laws which fix how the world should appear. It follows that, from how it appears we cannot infer how it works in itself. There is an uncertainty in our conception of how the transcendental world is which parallels that which is generally supposed to exist in our explanation of actions from beliefs and desires. It has been argued that different combinations of imputed beliefs and desires will explain the same action, and, as we have no independent way of fixing either parameter, the explanation is holistic and undecidable. Similarly, our experience is the product of (a) how the world-in-itself really works and (b) the laws transforming that into experience. *Ex hypothesi* we have no direct access to either of these things, for we experience the product, the intersubjective empirical world. Remember that the qualitative core of itself entails no particular laws, for the qualitative core intrinsically possesses no causal properties, not even of solidity. It is as if the transcendental world was in a code which is being interpreted by a machine to the internal working of which we can have no access. The messages that reach us are clear and consistent, but that is quite compatible with the original code being changed daily, so long as the principles on which the interpreting machine works also change. It follows that it is both epistemically and logically (or *metaphysically*, as some say in such contexts) possible that the transcendental world operates on laws quite different from those which a perfect science of the empirical world would generate. That it is logically (or metaphysically) possible follows from the fact that the intrinsic nature of the world (i.e. the unknown qualitative nature of its matter) entails nothing about the laws of its operation and hence provides no constraints on how it should operate and hence on whether its laws of operation should alter. (It is not reasonable to say that the identity of the transcendental world changes if its laws change, because the very same quality-bearing objects could come to be governed by different laws: if they are the same objects then it is the same world.) It is, therefore, not merely the case that we do not know whether the transcendental world follows the laws derivable from the empirical world, but that, even if it does, it is logically and metaphysically possible that it might cease to do so, without our being any the wiser.

This creates a problem for the physical realist. The physical realist's conception of the physical world has two components. The first is that the world is mind-independent; the second is that the physical world is what physical science investigates and hence its nomological structure is what physical science approximately uncovers. Both these are necessary truths for the physical realist. It is the former which distinguishes his position as realist, but the second condition is also essential, both (a) because it is a conceptual truth that the physical world is what physical science investigates, if it investigates anything real, and (b) because if mind-independence is severed from being the object of science then 'physicality' comes to mean simply 'non-mentality', and to have no positive content of its own. But the concept of physicality is not that thin. It combines both the idea of being 'out there' with that of being investigable by us in certain ways. A world not accessible to certain sorts of investigation—paradigmatically those exhibited by physical science—is not the physical world. Once naïve realism is refuted these two conditions come apart, for the following reasons.

The representative realist holds that the transcendental world is the physical world. It is a necessary condition for the truth of this that the transcendental world have approximately the same nomological structure as a developed physical science would attribute to the physical world. An argument against physical realism might initially proceed:

(1) As I have shown it is possible that the transcendental world does not realize, even approximately, physical laws.

(2) It has already been established that realizing physical laws, at least approximately, is a necessary condition for being the physical world.

Therefore

(3) It is possible that the transcendental world be not the physical world.

(4) Identities are necessary.

Therefore

(5) The transcendental world is not the physical world.

The necessity of identities is essential to the argument. The representative realist's natural inclination will be to say that the transcendental world is the physical world provided that the transcendental world embodies scientific laws; if it does not then there is no physical world, however things may appear. This could be maintained consistently with the necessity of identities provided that the realization (or not) of scientific laws were an essential feature of a given transcendental world, so that if the actual transcendental world embodies physical laws, it then qualifies essentially as physical. But the contingent connection between laws and ultimate objects means that it is a contingent feature of a given transcendental world whether or not it realizes a given set of laws. Suppose that the transcendental world did realize physical laws and thus itself counted as physical, it might cease to realize them. The realist would then have to say that the physical world had ceased to exist, though the transcendental world, which had been the physical world, endured. Wiggins has, I think, shown that identity cannot work in this way, provided that the referring expression in question (in this case 'the transcendental world' and 'the physical world') pick out a substantial and complete object.[27] The transcendental world could be, then cease to be, the physical world only if being the physical world was a matter of playing a certain role, like being Lord Mayor, not a matter of being a particular thing or substance. But if we adopt this view of being physical, then it follows that what is physical (what 'plays that role') is not essentially physical. First, this is not our normal (especially not our normal realist) conception of the physical world: and second it concedes to the non-realist that the physical world is a logically secondary product of the action of something not itself physical. Additionally, the representative realist's premiss that there is no physical world unless it is the transcendental world is not plausible. Suppose that initially the transcendental world realized physical laws, but then came not to do so, though the world remained unchanged from the viewpoint of all conscious beings within the natural or empirical realm. It seems wrong to say that the physical world would have ceased to exist just because the way it was sustained by the transcendental reality had changed. If that change were gradual, there would be no point at which it was natural to say that, unbeknownst to us, the physical world had ceased to exist. If this is accepted, then being the physical world is not just a role played by the

[27] D. R. P. Wiggins, in either *Identity and Spatio-Temporal Continuity* (Blackwell, Oxford, 1967), 1–25, or *Sameness and Substance* (Blackwell, Oxford, 1980), 15–44.

transcendental world because the physical world can continue when the transcendental world ceases to play that role.[28]

In sum, my position is this: acceptance that if there is a physical world then that is what physical science investigates, and observation of the logical features of identity, together show that what lies behind the veil of perception cannot be the physical world. Naïve realism, Berkeleian style, is correct; the physical world is the world of experience, irrespective of what more distant reality sustains it. And the world of experience is essentially mind-dependent because given the falsehood of the physical realist version of naïve realism the immediate objects of experience are mind-dependent.

VI THE TRANSCENDENTAL CAUSE OF EXPERIENCE

To complete the Berkeleian programme it is necessary to show that God is the transcendental reality which causes experience. The argument so far is neutral on this matter, being compatible with taking that reality to be, for example, a Kantian noumenal world. All that we have proved is that the transcendental cause of experience is not the physical world. What can be concluded, I think, is that, if one is a theist, then it is rational to assign God the Berkeleian role, because the only reason a theist resists this position is that he wishes God to create and use the physical world as an instrument, but we have proved that the phenomenal, not the transcendental world, is the physical world. To demonstrate the full conclusion it would probably be necessary to prove that only a mind can be an agent,

---

[28] My argument for idealism is a much simplified version of one employed by John Foster in *The Case for Idealism* (Routledge, London, 1982) Part III. My argument and Foster's both involve the claim that a transcendental world could have an essentially different nomological organization from the one we attribute to the physical world. To reach the idealist conclusion, I am content to appeal to the intuition that a physical world must realize the laws uncovered by a complete physical science, from which it follows that a transcendental world, not essentially possessing that organization, is not physical. Foster's argument does not rest on such an appeal to intuition, because he proves that the possible differences in nomological organization between the transcendental world and the world as pictured in physical science include possible differences in the geometries of their spaces. It follows from this that the space of a transcendental world could not be physical space and hence, *a fortiori*, that such a world is not the physical world. It will not have escaped some readers' notice that the claim that a transcendental world might fail to realize scientific law is challenged by Hilary Putnam in the final lecture of *Meaning and the Moral Sciences* (Routledge, London, 1980). It is not possible here to investigate the relationship between his form of anti-realism and the idealism for which I am arguing, except to say that they are entirely different.

hence nothing non-mental could cause our experience. Then it would be necessary to prove that there is just one such agent and he is God; or, perhaps, that God is the controlling principal among such agents. It would be disingenuous to suggest that lack of space is the only reason why I cannot prove this at present.

CHAPTER 10

THE SELF IN BERKELEY'S PHILOSOPHY

A. C. LLOYD

IT is well known that Berkeley intended to devote a Second Part of his *Principles* to the nature of God and of finite minds. The unfinished manuscript was lost in Italy; and no doubt his reluctance 'to do such a disagreeable thing as writing twice on the same subject' led him to add those laconic and puzzling references to 'notions of spirit' in the second edition of the *Principles*. That the self occupied for Berkeley an important place in his philosophy has hardly been questioned. Yet with a few recent exceptions his critics and exponents do not seem to have considered sufficiently and in the light of his extant writings what his account of it might have been. At the same time it has commonly been assumed that it must contradict the rest of his philosophy, and that this contradiction falls under two heads, which may be called ontological and epistemological. The first is the difficulty of squaring a description of a self which is not a bundle of perceptions with the interrelated rejections of abstraction and materialism; the second is the difficulty of squaring our possession of 'notions' with an otherwise nominalist theory of knowledge.

If such violent inconsistencies are to be admitted in the central doctrines of a philosophy, it is natural to wonder how so meticulous a philosopher as Berkeley should appear ignorant of them. Certainly there is an idealist viewpoint from which the history of philosophy is considered as the development of theories from premises which contain contradictions. In this view the development is not simply a logical one; for even the philosopher who tries to deny his predecessor's propositions does not really rid himself of them, since in denying them he remains tainted, so to speak, with the presuppositions which gave rise to them, and their 'dialectical' nature will appear in a new disguise elsewhere in his philosophy. The short answer to this is that it seems better to make sure first that the inconsistencies are there.

There is a second way of accounting at least in part for possible inconsistencies. This is the theory that there is a development in

Berkeley's philosophy and that he came to give up or emasculate his
nominalist doctrine of abstraction. If so, there is evidently no simple
system in which to place an account of the self and no body of
teaching from which to infer what was Berkeley's account of it. This
is, however, not a philosophical, but a historical theory, derived from
a study of his writings, and it is one which, though once popular, can
be shown to be very unlikely. His Notebooks, now usually called
Philosophical Commentaries and finished probably two years before
publication of the *Principles*, are crowded with entries describing the
self and our knowledge of it. A difficult, but on the whole self-
consistent account emerges, which is certainly the same as that
implied by the scattered references in the works he published. They
do not use 'notion' in Berkeley's special sense of it; the 1734 edition of
the *Principles* (140) read, 'In a large sense indeed, we may be said to
have an idea or rather a notion of *spirit*'; but it has been common
knowledge since T. E. Jessop's edition in 1937 that the words 'or
rather a notion', which were added in this edition, were also in the
1710 MS, but erased. As for abstraction, it used to be suggested that
the omission in the 1752 edition of *Alciphron* VII of the three sections
attacking abstract general ideas implied the weakening of an earlier
nominalism. But apart from removing an argument which is out of
place, the shorter version is if anything more nominalist by leaving
particular words or signs, instead of particular ideas, to denote other
particulars. In the least nominalist of his books, *Siris* (323), he still
points out the distinction between 'a really existing spirit' and 'an
abstract idea compounded of inconsistencies, and prescinded from
all real things, as some moderns understand abstraction'. Absolute
space and motion are also rejected along with 'the presumed evidence
of mathematical notions and reasonings' (281, 318). And if Berkeley
had *intended* a development of his epistemology would he have
republished, of all his works, the *De Motu* eight years later? In fact it
is because he is determined to remain faithful to his denial of abstract
ideas that his description of the mind is so difficult.

I have not argued that Berkeley's philosophy was not inconsistent,
only that if it was, he was unaware of it. It was necessary, however, to
suggest some prima-facie reasons why it should not be in the nature of
the case absurd to look for a single theory of the self which belonged
to that philosophy. The difficulties summarized earlier as ontological
and epistemological will still arise; and it is convenient to attempt an
account in that order, by separating as far as possible (i) the nature of

the self, together with its place in ethics, and its compatibility with immaterialism, from (ii) knowledge of the self and its compatibility with nominalism, or the denial of general ideas. Whether Berkeley's views are correct is of course a different question from the question what his views were, and I do not propose to discuss it. Many of the difficulties, however, may be thought of interest in themselves so far as they are difficulties which face any consistent empiricism or any description of the self given in terms of activity alone.

I   THE NATURE OF THE SELF

The self in Berkeley's writings is also called 'mind', 'spirit', and 'soul'. It is identified by him with the will or that which acts.[1] The Cartesian view of thought as the essence of mind is not rejected utterly (*De Motu*, 30). But it is the activity in thought which is essential; and this is the same activity, whether it is found in volition, in loving or hating, in memory, in imagination, or in perception.[2] It will be remembered that one (though only one) of the marks of distinction between ideas of imagination and ideas of perception, according to Berkeley, is that the former are self-evidently dependent on our will while the latter are self-evidently not. Now this at once presents a threat to the theory of immaterialism itself. For although objects of imagination may be 'suggested' by objects of perception, as the colour blue is by the sound of the word 'blue',[3] this does not imply any activity in an idea. For Berkeley the only conceivable activity is mental activity. Are there then acts as well as objects of cognition? The question arises acutely in cases of sense perception: since all my ideas are in the mind, but passive, how can they be called 'my' ideas at all unless (a) my mind is just a succession of ideas or (b) we separate my acts of perception from their objects? The first solution is certainly not Berkeley's. At the same time immaterialism requires us to reject solution (b).

The point may perhaps be elaborated because it has often been suggested (notably by Russell in *Problems of Philosophy*) that the failure to distinguish act and object was simply an oversight on Berkeley's part—that had he considered it, he might have concluded

---

[1] *PC*, 478a, 712, 788; *Principles*, 27; *De Motu* passim; Letter to Johnson 25. xi. 1729, *Works*, ii. 280; cf. *Siris*, 248.

[2] *PC*, 854; *Principles*, 49; cf. *Alciphron* VII Sect. 8 (sections of *Alciphron* are numbered here as in the 1st and 2nd editions), pp. 296–9.

[3] *Theory of Vision Vindicated* (henceforth *VV*) *Works*, i. Sects. 9, 10.

that it was the act, not the object, which was mental or alternatively that *percipi* is not to be identified with *esse* but is a necessary condition of it. It may still be worth quoting, however, the following passages which demonstrate that, rightly or wrongly, he was denying the distinction as consciously as Hume denied it.

(1) Consciousness, perception, existence of Ideas seem to be all one. (*PC*, 578)

(2) . . . wherein I pray you does the perception of white differ from white. (*PC*, 585)

(3) The Distinguishing betwixt an Idea and perception of the Idea has been one great cause of Imagining material substances. (*PC*, 609)

(4) PHIL. . . . You are at liberty to recover any slips you might have made, or offer whatever you have omitted, which makes for your first opinion.

HYL. One great oversight I take to be this: that I did not sufficiently distinguish the *object* from the *sensation.* . . . (*Dialogues*, 194.)

In the last passage Philonous does not simply ask Hylas (as one might have expected him to do) to find the distinction impossible by 'ransacking his understanding' but falls back on his regular *ad hominem* argument that primary and secondary qualities are equally inconceivable in an unthinking substance. Hylas rightly complains, 'You have an artful way, Philonous, of diverting our enquiry from the subject.' And Philonous goes on to say that sensation is intended by Hylas as an act of the mind, but the mind 'is to be accounted *active* in its perceptions so far forth as *volition* is included in them'. In plucking a flower and in applying it to the nose, replies Philonous, I am active—

But is either of these smelling? . . . I act too in drawing the air through my nose; because my breathing so rather than otherwise, is the effect of my volition. But neither can this be called *smelling* . . . But I do not find my will concerned any farther. (p. 196.)

We must return to this.

(5) In truth the object and the sensation are the same thing, and cannot therefore be abstracted from each other.

This statement in the 1710 edition of the *Principles* (5) was omitted from the second edition. The omission does not seem to indicate a change of position from that of the 'juvenile' Notebooks. The sentence in fact spoils the argument. For Berkeley is here arguing only that it is impossible to imagine the existence of a sensible thing apart from the perception of it; and this is not the same as to argue that the two are identical.

Leaving aside the validity of his position, I think in fact that the unsatisfactoriness of many of Berkeley's arguments is due to the combination of two factors—his intense desire to convert his readers and the necessity of avoiding a Humean theory of the self. And Berkeley clearly made up his mind at an early age that each of us has a direct knowledge of the activity which is his mind. But throughout the Notebooks he is puzzled how this is to be consistent with other equally strong convictions. He decided that will and our knowledge of it were not to be discussed at all in Part I of the *Principles*.[4] But when he comes to publish a second edition he has no design of rewriting the lost Second Part (the words 'Part I' are left off the title page). He is thus in the quandary of having to add too little or too much: too little if he is merely dogmatic, which he clearly is in not giving an account of 'notions' as he had done of 'general ideas', too much if he says sufficient about volition and the necessary relation of ideas to it to cast immediate doubts on the theory of abstraction which had been a mainstay of his immaterialism.

To return now to the question what it can mean to call ideas 'my' ideas, Berkeley's answer is naturally connected with his description of the relation of ideas to the mind. When it is objected that he makes the mind extended by making extension a mode which is predicated of the subject in which it inheres, he replies that qualities 'are in the mind only as they are perceived by it—that is, not by way of *mode* or *attribute*, but only by way of *idea*' (*Principles*, 49). But object and act of perception are indistinguishable, and to describe the relation as 'by way of *idea*' is simply to make it unique and indefinable. Berkeley's meaning is, I think, that *consciousness* is a characteristic of ideas themselves: 'Consciousness, perception, existence of Ideas seem to be all one'—only, 'consciousness' is misleading because the word appears to convey activity. Moreover each visual, tactile, olfactory idea and so on does not merely have the characteristic of consciousness or being perceived, but the determinate characteristic of being seen, touched, or smelt.[5] If this is called 'cognition', then cognition is wholly passive. But it can only be called 'passive' because we know

---

[4] *PC*, 792.

[5] To be strict, this should be pressed further, (i) by the removal of a distinction between a subject and its quality, (ii) by being made more determinate—e.g. a crimson colour, a tulip-like smell. But it is irrelevant here.

what activity is; and activity which is defined as the producing, discontinuing, or changing of anything is found in memory and imagination; and this too is always determinate—not recollection, but the recollection of a particular tulip or what not. This determinateness raises more difficulties which must be discussed shortly.

First, however, there is the objection which was implied by Philonous in text (4), that if cognition is itself passive, there is no place for the mind in mere sense perception—so that percepts are nobody's percepts. Berkeley's answer to this is to be found explicitly in two notes from the *Philosophical Commentaries*.

While I exist or have any Idea I am eternally, constantly willing, my acquiescing in the present State is willing. (791)

This is explained later:

It seems there can be no perception, no Idea without Will, being there are no Ideas so indifferent but one had rather Have them than annihilation, or annihilation than them. (833.)

This *acquiescing*, which must not be confused with the usually accompanying affective states of pleasure or pain, might nowadays be called 'attention'. And Berkeley's point is that, although the existence of sensible ideas does not depend on our will, we try either to prolong an idea or to remove it; this may take the form of effective action, in sniffing to create the condition under which the tulip will be smelt, or we may be unable to alter the sensations (as of some pains); but in every case, we adopt an attitude, which is not to be relegated to feeling, for it involves some effort or striving. This might be expressed by the assertion that there is no cognition without conation.[6]

We have thus a distinction between the self as activity, which is sometimes effective volition, sometimes the weak form of it called attention, and on the other hand ideas as passive experience, in which feelings, sense, and memory images are indistinguishable from the consciousness of them. Each is necessary to the other. For Berkeley— it will be more apparent later—it is of great importance that his account of the self should not be considered metaphysical, that is, inferring characteristics which are not experienced. He states at least in the *Philosophical Commentaries* and the *Principles* that neither understanding nor will could exist without ideas.[7]

---

[6] Cf. *PC*, 672a. I am here in agreement with I. C. Tipton, *Berkeley: The Philosophy of Immaterialism* (Methuen, London, 1974), pp. 268–9.

[7] *PC*, 547, 674, 841, 842; *Principles*, 98, 139.

How then is *the identity of the self* to be asserted? Am I annihilated by every dreamless sleep? No; for since time, independent of the succession of my ideas, is a meaningless abstraction, 'In Sleep & trances the mind exists not there is no time no succession of Ideas' (*PC*, 651). I make no assessment of this argument.[8]

His empiricism, however, causes Berkeley an equally serious difficulty. If we ask, 'Is the soul a substance?' we may distinguish between substance as (*a*) support of accidents and (*b*) something which persists through time. On neither point is he entirely unequivocal. As for (*a*) the question is not whether ideas are modes of the will—that has already been rejected—but whether willing is a mode of something which wills. Now it might be supposed that this cannot be asked of Berkeley who finds, as Hume does, the relation of subject and mode 'very groundless and unintelligible' (*Principles*, 49). Indeed, when he notes in the *Philosophical Commentaries* that a 'cause' means 'a Being which wills when the Effect follows the volition', he afterwards corrects this on the opposite blank page by writing 'it should be said nothing but a Will, a being *which* wills being unintelligible' (499, 499a); we are misled by the common form of language (ibid., 581). Yet none of this is mentioned in his published books. Presumably it would have appeared in the Second Part of the *Principles*, but he may not have thought it important enough to upset his readers, who already had to swallow the denial of 'corporeal substances'; in fact the printed text *adds* the description 'spiritual substance', which is not found in the manuscript.[9] For I take Berkeley's real view to be that, while we are directly conscious of our activity, to look for a subject of the activity distinct from the activity is no more possible than to look for the die distinct from its hardness, extension, and figure. As a late entry in the Notebooks states, 'Substance of a Spirit is that it acts, causes, wills, operates, or if you please (to avoid the quibble y^t may be made on ye word it) to act, cause, will, operate' (829). And when Hylas says 'It should follow that you are only a system of floating ideas, without any substance to support them', the retort is, 'I know or am conscious of my own being . . . I know that I, one and the same self, perceive both colours

---

[8] See also *Principles*, 98. The argument has recently been discussed by, e.g., Tipton, *Berkeley*, pp. 271 f., G. Pitcher, *Berkeley* (Routledge and Kegan Paul, London, 1977), pp. 205 f.

[9] Sect. 139. The MS had however called it 'one pure simple undivided being'; cf. Sect. 27.

and sounds'.[10] But this only pushes the difficulty to (*b*). How can Philonous know that it is the same activity which attends to the red and yellow on the tulip and to the sound of Hylas saying 'tulip'?

Berkeley's answer to this is of great importance for the squaring of his account of matter—the stumbling block of readers who feel, as Hylas did, that what is sauce for the goose is sauce for the gander. At first sight, he might be thought to be begging the question by maintaining as he does, that it is not he who is making an abstraction of will but his critics. For their difficulty is to see how a succession of various volitions can make one will; if there is no perceiving a tulip but only smelling this scent, seeing this crimson, and so on, surely there is no willing but only deciding to sniff now, recollecting that yellow and so on. But while the will, says Berkeley in at least one place, is not distinct from particular volitions (*PC*, 615), these can only be distinguished by their effects; 'Will, Understanding, desire, Hatred etc so far forth as they are acts or active differ not, all their difference consists in their objects, circumstances, etc.' (ibid., 854.) This (I think) is why he says, in no. 848, 'I must not say that the Understanding differs not from the particular Ideas, or the Will from particular Volitions.' He had already added a note, 'This alter'd hereafter', to an entry, 'The Will not distinct from Particular volitions' (*PC*, 615 and 615a). But I do not think that the 'alteration' is from an abandoned 'bundle' theory.[11] Berkeley would always have seen that a self which was a congeries of volitions was not on all fours with a material substance which was a congeries of sensations, if only for one of his own epistemological standpoint.

It follows first that what are called the faculties of the mind are but abstract ideas, nonentities.[12] But secondly it follows that, while the objects and circumstances are passive ideas, the identity of any will or mind is preserved because it is a *continuous* activity—and we have a direct experience of it as continuous. Ideas are necessary to will, but so is the presence of conative activity necessary to ideas or consciousness. Our question was a *question mal posée*; for we are not presented with a variety or succession which requires us to find a principle of unity, as Locke is required to do because he distinguishes

---

[10] *Dialogues*, 233–4.

[11] This is one of few disagreements which I have with R. M. Adams, 'Berkeley's "notion" of spiritual substance', *Archiv f. Gesch. der Philos.* 55 (1973), 47–69, although I do not find his conclusion altogether clear.

[12] *PC*, 867, 871; *Principles*, 143; *Alc.* VII Sect. 21, pp. 318–19.

'an idea of perception' from its object. All the variety and succession belongs to the ideas. Consequently the will or self must not be regarded as an empty concept; it has of itself and distinct from the changing stream of ideas a nature which is unique and can only be known by being experienced. The difficulty of this conception is best deferred until our knowledge of the self is considered, although it will also be apparent in Berkeley's ethics.

In the meantime, however, it may help to consider one of the two defences made by Berkeley against having 'mind' put in the same dock with 'material substance'. In the *Third Dialogue* (pp. 232 ff.) Philonous has two replies: (i) matter is neither a known nor an inferred entity, (ii) its existence involves a self-contradiction. If we are defending mind rather than attacking matter (i) is of course the more important for its implication, and will be considered later. As for (ii) Locke's material substratum only came to possess incompatible characteristics because it was a *general* idea, whether it meant prime matter or its species in things. For if only particulars or determinates are given in experience it is absurd to suppose a substance common to them—'Upon this supposition indeed, the objections from the change of colours in a pigeon's neck, or the appearances of a broken oar in the water, must be allowed to have weight.' (Ibid., 258.) But 'the self' is not a general concept formed from the particular, determinate acts of loving, hating, willing, etc. (determinables), as the substance of 'the pigeon' from its varying colours, shapes, sizes, etc; for, as we have seen, what varies in relation to the will is its objects and feelings, and these are ideas, which do not belong to its nature at all. ''Tis one Will, one Act.'[13] We are considering always *a* self— Hylas' or Philonous'—and this from a logical standpoint, Berkeley implies, is a particular; it may be the subject of a sentence in a fully analysed language where a pigeon may not.

The trouble with 'one Will, one Act' is underlined by another description of it as 'purus actus or rather pure Spirit . . . in no wise the object of yᵉ Understanding, no wise perceivable'.[14] It is that if any and every mental activity is inseparable from Ideas, then to make it a substance, or as Berkeley prefers to say a 'being' or a 'principle', seems to offend against his rule about abstract ideas.[15] Mind should be a compound of two kinds of being. For Berkeley it is not: of this

---

[13] *PC*, 788.
[14] *PC*, 828.
[15] See *Principles*, 5 and Intro., 10.

there can be no question. The problem however is not mentioned by him. Are there any reasons which could have occurred to him for supposing that the veto on abstraction was not applicable in this case? Of various possibilities there are two which are even probable and each of which would furnish in my opinion sufficient grounds.

In the first place Berkeley himself may have doubted that volitions were *necessarily* accompanied by ideas. The 'necessarily' is critical because the veto had not applied to parts or qualities found together but in whose case 'it is possible they may exist' apart. In fact he may have thought volitions did sometimes occur apart from ideas. For it could be the point of an affirmative answer (Berkeley gives none) to a Notebook query, 'whether perception must of necessity precede volition?'[16]

Secondly the veto referred to the abstraction of ideas from ideas. This is more than an *ad hoc* defence. Berkeley's approach to abstraction had been psychological—in terms of what he and other people can 'conceive' and 'frame an idea of'—while there is no question of doing any such thing with mind.

II   THE SELF IN ETHICS

The place of the self in Berkeley's ethics is only considered here so far as it brings out both the strength and the weakness of the account I have attributed to him. (But it has, I believe, been ignored in this connection.) Had Part II of the *Principles* survived its author's carelessness it is doubtful if its modern readers would have found either length or profundity in its treatment of ethics. Some confirmation, however, of the account of the self may be found in some of what Berkeley has to say on moral matters.

That the soul (will) is immortal follows from its not being an idea or ideas. But it is only 'natural immortality', that is to say, the soul 'is not liable to be broken or dissolved by the ordinary Laws of Nature or motion'.[17] After death it is presumed to be furnished with a new set of ideas, and there is no difficulty in conceiving these to come through 'new inlets of perception' without the use of bodily sense organs.[18] They will be necessary for the enjoyment of heavenly happiness.

In moral psychology Berkeley was an obedient child of his times.

[16] *PC*, 815.
[17] *Principles*, 141; Letter to Percival 6. ix. 1710 (*Works*, viii. 36).
[18] *Guardian* no. 27 (*Works*, vii. 184); Letter to Johnson 25. xi. 1729 (*Works*, ii. 282).

He held, if inconstantly, the common conviction that all deliberate action is determined by the prospect of happiness.[19] It is not easy to disentagle his own view of free will from those he is criticizing in the *Philosophical Commentaries*, but I think something as follows emerges. He does not accept the distinction as Locke drew it between desire and volition (no. 598), although he puts no such careful analysis in its place. But he saw, as other critics did, that in making uneasiness determine the will (by determining the mind) Locke was undermining moral freedom. For vice is then miscalculation only.[20] Berkeley retorts, 'Men impute their actions to themselves because they will'd them & that not out of ignorance but whereas they knew the consequences' (*PC*, 157). But he rejects the alternative extreme (William King's) according to which volition is preceded by a state of 'perfect indifferency';[21] this he finds not merely bad psychology, but bad ethics: 'Suppose an agent which is finite perfectly indifferent, & as to desiring not determin'd by any prospect or consideration of good I say, this Agent cannot do an action morally Good' (*PC*, 166); for the whole picture, it must be remembered, is coloured by consequentialism if not hedonism. 'Complacency seems rather to determine or precede or coincide w^th & constitute the Essence of volition than uneasiness.' (*PC*, 630.) Now 'complacency' cannot, I am sure, have the meaning given to it by Luce of 'hedonic indifference': on the contrary it means 'acquiescence' combined with 'satisfaction'.[22] Berkeley is accepting the 'greater good in view' theory, which is rejected by Locke but leaves room for moral value. To call complacency the *essence* of volition is of course quite inconsistent with his distinction of active will and passive feeling; but he is arguing on Locke's ground, where volition has been considered as *choice*.[23] The spontaneity of many of our acts is for Berkeley intuitively evident. I think Berkeley is blind to some of the difficulties because he finds the 'uneasiness' theory falsified by experience, and fails to see that there may as well be compulsion in a pleasurable feeling as in a painful feeling. At any rate, the outcome of the argument in the Seventh Dialogue of *Alciphron*, where Shaftesbury's description of

---

[19] *Alc.* VII, Sect. 14, p. 307; *Passive Obedience* Sect. 5. Cf. *PC*, 542; *Guardian* no. 83.

[20] *PC*, 149, 156, 166 [first sentence]. The last two entries are statements of *Locke's* view. (Cf. *Essay* II. xxi. Sect. 71. For 'miscalculation' *v.* Locke *loc. cit.* Sects. 56, 66).

[21] This is the meaning of *PC*, 158.

[22] I suggest Berkeley borrowed from Peter Browne (*v. sub.*), who described 'a secret *complacence* of mind' as the motive of good actions (*Human Understanding* p. 227).

[23] Locke, *loc. cit.* Sects. 21, 30.

the will as a football is discussed, is simply an appeal to introspection—just as 'walking before them was thought the proper way to confute' philosophers who tried to prove there was no such thing as motion.[24]

What is perhaps more constructive is the reasons he gives for his opponents' error. We are concerned only with their objection to free will on psychological grounds. And Berkeley implies that the objection rests on an invalid abstraction of faculties in the mind. Even will and judgement (as we learnt from his Notebooks) ought not to be distinguished.[25]

You say the appetites have by necessity of nature a tendency towards their respective objects. This we grant; and withal that appetite, if you please, is not free. But you go farther, and tell us the understanding cannot alter its idea, nor infer indifferently anything from anything. What then? Can we not act at all if we cannot alter the nature of objects, and may we not be free in other things if we are not at liberty to make absurd inferences? You take for granted that the mind is inactive, but that its ideas act upon it: as if the contrary were not evident to every man of common sense, who cannot but know that it is the mind which considers its ideas, chooses, rejects, examines, deliberates, decrees, in one word, acts about them, and not they about it. (Sect. 20, p. 317.)

It can be seen at once how this fits the description of mental activity that we extracted from his earlier writings. But let us glance at it in its historical position. It is remarkably reminiscent of the Stoics. In their psychology the psyche had a 'ruling centre' (*hegemonikon*); this was a unity which according only to its 'relational disposition' was either perception or judgement or assent and so on. It was sometimes equated with the person himself as subject of any activity, even walking. (Perception too is or involves an activity because it involves assent.) Epictetus extended the equation to 'choice' or 'will'. Just as Berkeley, when he claimed that willing entailed ideas, was clear that the claim meant '(x) (Ey) x is willed → y is perceived', not '(Ey) (x) x is willed → y is perceived',[26] the Stoics used Heraclitus' image of the river whose waters are ever changing to claim the self-identity of the psyche.

The primacy of the will or the understanding was a controversy which divided the Schoolmen and reappeared in Gassendi's objec-

[24] *Alc.* VII. Sects. 20, 21, pp. 316–19.
[25] *Alc.* VII. Sects. 21, 22, pp. 318–20.
[26] *PC*, 842.

tions to Descartes's voluntarism. The 'minute philosophers' naturally stressed the primacy of the understanding. Berkeley learnt on these matters, I think, from Malebranche. (Both, incidentally, were well read on Stoic doctrine.) For Malebranche judgement and reasoning were voluntary inasmuch as it is the will alone which acquiesces in what the understanding represents to it.[27] But since judgement needed the passive objects of acquiescence, deliberate action was composed of the two factors inseparably; and he called the scholastic controversy a futile question. In my view Berkeley either rejected this account of deliberate action (if we take it for the sake of argument to apply to what voluntarists call choice), or he accepted it but believed that an underlying *current*, as it were, of pure will or activity could be identified in the deliberate action. Either alternative is fraught with difficulty: but I think one can be confident that Malebranche's position cannot be attributed to him. That position makes a passive factor an *essential* part of will inasmuch as there can be no will without it. But despite his waverings there are two points on which Berkeley does not waver: the self is will and the essence of the self is to be active.

Against such a theory of pure will opponents could of course deal some heavy blows; they would raise familiar difficulties over attributing virtue and vice and even rationality to it. But our lightweight moral philosopher nowhere shows signs of taking them on. What he does show however is signs of a certain consistency in avoiding, at least on the surface, borrowing garments from the 'objects and circumstances' to clothe so bare a self. For example, sin lies not in physical actions 'but in the internal deviation of will from the laws of reason and religion'.[28] Or again,

From my Doctrine there follows a cure for Pride. we are only to be praised for those things wch are our own, or of our own Doing, Natural Abilitys are not consequences of Our Volitions. (*PC*, 694.)

III KNOWLEDGE OF THE SELF

Our awareness of this activity presents problems not the smallest of which is the terminology. (Even the term 'immediate' has been found obscure in modern commentary, though every eighteenth-century

---

[27] *Recherche* (1674) I. 2, Sect. 1.
[28] *Dialogues*, 237.

undergraduate would have known it meant 'not inferred'.) Our belief
in the existence of other minds is a different question, and it will not
be mentioned. In Berkeley's opinion it is self-evident that no *idea* of
the mind is possible. Ideas are passive perceptions, and Hobbes, he
implies, was more consistent than Locke in defining 'will' as 'the last
appetite'. For Locke had denied any active power to be perceptible in
the external world, so that 'ideas of reflection' should equally have
been inconceivable to him. Nor were ideas of reflection generally
accepted by contemporary and near contemporary writers. For our
present purpose perhaps the most interesting critic is Peter Browne,
Bishop of Cork and the author of *The Divine Analogy* (1733), whose
theology is roughly handled by Alciphron. When Berkeley was
studying at Trinity College, Browne was Provost and, in spite of his
work's appearing twenty years later, might therefore have had some
direct influence on the *Principles*. In 1728 he published anonymously
The Procedure, Extent and Limits of Human Understanding, and here
we find abstract general ideas described as 'the strangest and most
inconsistent *monsters* in the world'; an idea of thinking or willing
cannot be abstracted from what is thought of or willed.[29] Knowledge
of mental activities is said to be an immediate feeling or consciousness
without the mediation of ideas; it is quite certain:

> the *necessary* assent of the mind does not only follow of course upon this
> consciousness, as in the case of external sensation; but *falls in* with it. They
> are so closely connected that the *consciousness* is itself the *immediate* act of
> assent or knowledge.[30]

The same analogy is drawn from the *solvitur ambulando* proof of
motion as is drawn by Alciphron.[31] All of this in fact is Berkeley's
view.

Now Henry Lee, a much obscurer figure, had written similarly in
1702 (*Antiscepticism*). And for nearly a century after the Restoration
it is remarkable how many intellectual ideas, new as well as old,
appear independently in the writings of the great and of the lesser. If
Berkeley was not influenced by Peter Browne (and there are good
reasons against the influence being thought the other way about), his
belief in the knowledge of mind without ideas, is still not to be
considered original. What is original is the logical consistency with

---

[29] pp. 186, 64.
[30] Ibid., pp. 222 ff.
[31] Ibid., p. 76.

which he can be seen in his Notebooks working out the implications of this generic difference between active mind and passive ideas. In this difference is to be found the reason for his quarrel with Malebranche's account of self-consciousness. It is worth looking at because it seems to show how he is driven into an epistemology which he did not entirely recognize himself but which his predecessors might scarcely have recognized at all.

In the *Recherche de la vérité*, Malebranche distinguishes sharply our knowledge of the external world by the mediation of ideas from our knowledge of ourselves 'par notre conscience, ou par le sentiment intérieur que nous avons de nous-mêmes'.[32] Since Berkeley appears to have read the *Recherche* carefully it is puzzling to find these two remarks in his Notebooks:

Absurd that men should know the soul by idea ideas being inert, thoughtless, hence Malbranch confuted. (*PC*, 230.)
De Vries will have it we know the Mind [as we do Hunger not by Idea but sense or] Conscientia. So will Malbranch. This is a vain distinction. (*PC*, 888.)

The words in brackets are apparently not clear in the manuscript. Johnston for example read 'sensation' for 'sense or', but it does not follow that Berkeley's point cannot be understood. The objection to Malebranche, I suggest, is that he does not rest his distinction on the right ground. For Berkeley the line is drawn between what is passive, which is sensations, and what is active, of which there *cannot* be ideas. Malebranche says that knowledge of the mind is imperfect because without experience (e.g. of pain) we could not know whether it is 'capable' or not of a certain sensation (e.g. pain), but God, who is omniscient, is said to have 'une idée parfaitement intelligible' of our being.[33] The difference is thus to be only contingent. (*Sentiment* differs from *idée* of sense only in being confused and obscure.) This is possible because an idea is distinguished from the consciousness of it, and the latter is an activity of the mind proper. Now suppose that his contemporaries granted the inconclusiveness of introspection on this point and said, 'You are quite right to deny this distinction if you want to prove that *esse* is *percipi*: but we are not immaterialists'; Berkeley would retort, 'On your own terms it can still only be a *distinctio rationis*; and the nature of a mind will have then to include

[32] III. 2, ch. 7.
[33] *Loc. cit.* ch. I.

objects of perception or sensation because, unlike my volition, your acts of perceiving are completely characterless without their objects.' And this alternative was objectionable to the thought of the day on account of ethical implications which were seen in it. In fact if the self in Berkeley was thin, it should in the Cartesians, in Locke or in his followers who retained more of scholasticism, have been whittled by an examination of 'substance' to nothingness.

Whether Malebranche or even Descartes intended to represent the scholastic doctrine of *conscientia* is irrelevant. Berkeley does not, I think. His formula, 'we know what we mean by I' might suggest it. But the simplest objection is that it would contradict '*esse* is *percipi*'. For in its original, Aristotelian form, *conscientia* was a theory to explain the fact that when we see, say, a horse we do not merely see it but are aware that we do. If this were rewritten in Berkeleian terms as the fact that when there is an idea of something there is an awareness of it, it is no longer a fact to be explained by epistemology, but an empty tautology; for an idea of something is by definition an awareness of it. In its more familiar Augustinian form '*conscientia*' is knowledge of things *per se nota* (e.g. one's own anger), not *per signa* (your anger). But this would still be quite inadequate, for someone who did not have a representative theory of perception; it would not distinguish it from knowledge of ideas.

It is at this point that the terminology becomes difficult. Self-acquaintance is regarded as different in kind from acquaintance with ideas whether of toothache or of tulips, just because the self is activity and could not be contemplated without its essence being as it were frozen. In this respect it differs from all other processes, such as the motion of a billiard ball or the fading of a light; these can be contemplated in a single specious present, and their contemplation could be called, in an Irish manner, of the same kind as that of a toothache because in both cases the contemplation is indistinguishable from the objects; but this does not mean that the self which is misleadingly said to 'contemplate' is indistinguishable. Acquaintance with the self must therefore be given another name such as 'enjoyment' or *Erleben* as opposed to 'contemplation' or *Wahrnehmen*. Of course such acquaintance is often denied altogether: and some of those who deny it find it difficult to understand how it could in any case be a species of knowledge. But however this may be it is plausible to think Berkeley in the right at least against philosophers who consider that the two species overlap i.e. that acts of attention may be contemplated as well as enjoyed. For contemplation must then be either (i) simultaneous with enjoyment or (ii) after it in memory or (iii) at the last moment of the specious present like an after-image; (iii) however may be classed with (ii) because the objections to them are of the same kind. But (i) the 'reflex act', which Peter Browne (with Locke's ideas of reflection in mind) calls 'an unnatural squint', is self-contradictory since it is surely not possible to define 'attention' in such a way that it can attend to two objects at once, one of which is itself. As for (ii) attention as an act cannot be described except as *having* objects, so that as soon as it became an object it would lose its character as an act; for to think of myself thinking of x is indistinguishable either from thinking of x or alternatively from thinking of x and y and z, where y and z are additional characterizations of x. In Berkeley's language, it is not the volitions which drop into memory but their objects and circumstances, that is, if we try to recollect a particular volition as such it is in fact the muscular sensations and the like which we recollect. Thus what is present as a memory would not be a memory of what was said to be remembered.

How far these conclusions make the question whether the self is an object of *knowledge* a linguistic or a factual question, I do not wish to discuss. Berkeley himself thought it a major cause of confusion in philosophy that 'words signifying the operations of the mind are taken from sensible Ideas'.[34] And the significance of this is his realization that a Bergsonian 'intuition' is the only kind of self-knowledge consistent with the rest of his philosophy. That is why his appeal to *solvitur ambulando* in the dispute about free will is not just a burking of the issue. For the dispute falsified 'will' from the start because its definitions froze it, just as Zeno on his own ground was irrefutable for Bergson because on that ground 'motion' was frozen and therefore not *motion* at all. Many psychologists have said that we are aware of activity and they have given it a good deal of character— but only by not distinguishing it from physical and other sensations. The *thinness* of activity is due in Berkeley not to its being an abstraction but to the fact that our awareness of it is a different sort of awareness from that of sensations. When he implies that we know ourselves because we know what the term 'we' means, he intends to say that we can be conscious of our selves without being able to describe them, just as we know pink but can only give an 'ostensive definition' of it.[35] For we *are* aware of activity, he claims, so that it is out of place to suspect him, as one may suspect some apostles of a 'pure ego' of inferring a substance from a convention of language. His is a genuine theory of the self, an alternative to both a 'simple substance' and a 'bundle' theory.

Knowledge of spirits, as every reader knows, forms with that of relations a class of knowledge described as 'notions'.[36] There is here, I think, serious confusion, which is not confined to Berkeley. I propose to discuss two questions about notions: (i) Why is the term 'notion' used? (ii) Why are relations classed with spirits?

(i) *The term 'notion'*

It is clear that the enjoyment of mind must not be denoted by the same word as the contemplation of ideas. And this view of self-consciousness was on the whole a novelty in European thought. It might be supposed that if Berkeley had really meant this sort of *intuition* he could have borrowed from the terminology of Neoplatonists, with whom he was well acquainted. But their mysticism, although it involved being 'internal to one's self' was fundamentally the enjoyment of an indeterminate, universal divine thought. And for Berkeley's theism their language would have been seriously misleading.[37] How insistent he is to distinguish the favourite text of his Visual Language, 'In Him we live, and move, and have our being' from 'Seeing all things in God'! It has been seen that knowledge of the self without ideas was, verbally, not an uncommon theory, and that Berkeley himself called it 'an inward feeling': but this was a metaphorical dress and equally misleading. And correspondingly he has an occasional wide use of 'notion', as well as what we can call the technical one.[38]

The word 'notion' was still widely used even in 'the modern philosophy'. It was interchangeable with 'apprehension', 'conception', 'intention', or even 'meaning'; and to distinguish them from ideas, both Lee and Browne had applied these terms to mental acts. In

---

[35] The suggestion of *PC* 178, that this is due to the scantiness of language, is a bad one; and though it might have passed muster with contemporary readers, it is not reproduced in his published works.

[36] *Principles*, 89, 142.

[37] The derivation in *Siris* 347 of the unity of a finite soul from its participation in divine unity is claimed only as 'the Platonic philosophy'.

[38] E.g. as synonymous with 'abstract idea' (*Principles*, Intro., 6). See further *Principles*, 89.

this connection they were specially apt because the logic underlying the *Essay concerning human understanding* and indeed English philosophy of the period was heavily influenced by Ockham;[39] and Ockham had identified the concept or intention with the mind's *act* of understanding. So, as much from the association of the word as from any strict attention to its definition 'conception' and its synonym 'notion' came to be applied to knowledge which was held to involve an 'act of Understanding'. Locke crystallized it by giving this as the ground of its application to mixed modes.[40]

Here there is a danger for anyone who rejects abstraction except in a nominalist sense. For is 'notion' (*a*) the name of our intuition or enjoyment of mental activity, or (*b*) a concept of mental activity *derived from* the intuition? Browne for instance rejected abstraction but wrote in clear terms of (*b*).[41] Berkeley would probably have been uncertain if he had been asked: but I believe he intended to hold to (*a*). For the danger in (*b*) is that it implies either the overlapping of the two species of knowledge (contemplation and enjoyment), which Berkeley seems to have been unwilling to admit, or an impossible *tertium quid* between the two. But he might have been uncertain because it was never clear whether questions of this sort had a general or a particular reference; that is, whether they referred to 'mental activity' or 'my mental activity'. Berkeley's consistent account is that we have a notion of the operations of the mind inasmuch as we know the meanings of the words.[42] Philonous says he knows what he means by the term 'myself'.[43] But he knows presumably what he means by 'Hylas'—and this may imply knowledge by acquaintance and an 'ostensive definition' or knowledge by description and a definition in general terms. For Berkeley states rather awkwardly that I have a notion of my mind and of its acts of loving, hating, and so on:[44] but the definition of these acts involves also the use of general ideas. If, however, a notion is a (Bergsonian) intuition, it is nonsense to make a distinction between simple and general notions parallel to that between simple and general ideas. Now for other philosophers who

[39] A simplified version of his *Summa totius logicae* had been published at Oxford in 1675. But it is not necessary to claim that this or that philosopher had read it. Ideas are transmitted by other means, especially in universities.

[40] *Essay*, II. xxii. Sect. 2; III. v. Sect. 12; *Second letter* to Stillingfleet.

[41] *Human Understanding*, p. 66.

[42] E.g. *Principles*, 27, 140, 142.

[43] *Dialogues*, 231.

[44] *Principles*, 27, 142; *Siris*, 308.

talked of notions, there was no problem here, because a notion was by definition general—and many of Berkeley's modern commentators seem to have accepted this and simply regarded it in his case (to quote one of them) as 'an instance of letting in the waters that were destined to overflow the house'.[45] It would certainly imply the consequences which have been seen of definition (*b*)—consequences which I have tried to show Berkeley unwilling to accept.

Moreover, if his account of the self's nature is as I have suggested, there is another objection to the imputation of 'conceptual thinking': it would be to forget his motive in borrowing the term 'notion' at all and giving it its restricted denotation. For a self is an individual; and as a phenomenalist Berkeley naturally builds his philosophy from the materials of his own immediate experience. Alciphron must have his own intuition of free will. It does not appear that the original purpose of notions required them to have any but a particular reference. Some exponents of the concept interpretation have misled themselves by assuming that Berkeley simply took the self as substance in Locke's sense, and some have misled themselves by this confusion of general knowledge of *self* with particular knowledge of *this* self.

In fact the logical requirement is a greater nominalism. For the English empiricists suffered from a too narrow psychology of generalization. Locke and Hume both thought of universals in terms of an idea or impression standing for similar ideas, instead of admitting that at least sounds and sights of spoken and written words could equally stand for other ideas similar only to one another. Had they admitted this possibility at least some of the familiar difficulties about general ideas might have been avoided. It is interesting that in his last discussion of notional knowledge, in the third (1752) edition of *Alciphron*, this possibility is exactly what Berkeley emphasizes. In the Seventh Dialogue he considers arithmetic, which is about relations and expected therefore to be based on notions. The purpose of mathematics is practical, and when the mathematician applies the results of his sums to things he is of course applying them to the particular relations of particular things; he is taking an instance of what is universal; and he will only require (so to say) 'particular' notions of the relations. But when he is calculating his sums, notions are just what he does *not* concern himself with, but the figures on his paper. 'If I mistake not, all sciences, so far as they are universal and

---

[45] G. Dawes Hicks, *Berkeley* (Ernest Benn, London, 1942), p. 162.

demonstrable by human reason, will be found conversant about signs as their immediate object . . .' (Sect. 13, p. 305.)

For 'signs' here means written and spoken signs. This provides the exit from what would otherwise have been an impasse, unless one knocked down the greater part of Berkeley's theory of knowledge. Whenever a 'general notion' seems to be required, it is a symbol or word which supplies the generality. When he revised *Alciphron* for republication in the last year of his life, Berkeley was perhaps for the first time clear about the place of general ideas and notions in his logic. For there is even a suggestion that relations are as objective as qualities and known in the same way by ideas. But this is not to deny that his views must sometimes have wavered between the notion as an intuition and as a concept.

(ii) *Relations*

In describing our awareness of relations as 'notions' Berkeley, it might be thought, casts doubt on my account of his epistemology. When the reader of the *Principles* first meets the description (in Sect. 89) and even though he takes it in what I called the technical sense, he might suppose that Berkeley was making only a negative point; that is, he was concerned to distinguish notions as a mode of knowledge that was *not* that of ideas. For example—but only for example—they did not, perhaps, entail images or the possibility of images. But Sect. 142 makes it explicit that relations fall under notions for the same reason as minds do, namely that they entail mental activity.

An explanation of this is called for, and it may provide a little more light for what we are after, our awareness, according to Berkeley, of minds. He does not himself give an explanation. But Locke had treated relations as creatures of the understanding. In fact he made a valuable gift to empiricism when he saw their neglected importance.[46] But he never unlearnt the Aristotelian logic of subject and predicate on which their neglect had depended, so that failing to grasp consistently that they *are* relations he naturally hesitated to put them on an equal ontological footing with qualities. His grounds can be inferred from *Essay*, Book II, ch. 24, 'The understanding . . . can carry any idea, as it were beyond itself . . . and set it by another' (Sect.

---

[46] 'Lockiana Praedicamentorum divisio in Modos, Substantias et Relationes hodie receptissima est', Thomas Johnson can write in 1734, *Quaestiones philosophicae* ch. IX—a handbook for his pupils at Magdalene and a valuable but neglected guide to what was read and discussed in universities at the time.

1), and relation is the resulting 'way of comparing . . . two things together' (Sect. 7). So 'Caius, compared to several persons, may truly be said to be older and younger, stronger and weaker, &c.' (Sect. 5.) That Berkeley shared this strangely persistent view of relations when he wrote the *Principles* and *Three Dialogues* can be inferred from what he had to say about size. It accounts for his supposing that they depend, though only partially, on mental activity and choice.

I suggested that an account in *Alciphron* of mathematics as treating of symbols avoided the need of notions as concepts (corresponding to general ideas); and I mentioned Berkeley's suggestion that relations might be as real as qualities. The passage is an explanation which Berkeley added to his final edition:

The signs, indeed, do in their use imply relations or proportions of things; but these relations are not abstract general ideas, being founded in particular things, and not making of themselves distinct ideas to the mind, exclusive of the particular ideas and the signs. (VII Sect. 12, p. 305.)

This surprising addition has not received the attention it should. That it should be an inadvertent use of 'particular ideas' for 'notions' is out of keeping both with his nice use of terms and with the meticulousness with which he revised his text. For the same reason, it is unlikely that he is thinking only of the *relata* as supplying distinct ideas, for in that case the conjunction of particular ideas and *signs* would be muddling if not muddled. I think the context makes it clear that it is not the relations, but their generality which prevents the mathematician from dealing immediately with ideas—whether or not Berkeley was always clear on this. The passage means that we can have a simple idea, say of the relation, greater than, in the same way as we have a simple idea of black; so that we can form the atomic or purely categorical propositions 'this is greater than that', 'that is greater than that' and so on. One instance of these ideas—or as he prefers to say here, one instance of the words 'greater than' or the symbol ' > '—can stand for any idea of greater than, so that one can state significantly that the circumferences of all circles are greater than their diameters. Berkeley had never committed himself explicitly to the view that relations are creatures of the mind. In two places in the *Principles* our knowledge of them is called 'notions' because they include an act of the mind, but afterwards it is not, I believe, mentioned. The psychological rather than logical approach common to the empiricists might be said to lie behind the statements in the

Principles, but I should hesitate to say less than that it misled him.

To press the view of relations as notions would be to make judgements which contain them irreducibly compound. Whether they are spelt out as conditionals or as conjunctions, one of their elements will refer to the activity of the speaker/hearer. One might wonder whether Berkeley really recognized such judgements. A clue is to be found in some comments he made in his youth on Locke's chapter about 'particles'. These are syncategorematic words which (as prepositions) connect terms or (as conjunctions) connect sentences; both are 'marks of some action or intimation of the mind'.[47] Berkeley agreed that they do not stand for ideas: they stand for 'volitions and their concomitant Ideas'.[48] To put it roughly, hearing 'p although q' causes the hearer to have the ideas indicated by the words contained in 'p' and 'q' (or ideas resembling them) plus the notion or 'enjoyment' of attentive activity in connection with a felt break in the smooth train of ideas.

If 'p' and 'q' are empirical propositions all the elements of 'p although q' are matters of experience. Attentive activity has an intuitable character apart from its objects and circumstances; and this fact is a matter of experience. Berkeley, I have argued, believes that it is equivalent to the fact that knowledge of the self is a matter of experience. For attention is an exercise of will; and the nature of the self is to be a continuous exercise of will, or, what is the same thing, a continuously exercised will.

[47] Locke, *Essay*, III. Sect. 4.
[48] *PC*, 661a, 667.

ACTION AND INACTION IN BERKELEY[1]

C. C. W. TAYLOR

I BEGIN with a quotation from Wittgenstein's *Tractatus* (6.374):

Even if all that we wish for were to happen, still this would only be a favour granted by fate, so to speak: for there is no logical connection between the will and the world, which would guarantee it, and the supposed physical connection itself is surely not something that we could will.[2]

Substitute 'God' for 'fate' and this gives an exact description of the situation of human beings in Berkeley's metaphysical system. That system allows no role whatever for human agency, i.e. the production by human beings of changes in the external world. The nearest human beings can approach to acting is by exercising their imaginations and by wanting things to happen; but what actually makes anything happen is not the exercise of any finite will but always an act of the Divine will. To adapt Davidson's dictum 'All we ever do is move our wills: the rest is up to God.'

This is at first sight all the more surprising in view of Berkeley's emphasis on activity as one of the essential characteristics of spirits, of which human beings are a species. Ideas are differentiated from spirits primarily by the fact that the former are inert, i.e. lacking any causal power, whereas the latter are essentially active things (*Principles*, 25–7). Hence the well-known doctrines that 'the cause of ideas is an incorporeal active substance or spirit' (*Principles*, 26) and that

there can be no idea formed of a soul or spirit: for all ideas whatever, being passive and inert . . . they cannot represent unto us, by way of image or likeness, that which acts. A little attention will make it plain to any one, that to have an idea which shall be like that active principle of motion and change of ideas, is absolutely impossible. (*Principles*, 27).

---

[1] This discussion owes a great deal to those by Jonathan Bennett in *Locke, Berkeley, Hume* (Clarendon Press, Oxford, 1971), ch. 8 and Jennifer Hornsby in *Actions* (Routledge and Kegan Paul, London, Boston and Henley, 1980), ch. 4. I am also indebted to Dr. Hornsby for her comments on earlier drafts.

[2] Trans. D. F. Pears and B. F. McGuinness (Routledge and Kegan Paul, 1961).

It is clear from the *Commentaries* that Berkeley was at least inclined to make activity the sole essential characteristic of spirits, i.e. to maintain that just as for ideas to be is to be perceived, so for spirits to be is to be active. In several entries the soul or spirit is said to be the will: thus

The soul is the will properly speaking & as it is distinct from Ideas. (478a.)

It seems that the Soul taken for the Will is immortal, Incorruptible. (814.)

Substance of a Spirit is that it acts, causes, wills, operates, or if you please . . . to act, cause, will, operate its' substance is not knowable not being an Idea. (829.)

. . . our Ideas are distinct from the Mind, i.e. the Will, the Spirit. (847.)

Berkeley, however, corrects this tendency, first by his recognition of thought as well as volition as an essential aspect of the activity of spirits (*PC*, 812 '. . . there is in the Deity Understanding as well as Will. He is no Blind agent & in truth a blind Agent is a Contradiction'), and secondly by his recognition of the passive element in perception (*PC*, 301 '. . . it being that very having, that passive reception of ideas that denominates the mind perceiving. That being the very essence of perception . . .'; cf. *Dialogues*, 195–7). We thus reach the definitive statement of Berkeley's position, according to which thought, perception, and volition are distinct essential properties of a spirit. The clearest statement is perhaps *Principles*, 27: 'A spirit is one simple, undivided, active being: as it perceives ideas, it is called the *understanding*, and as it produces or otherwise operates about them, it is called the *will*' (cf. *Principles*, 2, *PC*, 429–429a, 848). But at the same time Berkeley recognized the logical interconnections of thought, perception, and volition: 'It seems to me that Will & understanding Volition & ideas cannot be severed, that either cannot be possibly without the other.' (*PC*, 841.)

This is correct; volition entails thought in the sense that I cannot decide to ϕ without thinking of ϕing, and while thought does not strictly entail volition, since I may find some thought occurring to me without any choice on my part, or obstinately lingering after I have decided to banish it, it is true that much of our thinking is intentional (in the sense of 'governed by intention') and that much, though not all free-floating thought involves volition in the minimal sense that we could get rid of the thoughts if we chose to. Similarly, perception involves thought and volition, in various ways. In most cases one recognizes what one perceives as an *F*, which is an exercise of the concept of an *F*, i.e. of the ability to think of things as *F*s. Again, much perception is the successful accomplishment of such intentional acts as looking for or at or listening to, and almost every perceptual item is such that one could eliminate it by moving one's position, closing one's eyes etc. Yet when all due allowance has been made for these and perhaps other connections between the concepts, it remains true that having the thought that *p*, wanting it to be the case that *p* or deciding to bring it about that *p* and perceiving that *p* are logically distinct states or events in the history of a person, and that the occurrence of events of any one of those kinds is no more central to what it is to be a person than the occurrence of events of any of the others. Berkeley was, then, right in his final position that to be a spirit is not just to be something which wills, but rather to be something which thinks, perceives, and wills (taking 'wills' to include 'wants, chooses, intends, and acts'). What we have now to consider is just how much scope he allowed to the human will.

In one respect he allows the will too much scope, and in another too little. In respect of thought and imagination the will is an absolute sovereign: 'I find I can excite ideas in my mind at pleasure, and vary and shift the scene as oft as I think fit. It is no more than willing, and straightway this or that idea arises in my fancy . . .' (*Principles*, 28). With regard to the senses, on the other hand 'the ideas imprinted on them are not creatures of my will' (*Principles*, 29). And since the class of real things just is the class of things perceived by sense (*Principles*, 33-4), it follows that real things are independent of the will. But if real things are independent of the will, it follows that we cannot, by the exercise of the will, bring about any change in real things. And since there is no way in which we can bring about a change in anything other than by an act of will,[3] it follows that we can bring about no change in the real world, i.e. we cannot act in it. We are absolute in the internal realm, impotent in the external.

As that argument may seem too swift for comfort, it is well to assure ourselves both that it is accurate in its account of Berkeley and that its conclusion is validly drawn. First, with regard to the thesis that the will is absolute in the internal realm, it is true that Berkeley does not explicitly say that *all* ideas in the imagination are under the control of the will. The sentence quoted above from *Principles*, 28, 'It

---

[3] Phil.. . . I desire to know . . . whether . . . you can conceive any action besides volition . . . Hyl. I give up the point entirely. (*Dialogues*, 217.)

is no more than willing, and straightway this or that idea arises in my fancy . . .' is most naturally taken as saying not that whatever ideas of imagination I have, I have because I choose to, but rather that whatever ideas of imagination I choose to have, I do have. In that case Berkeley would have differentiated ideas of sense from those of imagination by some other tests, presumably by the tests of vividness and coherence mentioned in *Principles*, 30:

The ideas of sense are more strong, lively and distinct than those of the imagination; they have likewise a steadiness, order, and coherence, and are not excited at random, as those which are the effects of human wills often are, but in a regular train or series . . .

These tests are no doubt of questionable value. Vividness obviously provides no test at all, since some hallucinations are at least as vivid as veridical perception. Coherence fares better, particularly if we separate the notion of 'differentiation' into (i) the conditions logically necessary and sufficient to differentiate perception from imagination and (ii) the tests which one would apply to tell whether a given experience was a bit of perception or a bit of imagination. Under (i) we have to specify that causal process, involving the activity of a sense organ, which constitutes a given experience as the exercise of a specific sort of perception. Since Berkeley has to recast any description of a causal process as a description of a regular sequence of ideas, his statement of the causal conditions which constitute an experience as an act of perception would be a description of sets of ideas occurring 'in a regular train or series'. With regard to (ii), any test which could apply to check whether a given experience is an act of perception or not will rely on coherence, whether with the testimony of others or with further experiential data, assumed to be themselves perceptual. There is, then, some philosophical merit in the claim that we tell perception from imagination by applying a test of coherence. But more directly relevant to our present question is the fact that Berkeley's account of causation leads to the conclusion that perception is differentiated from imagination by the fact that the former displays a type of coherence which the latter lacks. Hence he could consistently hold that the thesis that the imagination is under the control of the will is not necessarily true, and perhaps not even universally true, and thus escape the accusation that his theory requires the absurdity that 'dreams, phrensies, and the like' (*Principles*, 18) are under voluntary control. There is, however, pretty clear evidence that he held that the class of ideas of the imagination is in fact coextensive with that of ideas under the control of the will, and similarly that the class of ideas of sense is coextensive with that of ideas not under the control of the (finite) will. Thus in *Principles*, 30, having distinguished ideas of sense from those of imagination by the test of vividness, he continues 'they have likewise a steadiness, order, and coherence, and are not excited at random, as those which are the effects of human wills often are . . .' It seems plain that he is here making a further contrast between the same two sets of items, viz. ideas of sense and ideas of imagination, rather than introducing a new contrast between ideas of sense and ideas of *voluntary* imagination, i.e. 'those which are the effects of human wills' is here coextensive with 'those of the imagination'. Further, on Berkeley's principles the occurrence of any idea is the effect of an act of some will, since acts of will are the only causes (*Principles*, 26, 105; *PC*, 499) and there are (apparently) no uncaused events. His argument in *Principles*, 29, repeated in *Dialogues* (II), 212–14, that, because I find that some ideas are not dependent on my will, i.e. that they 'have an existence distinct from being perceived by me' (p. 212), therefore I conclude that they have real existence, i.e. that 'there must be some other mind wherein they exist' (ibid.), is best understood as resting on the assumption that there are no ideas of my imagination which are independent of my will. For if there were any such ideas, by this argument Berkeley ought to attribute real existence to them. But then the contents of dreams and hallucinations would have to be counted as real things, which would be a *reductio* of the system. Berkeley could, of course, avoid that criticism by distinguishing between 'caused by the will of *A*' and 'existing in the mind of *A*'. Dreams and hallucinations would then be independent of the will of the person having them, from which it would follow that their occurrence is to be ascribed to the Divine will, but they would exist only as states of particular finite minds. But not merely is it the case that Berkeley does not make that distinction; his argument turns on his failure to make it, as is clear from the following passage (p. 214):

. . . these ideas or things by me perceived, either themselves or their archetypes, exist independently of my mind, since I know myself not to be their author, it being out of my power to determine at pleasure, what particular ideas I shall be affected with upon opening my eyes or ears. They must therefore exist in some other mind, whose will it is that they should be exhibited to me.

Hence the defence just proposed is not available to Berkeley, and it therefore seems best to assume that he preserved the consistency of his system by the assumption that all and only ideas of the imagination are under voluntary control.

Though in fact the evidence thus suggests that Berkeley accepted the material equivalence of the expressions 'ideas of the imagination' and 'ideas under the control of the will', the main argument of this paper does not require that, but merely that he held that only ideas of the imagination are under voluntary control. For even if some ideas of imagination are not under voluntary control, it remains Berkeley's thesis that no ideas of sense are under the control of the will. And from that our conclusion follows by the reasoning stated earlier. Berkeley can, then, be rescued from this situation only if one can succeed in showing that his thesis that our ideas of sense are independent of our will does not lead to the conclusion that we can bring about no change in the real world.

An argument to that effect may be stated as follows. 'The argument proposed above depends on an equivocation in the expression "independent of the will". If the premiss "ideas of sense are independent of the will" is to represent Berkeley's actual position, the expression "independent of the will" must be understood as "not *totally* dependent on the will". But the inference "If real things are independent of the will, we cannot bring about any change in them" is valid only if "independent of the will" means "totally independent of the will". But from the fact that something is not totally dependent on the will, i.e. cannot be created, altered, or destroyed *at will,* it does not follow that it is totally *in*dependent of the will, i.e. is such that the will cannot affect it at all. Hence the argument fails. In fact Berkeley's position is quite tenable. Instead of the absurd contrast between absolutism in the internal realm and impotence in the external we have a sensible contrast between absolutism and constitutional monarchy. Whereas we can do just as we like in our imagination (which is what makes the exercise of that faculty such fun), if we are to do anything in the external world we have to operate by the proper procedures, i.e. by conforming our wills to those regular sequences of ideas, vulgarly called causal laws, which God has in this goodness established for our guidance.'

It is indeed possible to read some of Berkeley's text in the way which this defence requires. Thus *Principles*, 28 can be read as putting particular stress, not just on the control of the imagination by the will, but on the unrestricted nature of that control. 'I find I can excite ideas in my mind *at pleasure*, and vary and shift the scene *as oft as I think fit*. It is *no more than willing*, and *straightway* this or that idea arises in my fancy . . .' (my italics). And when in the next paragraph he says that 'I find the ideas actually perceived by sense have not a like dependence on my will', the phrase 'have not a like dependence' may be read as 'do not have the same sort of dependence' (i.e. unrestricted dependence), rather than as 'are not like ideas of imagination in being dependent' as required by the anti-Berkeleian reading. The corresponding passages in *Dialogues* II (referred to above) can also be read in the light of this defence; but since both sets of passages also fit the anti-Berkeleian interpretation, the question of which interpretation is correct cannot be settled by appeal to those passages alone, but must depend on wider considerations. Berkeley's defence requires him to hold that, while we do not have unrestricted control over what ideas of sense we have, nevertheless we have some control. Thus suppose I am sitting with my back to the window. I can imagine the view from the window purely at will, and vary the imagined view as I please. My control over what I see is much more limited, in that (a) if I am to see the view I must first turn round, and (b) I cannot alter the actual view at will, but, if at all, only by taking certain specific steps, e.g. by having someone remove the wheelbarrow from the middle of the lawn. Nevertheless, subject to these restrictions, I do have some voluntary control over what I see. Specifically, I can make a difference to my ideas of sense by initiating one or other of a number of possible causal sequences which have different ideas of sense among their members. The central question then is: can Berkeley consistently allow that we can initiate causal sequences?

The question has only to be put for it to be clear that the alleged escape-route is a blind alley. The suggestion is that, while I cannot cause myself to see the lawn *just* by willing it, I can cause myself to see it by willing it, provided that I will that I turn round before I see it, i.e. in Berkeleian terms, provided that I will that I have a sequence of ideas beginning with the visual etc. ideas of the interior of the room, continuing with the visual and kinaesthetic data of my turning round and ending with the visual ideas of the view from the window. But what about the first item of the sequence? It is plainly absurd to suggest that I can cause myself to have an idea of sense, as opposed to an idea of imagination, by first causing myself to have another idea of sense which precedes the first in a causal sequence, for in that case the sequence can never start. But if the sequence begins with my causing myself to have an idea over which my control is not limited by the necessity for the prior occurrence of some other idea, then the sequence begins with an idea of imagination. For instance, if I do not have to will that I have any other idea first in order to have the idea of my hand's moving, but can have that idea merely by willing it, then the occurrence or non-occurrence of that idea is totally under the control of my will. But in that case the distinction between actually moving my hand and merely imagining a movement of my hand disappears. And if there is no difference between actually moving my hand and imagining a movement of my hand, then in general the concept of action collapses into that of imagining occurrences. For if the difference between, for example, my picking up a stick and my imagining the stick's moving from the ground in my hand lies in the fact that the former requires me actually to move my hand, while the latter requires merely that I imagine a movement of my hand, then the collapse of the action/imagination distinction for changes I make to the position of parts of my body entails its collapse also for changes I make to things beyond my body.

The defender of Berkeley can now object that, while the having of that congeries of ideas which constitutes a movement of the body is under the unrestricted control of the will, that does not obliterate the distinction between action and imagination, since the former is publicly observable, whereas the latter is private. Again in Berkeleian terms, what I cause by my act of will is not merely that I have a certain sequence of ideas. If that were all, then no matter how lively and coherent the sequence, what I should be doing would be imagining, not acting. In addition, I bring it about both that any finite spirits actually in the vicinity do have corresponding sequences of ideas, and also that if any finite spirit were in the vicinity it would, subject to the appropriate conditions, have a corresponding sequence (cf. *Principles*, 3 and 58). (I omit consideration of whether I may also be said to cause God to have certain ideas.[4]) But this defence merely makes matters worse, since it adds to the obscurity surrounding the notion of an act of will which accounts for bodily movements the deeper obscurity of the suggestion that one might be able to affect the sensory states of other persons purely by an act of will.

The difficulty in the suggestion that an act of will might be

---

[4] For discussion of that issue see my 'Berkeley on Archetypes', *Archiv für Geschichte der Philosophie* 67 (1985) 65–79, especially p. 75.

sufficient to cause a bodily movement is brought out in a well-known quotation from Professor Anscombe:

People sometimes say that one can get one's arm to move by an act of will but not a matchbox; but if they mean 'Will a matchbox to move and it won't', the answer is 'If I will to move my arm in that way, it won't', and if they mean 'I can move my arm but not the matchbox', the answer is that I can move the matchbox—nothing easier.'[5]

In order to get my hand to move all that I have to do is to move it, and if I can't move it, all the willing in the world won't get it to move. But that is just the situation of Berkeleian man; he can't actually move his hand, but can merely will that it should move. But surely he *can* move his hand; he moves it by willing that it should move. But that is miraculous; for he has no means of giving effect to his acts of will, but is supposed to give them effect just by making them. Someone who can act can give effect to desires, decisions, and intentions by acting; the description of someone whose only way of acting is to desire, decide or intend is totally mysterious.[6]

What Berkeleian man has the power to do, just by willing it, is to cause other Berkeleian men to have certain ideas. How does he do it? We might of course say, using our ordinary concepts, that I can cause it to seem to you that my hand is moving by moving my hand within the range of your vision. (I might also, if I were skilful enough, cause the same effect by some other means, e.g. by staging some clever illusion.) But we should find quite baffling the assertion that I produce that effect just by willing that that effect should be produced. That might perhaps be taken as attributing to me some extraordinary telepathic powers, but could not conceivably represent what we ordinarily mean by, for example, 'He moved his hand'. So Berkeley's account would have to represent a radical revision of our concept of action, not a description of it. And what an extraordinary revision it

---

[5] *Intention* (Blackwell, Oxford, 1957), §29, p. 52.

[6] Cf. Bennett, *Locke, Berkeley, Hume*, p. 208. '. . . it is obviously false that what happens in intentional action is that (*a*) one wants certain events to happen, and (*b*) in consequence of that want events do happen. By mere wanting I can no more get my fingers crossed than I can move mountains'; and Hornsby, *Actions*, pp. 56–7: 'The idea that someone's body should move just because he thought that it would, or preferred it to, or willed it to move, is no less baffling than the idea that a desire should move his body. A man who knows he has become paralysed may be able to think as well as anyone else of his body's moving, and he can will as hard as he likes that it move. Thought or willing alone is not what brought about movements when he could make them. If you simply think of your body's moving, or will that it move, nothing happens.'

would be. Surely one would have to be God to be able to control the sensory states of others just by one's will.

In fact, Berkeley's view is that it is God alone who produces those causal sequences, i.e. sequences of ideas in finite minds, which we call changes in the natural world, of which the movements of human bodies are a sort. *Principles*, 30 gives a typical statement of this view:

> The ideas of sense . . . are not excited at random . . . but in a regular train or series, the admirable connexion whereof sufficiently testifies the wisdom and benevolence of its Author. Now the set rules . . . wherein the mind we depend on excites in us the ideas of sense, are called the *Laws of Nature* . . . .

These rules are in fact the rules of a conventional system of signs, a Divine language by which God signifies his intention of producing certain ideas by correlating them with certain others which enable us to predict the occurrence of the former (*Principles*, 65; cf. *Alciphron*, Dialogue IV). We find the view that God alone is the cause of our ideas of sense also in *PC*, 433: 'One idea not the cause of another, one power not the cause of another. The cause of all natural things is onely God';[7] and in *Dialogues*, 220:

> PHIL. You acknowledge then God alone to be the cause of our ideas . . .
>
> HYL. That is my opinion.

Berkeley also explicitly asserts that the ability of one finite spirit to produce ideas in another, which we saw to be necessary to the supposed production of real changes in the world, cannot be explained otherwise than by appeal to the power of God:

> There is not any one mark that denotes a man, or effect produced by him, which doth not more strongly evince the being of that spirit who is the *Author of Nature*. For it is evident that in affecting other persons, the will of man hath no other object, than barely the motion of the limbs of his body; but that such a motion should be attended by, or excite any idea in the mind of another, depends wholly on the will of the Creator. He alone it is who *upholding all things by the Word of his Power*, maintains that intercourse between spirits, whereby they are able to perceive the existence of each other. (*Principles*, 147.)

In making the central point that our 'causation' of ideas in the minds of others is in fact a special case of the universal process of

---

[7] This passage has the marginal + sign, which sometimes, though not always, indicates rejection.

Divine causation Berkeley reveals two areas of incoherence in his system. First, he here assumes the ordinary, true account of action, viz. that we move our bodies and by so doing bring about further effects, including effects on the sensory states of others.[8] But that conflicts with the doctrine that our bodies are collections of ideas of sense just as much as any other physical object, and are therefore under the exclusive control of God.[9] Again, the occurrence in the mind of another of, for example, the visual impression of my hand's moving cannot be an event which attends or is excited by that motion itself, since that occurrence is itself partly constitutive of that motion; what is taking place would not be an actual case of my hand's moving were not that visual impression occurring. Secondly, Berkeley here talks of effects produced by finite spirits, which yet more strongly evince the being of the Author of Nature. But while we may be familiar with the idea that two conditions may be jointly sufficient and severally necessary, though neither is by itself sufficient for the production of a given effect, it does not seem that Berkeley can make use of that concept here. For since in this very passage he says that the occurrence of ideas associated with any bodily movement depends *wholly* on the will of the Creator, he could not consistently maintain that the Divine will is by itself insufficient to produce those ideas, requiring in addition the exercise of a finite will. Yet at the same time he holds that, just as we have sufficient evidence of the existence of God in the character of the ideas which he produces in us (*Principles*, 30–2, 72, 147–8, etc.), so we have sufficient evidence of the existence of other finite spirits in the character of the ideas which *they* produce in us (*Principles*, 145, 148). So he must either accept that some of our ideas of sense are produced by the unmediated action of one finite spirit on another, or, while maintaining the causal dependence of all ideas of sense on God alone, abandon the claim that any ideas are evidence of the causal activity and hence of the existence of other finite spirits.

[8] Cf. *PC*, 548: 'We move our Legs our selves. 'tis we that will their movement. Herein I differ from Malbranch.'

[9] This passage suggests that Berkeley may have thought that he could resolve the inconsistency by holding that while the movement of my hand is, *qua* perceived by me, caused by my will, it is, *qua* perceived by another, caused by God's will. (I owe this suggestion to Jennifer Hornsby.) This would appear to have the consequence that a bodily movement is a kind of logical construction of (*a*) imaginative states of the agent and (*b*) actual and possible sensory states of other finite spirits, which seems to amount to saying that human bodies are partly real (i.e. sensible) things and partly imaginary. I doubt the coherence of that suggestion.

Neither alternative is acceptable to Berkeley. His dilemma emerges clearly from comparison of two passages, first *Principles*, 145: 'we cannot know the existence of other spirits, otherwise than by their operations, or the ideas by them excited in us. I perceive several motions, changes, and combinations of ideas, that inform me there are certain particular agents like my self, which accompany them, and concur in their production'; and secondly *Principles*, 72: 'To me, I say, it is evident that the being of a *spirit infinitely wise, good, and powerful* is abundantly sufficient to explain all the appearances of Nature.' The doctrine of *Principles* 147–8, that our perception of the motions produced by men, i.e. of the movements of human bodies other than our own, is, in common with every other perception, a sign or effect of the power of God, may be seen as Berkeley's attempt to evade this dilemma. But that attempt has no hope of success. For once the actual production of the perception has been wholly ascribed to Divine power, the only role left for the act of the human will is to serve as a sort of signal to God that now is the moment for Him to exercise his causal power in a particular way. But that is to revert to the doctrine of occasionalism, which Berkeley firmly rejects in *Principles*, 68–72 and *Dialogues*, 220. It is true that his attack is directed against the thesis that material substances serve as occasions of God's producing ideas in human minds, i.e. 'as it were so many occasions to remind him when and what ideas to imprint on our minds' (*Principles*, 70) but his concluding argument against that view tells equally against what we might call the occasionalist theory of volitions:

I only ask whether the order and regularity observable in the series of our ideas, or the course of Nature, be not sufficiently accounted for by the wisdom and power of God; and whether it doth not derogate from those attributes, to suppose He is influenced, directed, or put in mind, when and what He is to act, by any unthinking substance. (*Dialogues*, 220.)

The substitution of 'thinking' or 'willing' for 'unthinking' in the last sentence leaves the argument unimpaired. It is surely blasphemous to suppose that God can be instructed to act by any of his creatures and absurd to suggest that He needs to be reminded to do so. Berkeley might perhaps reply that these difficulties arise from too literal an insistence on 'direct' and 'put in mind'. Rather, our acts of volition are to be understood as petitions, expressive of desires which we ourselves are powerless to put into effect, but which God in his goodness actualizes on our behalf. Prayer, rather than command, is thus the appropriate model for the occasionalist theory of volition. That model is certainly intelligible, but merely transforms the difficulty which I have mentioned into the general theological problem of the function of petitionary prayer. It is absurd to suggest that an omnipotent and benevolent God needs to be stimulated into action by any act whatever on our part, even the act of wishing that He should act. A first reply might be to suggest that God's power and benevolence is exercised precisely in creating a world in which He does some things because we want Him to, rather than immediately because it is best that He should do them. I cannot pursue that topic here, but shall instead mention one further difficulty, which Berkeley himself tried to answer. This is the problem of God's responsibility for the evil acts of human beings, which the occasionalist theory poses in a particularly challenging way. If it is God, and not we, who gives effect to our volitions, then it is God who gives effect to wicked volitions; man desires to murder and steal, but it is literally God who commits those crimes. Berkeley has no adequate reply to this objection. In the *Third Dialogue* (pp. 236–7) and again in his first letter to Johnson (*Works*, ii. 281) he observes correctly that this difficulty tells equally against the materialist version of occasionalism; but the correct conclusion to draw from that is that any variety of occasionalism, including his own, is inconsistent with his theological principles. In the *Dialogue* he adds two further arguments. First, moral guilt does not apply to the 'outward physical action or motion' but only to the act of will which gives rise to it. The evidence is that 'the killing an enemy in a battle, or putting a criminal legally to death, is not thought sinful, though the outward act be the very same with that in the case of murder'. Hence, since sin does not attach to 'physical action', in making God the cause of such actions we do not make him the author of sin. Berkeley's support for his first premiss involves a fallacy; from the fact that a predicate F characterizes an action only if that action issues from a given intention it does not follow that F characterizes only the intention, not the action. But his argument can stand without that support, for on his theory our only actions, and hence our only sinful actions, are volitions, but God is the cause, not of our volitions, but of the bodily movements which we ordinarily, though mistakenly, believe to be caused by those volitions. Hence God is not the cause of our sins. But though valid and consistent with his theory as a whole, the argument does not meet the objection; for the objection is not that on Berkeley's theory God causes us to do the wicked things we do, but that on that theory God does the wicked things which we want to do but are unable to do.[10]

Berkeley's second argument is that he allows human beings limited powers in the production of motions 'ultimately indeed derived from God, but immediately under the direction of their own wills, which is sufficient to entitle them to all the guilt of their actions'. On the general question of the consistency of this position with Berkeley's system, see above, pp. 220–3. On the particular question of the allocation of guilt for wicked actions, if, as the system requires, God is the agent of the wicked designs of which we are principals, then surely the guilt is shared between principal and agent, i.e. we are not entitled to *all* the guilt of our actions. Berkeley seems unclear on this point. In his reply to Johnson he says, 'As to guilt, it is the same thing whether I kill a man with my hands or an instrument; whether I do it myself or make use of a ruffian.' (*Works*, ii. 281.) This is to this extent correct, that if *A* intentionally brings about the death of *B*, he is no less guilty if he arranges for someone else to kill him than if he kills him by his own hand. But there is the crucial difference that if *A* uses an instrument there is only one guilty party, whereas if he makes use of a ruffian there are two. Suppose (i) *A* causes *C* to fall to his death over a cliff by intentionally pushing *B* against him, so that *C* is pushed over; (ii) *A* asks *B* to push *C* over, and *B* complies. In case (i) *A* pushes *C* over, and *A* kills *C*, while *B* is not an agent, but merely an instrument which *A* uses to push *C*. In case (ii) both *A* and *B* are agents, but *A* does not push *C* over, nor does he (it seems natural to say) kill *C*. What *A* does is cause *B* to push *C* over, and to kill him. Neither model of agency, when applied to our relation to God in Berkeley's system, gives a result which is morally or theologically satisfactory. On model (i) we are literally agents, but God is (absurdly) reduced to the status of an instrument. On model (ii), which is Berkeley's actual model, we are not literally the agents of our crimes, and God is the ruffian who carries out the wicked designs we are helpless to execute.

We can now see how precisely Berkeley's account of action fits the quotation from Wittgenstein with which I began. If anything that we

---

[10] Malebranche drew this conclusion explicitly: 'Il remue même notre bras lorsque nous en servons contre ses ordres; car il se plaint par son prophète que nous le faisons servir à nos désirs injustes et criminels' (*Recherche* VI. ii. 3 (*Œuvres de Malebranche*, ed. Simon (Paris, 1871), vol. IV, p. 332)).

wish for does in fact happen, that is a favour granted by God. There is no logical connection between our will and the world, and the physical connection, which consists in the fact that what happens is not a private imaginative experience but the correlated occurrence of a set of actual and possible ideas in different finite minds, is not something that we can bring about by willing. 'That intercourse between spirits, whereby they are able to perceive the existence of each other' (*Principles*, 147) holds solely by the grace of God. This position fits well the striking phraseology of *PC*, 107:

Strange impotence of men. Man without God. Wretcheder than a stone or tree, he having onely the power to be miserable by his unperformed wills, these having no power at all.

Yet Berkeley could not rest happily in that position, since it is inconsistent with the anti-Malebranchean position (viz. that we move our own bodies) to which he was equally firmly committed.[11] Agency is essential to our nature as spirits, but is made impossible by Berkeley's account of the nature of the world in which those spirits are active. Berkeley has no escape from this dilemma; in his world we are made for action, but condemned to inaction.

[11] This may account for the fact that 107 has the marginal + sign; see I. C. Tipton, *Berkeley, The Philosophy of Immaterialism* (Methuen, London, 1974), pp. 305-9.

CHAPTER 12

BERKELEY ON BEAUTY

J. O. URMSON

IN the history of thought it is almost always pointless to ascribe even an approximate date to the beginning of any movement or enterprise, both because antecedents can always be found and because such movements and enterprises are not easily individuated. But, with such an acknowledgement and allowing ourselves the licence of including 1699, the year of publication of Shaftesbury's *Inquiry Concerning Virtue*, in the eighteenth century, we may reasonably ascribe the beginnings of aesthetics as we know the discipline today to British philosophers of the eighteenth century, most notably to Shaftesbury, Hutcheson, Hume, and Reid. It was these philosophers who first systematically discussed such questions as what in the twentieth century might be called the analysis of aesthetic judgements and the criteria of aesthetic excellence, though they would more likely have framed their questions as being concerned with the definition of beauty and of the standard of taste. Our modern discussions of aesthetics are no doubt in many ways different from but are surely continuous with theirs to a degree far greater than with any earlier work.

Berkeley contributed briefly to this movement of thought. While his discussion of the nature of beauty and of criteria of judgement of aesthetic merit is motivated by theological considerations and put to theological use, and while he makes no contribution not found elsewhere in the philosophers of the eighteenth century, nevertheless the major problems are there raised in an acute form with all Berkeley's familar clarity and directness. At least in a tercentennial year his contribution is worthy of notice.

In the earlier portion of the Third Dialogue of the *Alciphron* Alciphron presents the views of those free-thinkers whom he regards as 'men of curious contemplation, not governed by such gross things as sense and custom' (116) on morality and beauty. He offers a version of the position taken by Shaftesbury and Hutcheson; but it is surely wrong for Jessop to claim, as he does in his edition of the *Alciphron* (116), that Alciphron either faithfully presents or is meant faithfully to present the ideas of Shaftesbury, though Shaftesbury, clearly referred to under the name of Cratylus in the dialogue, is represented as being of the same school of thought. Berkeley makes no clear reference to Hutcheson's *Inquiry into the Origin of Ideas of Beauty and Virtue* which had been published seven years before *Alciphron* and he appears to have, at any rate, made no close study of it.

Alciphron commences by claiming that 'there is an idea of Beauty natural to the mind of man' (117). Beauty is discerned by all men by instinct and it 'attracts without a reason' (117). There is corporeal beauty and there is moral beauty, and 'as the eye perceiveth the one, so the mind doth, by a certain inner sense, perceive the other' (117). Thus moral beauty is rather to be felt than understood, it is 'an object, not of the discursive faculty, but of a peculiar sense, which is properly called the *moral sense*, being adapted to the perception of moral beauty as the eye to colours, or the ear to sounds' (120). There is an odd asymmetry in this; while there is a peculiar, i.e. special, sense of moral beauty which feels rather than understands, physical beauty is said to be directly perceived by the eye and should therefore be a, no doubt, complex idea of sense alongside of such ideas as those of colour and shape. This asymmetry, not found in Shaftesbury, Hutcheson, and Hume, will, as we shall see, be disastrous for Alciphron.

In the dialogue Alciphron is motivated largely by a desire to explain morality without an appeal to theology; for Alciphron morality is not, as it is for Berkeley, obedience to the will of God and motivated by a desire to avoid punishment for transgressions against that will. It is a brute fact of human nature that moral beauty is perceived in some things by men and pleases them, even if they are sometimes led by self-seeking to disregard it. Like Shaftesbury, Alciphron claims that his morality is true morality, while theocentric morality, so called, is mercenary and banausic. But the view had also other attractions and it is quite similar to Hume's discussion of the perception of virtue and vice in his *Treatise of Human Nature*, Book III, Part 1.[1] The theological motivation is dispensable.

At this stage Euphranor, the Christian apologist, professes himself

---

[1] References to Hume's *Treatise* are to the Selby-Bigge edition (Clarendon Press, Oxford, 1888).

unable to understand this claim to a physical sense of corporeal beauty and an internal sense of moral beauty. Regarding it as unwise to attempt to discuss both claims at once, Euphranor proposes that they should discuss only the sense of corporeal beauty, and asks what it is that we call beauty in objects of sense. Alciphron feels compelled to answer the question, and, having already incautiously spoken of moral beauty as being 'an order, a symmetry, and comeliness, in the moral world' (117), now answers analogously that corporeal beauty is a 'certain symmetry or proportion pleasing to the eye' (123).

Why, one might reasonably ask, only to the eye? At Euphranor's prompting Alciphron has ruled out mere pleasing smells and tastes as not beautiful, since they scarcely could be said to have symmetry and proportion, thus reminding us of Kant's rejection of such pleasures as not aesthetic. So Alciphron says that 'beauty is, to speak properly, perceived only by the eye.' (123.) This clearly rules out beauty in music and in literature, which is surely arbitrary and not required by the argument to date, since it is not unreasonable to claim that symmetry and proportion may be discerned in both these fields as well as by vision. The explanation seems to be that Berkeley limits his discussion to natural beauty, and the beauty of artefacts, a contrary limitation to that of many modern writers on aesthetics who limit their discussion to the arts. Berkeley's limitation clearly excludes literature, and natural sounds might be thought to lack the necessary structure.

But, to return to exposition, Alciphron now agrees that symmetry and proportion vary with different kinds of object and that symmetry and proportion is what makes 'the whole complete and perfect in its kind' (124). Thus the proportions we admire in a horse are different from those we admire in a door and in each case appropriate to the perfection of its kind. Euphranor now leads Alciphron to agree that a thing is 'perfect in its kind when it answers the end for which it was made' (124). This disastrous admission completes Alciphron's downfall; he cannot possibly claim that the eye determines whether a thing answers to the end for which it was made and admits that this is the work of reason. Euphranor can now claim that 'beauty, in your sense of it, is an object, not of the eye, but of the mind' (124); we see the object but discern its beauty with the aid of reason.

Euphranor's theological strategy now becomes clear; by analogy the notion of moral beauty, based on order and symmetry in social and personal relationships, must require the notions of end and purpose. So we cannot interpret the world in terms of chance, but must allow a providence that has ends and purposes.

In some respects, no doubt, this is an unsatisfactory and contrived end to the discussion. If beauty is, indeed, fitness for an end, then our perception of beauty has to be limited not merely to objects of the eye but to such of those which we may discern by reason to answer to an end. Even by highly anthropocentric criteria this is limiting. If we allow that a horse is made for an end discernible by Berkeley and Euphranor, and if the atheist Alciphron can at any rate allow that men treat horses as serving a human purpose, it is hard to see that we have here an account of beauty applicable to sunsets and roses. Berkeley and Euphranor may be sure that God made them for a purpose, but would be surely arrogant to claim that they knew what it was.

But we cannot simply dismiss Alciphron's view as merely contrived by Berkeley to give Euphranor an easy theological victory. No doubt Alciphron was disastrously incautious to identify symmetry and order with being made for an end, but much of his view was to remain standard in the eighteenth century. Thus Hume in his Treatise says that 'if we consider all the hypotheses which have been formed either by philosophy or common reason, to explain the difference betwixt beauty and deformity, we shall find that all of them resolve into this, that beauty is such an order and construction of parts, as, either by the *primary constitution* of our nature, by *custom*, or by *caprice*, is fitted to give pleasure and satisfaction to the soul' (299). If Hume would not dream of specifying the order and construction of which he speaks in terms of being made for an end, as Alciphron was led to do, he is ready enough to specify it in terms of utility, of it serving our ends, or, in the case of animals, their welfare. Thus 'that shape which produces strength is beautiful in one animal; and that which is a sign of agility, in another' (299). This remained Hume's view to the end, and in the *Enquiry concerning the Principles of Morals* the beauty of certain forms of ships, buildings, doors and windows is explained in terms of their utility.[2] Hume is also too canny a Scot to identify beauty simply with rationally discerned utility, as Euphranor persuades Alciphron to do; 'the power of producing pain and pleasure', he tells us, 'makes . . . the essence of beauty and deformity' (299). Thus for Hume beauty is something other than order and construction of parts and other than utility; it is merely a well-

_____
[2] *Enquiries*, ed. Selby-Bigge (Clarendon Press, Oxford, 1902), 212–13.

founded observation that these bring about that special kind of pleasure in which the sense of beauty consists. In this Hume was following in the steps of Hutcheson. Hutcheson recognized two special senses; the moral sense which Alciphron following Shaftesbury, had also recognized, and also a sense of beauty.

Euphranor's attack against Alciphron would have been ineffective against Hutcheson and Hume. They could readily have admitted that reason, reflecting on the evidence of sense-perception, recognized order, symmetry, unity amidst variety (Hutcheson's preferred version) or whatever else was the ground of the peculiar aesthetic pleasure; but the pleasure itself was an ultimate fact of human nature and not to be explained by theological or any other considerations. Euphranor's attack would indeed have been ineffective if it had been launched directly against Alciphron's account of morality. For Alciphron had postulated, like Shaftesbury, Hutcheson and Hume, a special moral sense; so he could have readily agreed with Euphranor that social order and harmony were recognized by reason and still claimed that morality was a matter of sense, something 'rather to be felt than understood'.

Alciphron, in fact, misstates the position he is supposed to defend; he fails to make a true parallel between the sense of beauty and the moral sense. Having claimed that order and symmetry are the ground both of aesthetic and/or moral delight, he appears to present a neat parallel: 'as the eye perceiveth the one, so the mind doth, by a certain interior sense, perceive the other' (117). But it is clear that Alciphron's interior sense does not perceive order and symmetry in the social world—if it did it would not be an interior sense—but is rather the feeling induced by this order and symmetry; by making the sense of beauty a matter of sense-perception he brings ruin on himself and he is forced to identify beauty with something external to himself. The true parallel would be to have two inner senses, the moral sense and the sense of beauty, each triggered by a different kind of symmetry and order.

So Berkeley failed to state the theory of the peculiar senses of beauty and morality, through Alciphron's mouth, in a satisfactory form. So Euphranor's attack, whatever force it may have against Alciphron, leads only to an unsatisfactory victory. It was to be left to Reid to begin the assault on this characteristic eighteenth-century theory which eventually led to its disappearance.

One final reflection. We have seen how not merely Alciphron and

Euphranor, in Berkeley's writings, but also Hume, linked the order that brought the response of the sense of beauty or the moral sense with finality—the notion of an end or purpose. We have seen how Hume avoided the theological implications suggested by Euphranor by relativizing the notion of utility; we use horses for an end and there is no need to inquire into the end or function of a horse *sub specie aeternitatis*. But still the notion of an end was powerless to deal with the beauty of the many things which we find beautiful but for which we have no use and which scarcely have ends of their own—flowers and the creations of the fine arts, for example. Can it be that Kant's doctrine of the beautiful having the form of finality can be seen as a sophistication and generalization of the line of thought which had appealed to the British philosophers of the eighteenth century? If so, it would not be an isolated case.

CHAPTER 13

GOD-APPOINTED BERKELEY AND THE GENERAL GOOD

STEPHEN R. L. CLARK

I

'GOD-appointed Berkeley that proved all things a dream'[1] is usually remembered as a 'mystical and visionary idealist', author of an ideology that justified neglect of the material conditions of human life. His being known as 'Bishop Berkeley' does not convey to modern minds the information that he successfully cared for the spiritual and material necessities of an impoverished diocese, but that he was a comic clergyman, even a 'hypochondriacal recluse'.[2] His metaphysical idealism, expounded in his twenties, is generally studied as an episode in the development of 'British empiricism', although he was himself at pains to distinguish his thought from that of the 'minute philosophers', and is more accurately classified as an 'Irish Cartesian'.[3] His contributions to ethical theory have been dismissed, if they are noticed at all, as 'not important',[4] or are, at best, acknowledged as a curious anticipation of utilitarian theory. 'If he had given to the question the thought necessary to produce a systematic work, he might have been the first Utilitarian.'[5]

This ignorance of Berkeley's life and works has not, of course, been universal. Some philosophers have examined his theory of morals, especially as represented in another early work, the sermon on Passive Obedience (1713: vi. 15 ff.). Some non-philosophers have remembered other writings: with *The Querist* (1735–7: vi. 89 ff.) especially in mind, Johnston has contended that 'every national

[1] W. B. Yeats, 'Blood and the Moon' II, *Collected Poems* (Macmillan, London, 1933), p. 268.

[2] J. M. Hone and M. M. Rossi, *Bishop Berkeley: his life, writings and philosophy* (Faber, London, 1931), p. 197; cf. E. D. Leyburn, 'Bishop Berkeley: the Querist', *Proceedings Royal Irish Academy* 44.C (1937–8), pp. 75 ff.

[3] H. M. Bracken, *Berkeley* (Macmillan, London, 1974), ch. 7.

[4] G. D. Hicks, *Berkeley* (Ernest Benn, London, 1932), p. 181.

[5] G. A. Johnston, 'The development of Berkeley's ethical theory', *Philosophical Review* 24 (1915), p. 430.

leader who had a comprehensive concept of Irish nationhood was influenced consciously or unconsciously by the spirit of George Berkeley'.[6] American scholars, conscious of his generous gifts to Harvard and to Yale and of his optimistic assessment of the prospects for the young American civilization ('Time's noblest offspring is the last': *Works*, vii. 373), recognize him as a 'man of action bent upon promoting the common weal in all things, upon reestablishing public spirit, correcting the excesses of immoderation in society, and directing education toward workable public and private ends'.[7] The recent work by Paul Olscamp (1968, 1970) has done something to re-establish Berkeley in the moral tradition—though Olscamp himself is so far out of sympathy with Berkeley's God-centredness as not to do him perfect justice. But there is still a general assumption that Berkeley was an ingenious sophist, without even the courage of his sceptical convictions to abandon God and the soul (as Hume did after him). Samuel Johnson's 'refutation' is remembered, not his considered admission that 'Berkeley was a profound scholar, as well as a man of fine imagination'.[8] A profound scholar, and a very persuasive politician: how many of his detractors could have persuaded the King and Parliament (and many private individuals) to fund a college in the Summer Isles, for the better education of planters and Indians alike? This latter project, of course, was stillborn—partly because he had been misinformed about conditions in Bermuda, and largely because Sir Robert Walpole so delayed payment and blocked Berkeley's effort to transfer the charter to Rhode Island that Berkeley had to abandon hope. It is a minor irony of history that the colony founded with the moneys earmarked for St Paul's College was also supported by money bequeathed for the specific benefit of blacks, and intended to manage entirely without slaves—its name was Georgia.[9]

Berkeley was a man of action, a mover of great affairs, and one entranced by the details of material life (in the common, not the metaphysical sense). Long before he was convinced—by trial—of the

[6] J. D. Johnston, 'Berkeley's influence as an economist', *Hermathena* 82 (1953), p. 88; see also J. M. Hone, 'Berkeley and Swift as National Economists', *Studies* 23 (1934), p. 422.

[7] G. P. Conray, 'Berkeley and education in America', *Journal of the History of Ideas* 21 (1960), p. 211.

[8] J. Boswell, *Life of Samuel Johnson* (Clarendon Press, Oxford, 1963), p. 448 (1770), p. 333 (6 Aug. 1763).

[9] E. S. Gaustad, *George Berkeley in America* (Yale University Press, New Haven/London, 1979).

merits of tar-water (on which he wrote his second recorded poem, beginning 'Hail, vulgar juice of never-fading pine . . .': *Works*, vi. 225), he had speculated on the superiority of strong coffee to laudanum for the relief of colic, and the virtues of 'Jesuit's bark'.[10] The hypochondria that Hone and Rossi impute to him is a careful eye for the management of Brother Ass. He was, with his wife, 'one of the few progressive landlords in at least southern Ireland, employing a hundred men on his glebe, teaching his people how to spin, and building and minding a workhouse for vagrants'.[11] According to Thomas Blackwell, he knew more than any ordinary craftsman of any liberal or mechanical art, and especially loved sitting attentively by foundries.[12] There is even some slight evidence that he or his wife invented a washing-machine—it would at least have been in character.[13]

He was a man of action: not the sort of 'practical man' who shows practicality by being ignorant of the principles on which he acts, and careless of the long-term consequences of what he does.[14] He delighted in the detail of the natural universe, admiring it as God's speech to humankind, His foretaste of heaven. 'Green fields and groves, flowery meadows and purling streams, are nowhere in such perfection as in England, but if you would know lightsome days, warm suns and blue skies, you must come to Italy; and to enable a man to describe rocks and precipices, it is absolutely necessary that he pass the Alps' (*Works*, viii. 83). 'He is the true possessor of a thing,' he wrote in Steele's *Guardian*, 'who enjoys it, and not he that owns it without the enjoyment of it', condemning in these words all absentee landlords who sought the 'fantastical' pleasures of court (vii. 195).[15] The *Summum Bonum* lay in sensual pleasure (*PC*, 769), of the kind that we might know in loving appreciation of God's bounty, and 'he that acts not in order to the obtaining of eternal Happyness must be an infidel' (*PC*, 776). That 'eternal Happyness' is as 'large as our desires, & those desires not stinted to ye few objects we at present receive from some dull inlets of perception, but proportionate to wt

---

[10] B. Rand, *Berkeley and Percival* (Cambridge University Press, Cambridge, 1914), p. 226 (28. 12. 1725), p. 179 (12. 10. 1721).
[11] T. E. Jessop, 'George Berkeley 1685–1753', *Hermathena* 82 (1953), p. 9.
[12] T. Blackwell, *Memoirs of Court of Augustus* (1775), vol. 2, p. 277; cited by Jessop.
[13] I. C. Tipton and E. J. Furlong, 'Mrs George Berkeley and her washing machine', *Hermathena* 101 (1965), pp. 38 ff.
[14] H. Belloc, *The Servile State* (Constable, London, 1927), p. 131.
[15] This has the air of a Horatian tag: I have not yet located its source.

our faculties shall be wn God has given the finishing stroke to our nature & made us fit inhabitants for heaven' (*Works*, vii. 12). Berkeley's heaven was not an abstract realm to which he hoped to escape from natural living: it was an intensity of sensual perception for which we might be prepared even in this dull age.

'On meeting Berkeley Bishop Atterbury said of him: "So much understanding, so much knowledge, so much innocence, and such humility, I did not think had been the portion of any but angels till I saw this gentleman."' (*Works*, vii. 177.) Allowance must be made for eighteenth-century style, and Berkeley's persuasive presence, but there is no good evidence that the Bishop's judgement was all that awry. Berkeley's enemies were those who knew him by reputation only, not personal acquaintance. 'Whatever the world thinks,' Berkeley wrote in *Siris* (v. 350), 'he who hath not much meditated upon God, the human mind, and the *summum bonum*, may possibly make a thriving earthworm, but will most indubitably make a sorry patriot and a sorry statesman.' The contrary implication does not always hold, but there can be few with any large acquaintance with Berkeley's life and works to doubt that he was a sound patriot, a sound statesman, and as honourable in his life as in his philosophy.

'To feed the hungry and clothe the naked, by promoting an honest industry, will, perhaps, be deemed no improper employment for a clergyman who still thinks himself a member of the commonwealth.' (*Works*, vi. 103.) Now that it is fashionable to decry the involvement of 'the Church' with 'politics', we could do worse than remember Berkeley's query: 'Whether there can be a greater reproach on the leading men and the patriots of a country, than that the people should want employment?' (vi. 135). And the patriots might also remember his answer:

. . . General corruption of manners never faileth to draw after it some heavy judgment of war, famine, or pestilence . . . The same atheistical narrow spirit, centering all our cares upon private interest, and contracting all our hopes within the enjoyment of this present life, equally produceth a neglect of what we owe to God and our country. (vi. 78 f.)

After this preamble, what can be said of Berkeley's moral purpose, and his arguments? That his was not a systematic intellect is well known. His wife, indeed, remarked to her son that 'had he *built* as he has *pulled down* he had been then a *Master builder* indeed but unto every Man his Work' (vii. 388 f.). Part of the apparent lack of system is due to the loss, in Italy, of the second volume of his *Principles* (ii. 282), which was to handle 'the 2 great Principles of Morality. the Being of a God & the Freedom of Man' (*PC*, 508). In its absence we have no definitive statement of Berkeley's moral theory, but must piece it together from the *Philosophical Commentaries*, his sermons (especially those on Passive Obedience, Immortality, and the Will of God) and essays (especially those on 'Preventing the Ruin of Great Britain', 'Pleasure', and 'The Bond of Society'), *Alciphron*, and *The Querist*. This task faces two further difficulties. First, that in his moral, as well as his epistemological theory, Berkeley often argues from a thesis that he attributes to his opponents, believing that 'the same principles which at first view lead to *scepticism* [or amoralism], pursued to a certain point, bring men back to common sense' (*Dialogues*, 263). Secondly, that it is all too easy to apply the catchwords of a later generation to Berkeleian texts, and see nothing there that we do not know already, particularly if we concentrate (as general studies of Berkeley usually do[16]) on the early sermon on Passive Obedience.

'Socrates' whole employment was the turning men aside from vice, impertinence, and trifling speculations to the study of solid wisdom, temperance, justice and piety, which is the true business of a philosopher.'[17] That is how Berkeley conceived of his own business, as philosopher and cleric. In pursuit of this goal, he concerned himself especially with the relationship between self and society. 'To be a real patriot, a man must consider his countrymen as God's creatures, and himself as accountable for his acting towards them. . . . The patriot aims at his private good in the public. The knave makes the public subservient to his private interest. The former considers himself as part of a whole, the latter considers himself as the whole.'[18] To explain the force of these maxims I shall discuss Berkeley's moral theory under the following six heads: (i) the Freedom of Man; (ii) the strict indemonstrability of substantive moral judgements; (iii) the Summum Bonum as Sensual Pleasure; (iv) the virtue of obedience and the vice of 'going it alone'; (v) social attraction, mutual connection, and 'the Great City'; (vi) the Being of God. The first three

---

[16] G. Pitcher, *Berkeley* (RKP, London, 1977), pp. 228 ff.; J. O. Urmson, *Berkeley* (Oxford University Press, Oxford, 1982), pp. 72 ff.; see H. W. Orange, 'Berkeley as a moral philosopher', *Mind* o.s. 15 (1890), p. 515 re A. Campbell Fraser.

[17] Rand, *Berkeley and Percival*, p. 68 (27. 12. 1709).

[18] *Maxims* (1750), *Works*, vi. 253 f.; possibly by Anne Berkeley.

topics could be considered as the rising water of Philonous's fountain, 'how it is forced upwards, in a round column, to a certain height; at which it breaks and falls back into the basin from whence it rose' (*Dialogues*, 262); the last three topics are the water's fall, and Berkeley's answer to the amoralists.

II

The Philosophical Commentaries record Berkeley's debate with himself whether 'uneasiness be necessary to set the will at work' (*PC*, 423), and so whether precise prediction of our acts be possible (*PC*, 145). He concluded, 'That God & Blessed Spirits have Will is a manifest Argument against Lockes proofs that the will cannot be conceiv'd put into action without a Previous Uneasiness' (*PC*, 610). 'Uneasiness', as a matter of experience, 'precedes not every volition' (*PC*, 628), nor can it ever be supposed to be a genuine cause of volition, since 'ideas' or the contents of consciousness (and uneasiness is such a content) cannot bring about the emergence of any other idea, or any act (*PC*, 653). 'What means Cause as distinguish'd from Occasion? nothing but a Being wch wills w^h the Effect follows the volition.' (*PC*, 499.) Our only notion of true causation, for Berkeley, is derived from the experience of volitionally bringing about an effect: 'We move our legs our selves. 'tis we that will their movement.' (*PC*, 548) That there is a real difficulty here for Berkeley's understanding of the relations between God's agency and ours, our ideas and those of other creatures and those of God, is clear, and I shall not attempt to resolve it here. It is enough that Berkeley reckons that our freedom lies in our capacity to do as we will (*Alc.*, 316), and that our will, our volition is not determined by anything but itself.

If our soul was an entity with a definable nature, it might be possible to argue that being so it could not but will the way it did. But the soul, for Berkeley, 'is the will properly speaking' (*PC*, 478a). The very being of a soul lies in 'percipere (or velle i.e. agere)' (*PC*, 429), and while it exists at all it cannot fail to be acting. 'In Sleep & trances the mind exists not' (*PC*, 651; see *Principles*, 98). There is no substantial entity that has any prior existence of a kind that could determine what sort of effects it could will. '. . . tis no thing at all that wills' (*PC*, 658). Berkeley asks 'Whether Identity of Person consists not in the Will' (*PC*, 194a): who I am, or what I am, is a matter of what Will is operative. Identity of person does not rest in the ideas that the Will contemplates ('memory'), still less in those that others also contemplate ('the body'). In this Berkeley recalls Aristotle, who also (though obscurely) rested identity in *prohairesis*, deliberate choice, and denied that 'human nature' could be anything but indeterminate.[19] Our nature as rational souls is to have no determining nature: what we are is the will with which we will to have certain ideas, not to entertain others.

In other contexts, of course, Berkeley acknowledged that 'the Soul is so constituted, in her original state, that certain dispositions and tendencies will not fail to shew themselves, at proper periods, and in certain circumstances; which affections . . . are properly said to be natural or innate' ('On the Will of God': *Works*, vii. 130). Such innate affections, though, still do not determine the soul's volition, but only speak to entice it on the narrow way. They are part of God's address to us, and do not compel. Following God's example (as it were), Berkeley's usual technique for altering the behaviour of his fellow countrymen is to try and present to them such images as may awaken their will, or their reason. 'Rational desires are vigorous in proportion to the goodness &, if I may so speak attainableness of their objects.' (On Immortality: *Works*, vii. 11.) To will rationally is to proportion one's behaviour by the 'direct compounded reason of the excellency and certainty of the objects'. Not that there is any natural necessity that one will do this, but that anything less seems silly. The welfare of the Gaelic poor will be best served by showing them new reasons for industry, coaxing them from penury by the prospect of a decent patrimony (*Works*, vi. 110 f.). Architecture, sculpture, and painting have as their office the task of filling minds with great ideas, 'spurring them up to an emulation of worthy actions' (vi. 80). But these ideas, being 'absolutely inert' (*Alc.*, 314), do not strictly cause our response.

Our freedom rests upon the fact that we are naked wills, not to be equated with any object of consciousness (*PC*, 478a, 643). 'The only original true notions that we have of freedom, agent, or action are obtained by reflecting on ourselves, and the operation of our own minds.' (*Alc.*, 318) We have no IDEA of what it is we are; our being can never be an object of consciousness even to ourselves, although we have a use for language that looks as if it describes our being. Similarly, we have 'no Ideas of vertues & vices, no Ideas of Moral

---

[19] Aristotle, *Nicomachean Ethics* I. 1098a 3 ff.; see my *Aristotle's Man* (Clarendon Press, Oxford, 1975), ch. 2. 1.

Actions wherefore it may be Question'd whether we are capable of arriving at Demonstration about them, the morality consisting in the Volition chiefly' (*PC*, 660). There is nothing, that is, which we could bring before our consciousness that is what it is to be virtuous or vicious:[20] 'sin or moral turpitude doth not consist in the outward physical action or motion, but in the internal deviation of the will from the laws of reason and religion' (*Dialogues*, 237), and this deviation cannot be detected by any but the active will itself (and the 'watchful, active, intelligent, free Spirit . . . in whom we live and move and have our being': *Works*, i. 251). Being good, accordingly, cannot be equated with being any idea, despite Broad's understandable assertion that, to Berkeley, 'nothing is intrinsically good except pleasant experience or intrinsically bad except unpleasant experience.[21] On the contrary, such ideas as these cannot be 'intrinsically good or bad', although they may serve, for well-appointed souls, to awaken the will that points to Heaven. 'Actions leading to heaven are in my power if I will them, therefore I will will them' (*PC*, 160, obelized)—but outward acts are not to the purpose, only the inner direction of the will.

Having no idea of goodness, when we speak of persons or of God as good, or of others as bad, we mean only to excite 'the passions of fear, love, hatred, admiration, disdain, and the like' (*Principles*, Intro. 20). What we say of God particularly is correct not in that it is 'true' (for we can have no idea of what God is), but in that it 'makes proper impressions on [the] mind, producing therein love, hope, gratitude, and obedience, and thereby becomes a lively operative principle, influencing [our] life and actions, agreeably to that notion of saving faith which is required in a Christian' (*Alc.*, 297). 'So likewise, a man may be just and virtuous, without having precise ideas of *justice* and *virtue*' (*Principles*, 100), for there are no such ideas. That conformity to the will of the creator spirit is, in the abstract, 'right' is not a thought for which Berkeley's analysis makes room, let alone one that he purports to demonstrate. It is, on the contrary, part of his attack on the 'minute philosophers' that they pretend to an 'abstract idea of moral fitness' and 'an adequate idea of the divine economy' with a view to measuring the one by the other (*Alc.*, 252).

---

[20] See my paper on 'Morals, Moore and MacIntyre', *Inquiry* 26 (1984), pp. 425 ff. A. MacIntyre's own *After Virtue* (Duckworth, London, 1982) is as opposed as Berkeley was to abstract ideas in morals, and as concerned for tradition.

[21] C. D. Broad, 'Berkeley's theory of morals', *Revue Internationale de Philosophie* 7 (1953), p. 84.

What appear to be demonstrations of moral truth turn out to be making 'a dictionary of words' (*PC*, 690). 'God Ought to be worship'd. This Easily demonstrated when we ascertain the signification of the word God, worship, ought.' (*PC*, 705.) The law of absolute passive obedience to civil authority does not apply 'where a government is unhinged or the supreme power disputed' (*Works*, vi. 45), any more than theorems about triangles apply to figures that are not triangular. Such demonstrations (as that there is a contradiction in acknowledging a prince as supreme authority while also pretending to reserve the right of rebellion) may be significant, but they do not establish the first principles of moral judgement—as that it is the LORD that is God, or that there is a 'happyness large as our desires . . . wch we narrow-sighted mortals wretchedly point out to our selves by green meadows, fragrant groves, refreshing shades, crystal streams & wt other pleasant ideas our fancys can glean up in this Vale of misery, but in vain' (*Works*, vii. 12). We have no idea of God, nor of that eternal happiness, and the first principles of our actions cannot be understood as statements of what ideas are found with what other ideas. They are simply ways of exciting and preserving in ourselves a particular direction of the will. 'Moral truth' is of a different kind from 'mathematical' or 'natural truth' (*PC*, 676), and its 'recognition' depends on our not being indifferent: 'Suppose an agent which is finite perfectly indifferent, & as to desiring not determin'd by any prospect or consideration of good I say, this Agent cannot do an action morally Good.' (*PC*, 166.) To think something intrinsically good is to 'move' towards it, not to have a distinct idea of its 'goodness'.

Accordingly, Berkeley 'allow[s] not of the Distinction there is made twix't Profit & Pleasure' (*PC*, 541). 'I'd never blame a Man for acting upon Interest. he's a fool that acts on any other Principle. the not understanding these things has been of ill consequence in Morality.' (*PC* 542: 1.68.) 'Sensual Pleasure qua Pleasure is Good & desirable. by a Wise Man. but if it be Contemptible tis not qua pleasure but qua pain or . . . loss of greater pleasure.' (*PC*, 773.) Berkeley here adopts the hedonism of Plato's Protagoras: it is desire and enjoyment that mark things out as 'good', and the wise man's task is so to calculate consequences (in accordance with the warnings displayed before him in nature) as not to end up in a state that cannot be enjoyed. People can be misled: 'In Valuing Good we reckon too much on ye present & our own.' (*PC*, 851) Also we forget that there are 'two sorts of

Pleasure the one is ordained as a spur or incitement to somewhat else . . . the other is not. Thus the pleasure of eating is of the former sort, of Musick is ye later sort. These may be used for recreation, those not but in order to their End.' (*PC*, 852.) Berkeley further distinguishes between 'natural' and 'fantastical' pleasures:

It is evident that a desire terminated in money is fantastical; so is the desire of outward distinctions, which bring no delight of sense, nor recommend us as useful to mankind; and the desire of things meerly because they are new or foreign. Men who are indisposed to a due exertion of their higher parts are driven to such pursuits as these from the restlessness of the mind, and the sensitive appetites being easily satisfied. It is, in some sort, owing to the bounty of Providence that, disdaining a cheap and vulgar happiness, they frame to themselves imaginary goods, in which there is nothing can raise desire, but the difficulty of obtaining them. Thus men become the contrivers of their own misery, as a punishment on themselves for departing from the measures of nature. (*Works*, vii. 194.)

Berkeley sometimes seems to think that this 'vulgar happiness', delight in the ideas presented to the soul that is set upon the right way, is easy, and a superficial reading of the texts may suggest the image of a complacent clergyman. Later moralists, more high-minded maybe, are also inclined to think his view intolerably egoistical. Orange, for example, summarizes Fraser's interpretation of Berkeley's 'theological utilitarianism' (itself a misnomer) as the claim that what is good is 'that which will enable me to avoid the pit and clutch the crown'.[22] Generations of high-minded moralists have contended that 'really moral' persons do not act for their own well-being, but for some other good, not their own. Berkeley was in the older (and sounder) tradition, in thinking that one could only have others' happiness as one's goal in so far as one identified oneself with the whole of which both one and others were parts. But the extent of his egoism will concern me later; here it is necessary to observe that Berkeley knew the struggle that was needed to hang on to real happiness. 'Strange impotence of men. Man without God. Wretcheder than a stone or tree, he having onely the power to be miserable by his unperformed wills, these having no power at all . . .' (*PC*, 107, obelized). Well aware of pestilence, famine, death, and horror,[23] and of the impending ruin of his country if its ways did not change, Berkeley saw

---

[22] Orange, 'Berkeley as a moral philosopher', p. 516.

[23] J. P. Hershbell, 'Berkeley and the Problem of Evil', *Journal of the History of Ideas* 31 (1970), p. 545.

our only hope in true religion. Without the 'sense that we act in the eye of infinite wisdom, power, and goodness', and the hope of immortality, 'the highest state of life is insipid' (*Works*, vii. 196).

'What beauty can be found', Euphranor enquires in criticism of the high-minded atheist, 'in a moral system, formed, connected, and governed by chance, fate, or any other blind unthinking principle?' (*Alc.*, 128.) Without hope, Berkeley could hardly have held his will to enjoy natural beauty when his son William died: 'not content to be fond of him', he mourned, 'I was vain of him' (*Works*, viii. 304).

Happiness must rest in, somehow, welcoming the ideas presented to us as rational beings. 'God May comprehend . . . the Ideas wch are painfull & unpleasant without being in any degree pained thereby. Thus we our selves can imagine the pain of a burn etc without any misery or uneasiness at all.' (*PC*, 675.) We can, with effort and by the grace of God, so far conform ourselves to His will as to enjoy His long-term plan, and not be lost either in the pleasures or the pains of our merely animal natures.

We should propose to our selves nobler views, such as to recreate and exalt the mind, with a prospect of the beauty, order, extent, and variety of natural things: hence, by proper inferences, to enlarge our notions of the grandeur, wisdom, and beneficence of the Creator: and lastly, (3) to make the several parts of the Creation, so far as in us lies, subservient to the ends they were designed for, God's glory, and the sustentation and comfort of our selves and fellow-creatures. (*Principles*, 109)

In his *Guardian* essays II and III, Berkeley devised a piece of early science fiction: philosophical snuff, whereby one might enter another's pineal gland and 'being so placed, become spectator of all the ideas in his mind' (*Works*, vii. 186). Entering the gland of a Free-thinker, Ulysses Cosmopolita finds a castle with racks, dungeons, and 'certain men in black, of gigantick size, and most terrifick forms'. On closer inspection the appearance turns out to be a church with bells, ropes, and gravestones, and 'the terrible Giants in black shrunk into a few innocent clergymen' (vii. 188 f.). The difference between the destinies of the faithful and the infidel is similar, resting not upon external rewards and punishments, but on the ideas each chooses to receive, and the enjoyments each wills to cultivate. Ulysses

could see no manner of relief or comfort in the soul of [a voluptuary], but what consisted in preventing his cure, by inflaming his passions and suppressing his reason. But tho' it must be owned he had almost quenched that light which his Creator had set in his soul, yet in spight of all his efforts, I observed at certain seasons frequent flashes of remorse strike thro' the gloom, and interrupt that satisfaction he enjoyed in hiding his own deformities from himself.' (vii. 187.)

In that human beings are rational, they may not live by sense and appetite and still be happy: to live like a brute is 'to be defrauded of true happiness' (*Alc.*, 85). Every kind of creature has its own pleasures: 'you can easily conceive that the sort of life which makes the happiness of a mole or a bat would be a very wretched one for an eagle.' (86.) Alciphron supposes that 'every wise man looks upon himself, or his own bodily existence in this present world, as the centre and ultimate end of all his actions and regards. He considers his appetites as natural guides directing to his proper good, his passions and senses as the natural true means of enjoying this good.' (45.) Berkeley did not wholly disagree, any more than he wholly disagreed with Lysicles' claim that the life of business is in 'the circulation of money' (67).[24] Their error lies in restricting their interest to this world, and their major pleasures to the fantastical. 'He yt will enjoy heaven in ye next life must think on it in this.' (*Works*, vii. 15)

So Berkeley, though he used these principles to his own effect, was a voluntarist, emotivist, and hedonist. Neither natural nor logical necessity requires us to set out on the road to Heaven. The first principles of our action are not strictly statements, but expressions and evocations of our devotion. What all but fools aim at is a real increase of their own pleasure.

III

Although substantive moral judgements cannot be strictly demonstrated, it is possible of course to unfold the implications of a system in such a way that people may find that it embodies what they already will. That is what Berkeley especially seeks to do in his sermon on Passive Obedience (*Works*, vi. 15 ff.). Such demonstrations rest upon 'making a dictionary of words', and run the risk of being merely 'trifling' (like Locke's: *PC* 690 f.) or wilfully absurd (like Spinoza's: *Alc.*, 324). We should not define words just as we choose, nor yet imagine that anyone of us can by ourselves construct a workable system in ethics or in physics, 'so swift is our progress from the womb

[24] See T. W. Hutchison, 'Berkeley's Querist and its place in economic thought', *British Journal of the Philosophy of Science* 4 (1953–4), p. 70.

to the grave' (*Works*, vii. 14). Nor can we rely upon our judgement to determine exactly what on any given occasion would have the best results for us, or for our country (*Works*, vi. 21). If our only hope of happiness lies in conformity to the will of God (vi. 20), we need to know what that will is.

That our understanding is in its own nature not only very weak and imperfect, but also much obscured by passion and prejudice, is a point too plain to need proof.

From all which, we may certainly conclude, it is not our true interest to be governed by our own carnal and irregular wills, but rather to square and suit our actions, to the supreme will of him, whose understanding is infinite, comprehending in one clear view the remotest events and consequences of things. (*Works*, vii. 135.)

That virtue lies in conformity and obedience is a thought to which we have grown unaccustomed. It is generally thought that 'mature' human beings can only act out of their own judgement of what's best to do, that ancestral prejudice and sovereign authority can only constrain the free spirit. This view is often conjoined, as in the minute philosophers, with the view that liberty consists in not being prevented from doing what one wants, while one's wants are themselves determined by blind unthinking principle. Berkeley disagreed.

To insist on acting only on one's own judgement is absurd, for the only context in which it makes sense to give such respect to this 'little agitation of the brain known as thought'[25] is when it is conceived to be the child of eternal Reason. If thought and judgement are only a sort of cranial perspiration, what respect do they merit? But if they are the voice of reason, why should we despise tradition and sovereign law, equally the offspring of that reason? Berkeley applies this thought in two areas. First, in the field of belief: tradition, custom, authority, and law ensure that belief in God is 'entrenched', only to be abandoned for clear reason even if we cannot provide clear reason for adopting such a belief in the abstract (*Alc.*, 143). He was perhaps the first philosopher to see clearly that the failure of the Cartesian enterprise could not be patched up by appealing to supposedly uncontested experience instead of incontrovertible logic. We cannot sensibly adopt the epistemological rule, 'Believe only what you can

[25] D. Hume, 'Dialogues concerning Natural Religion', in *Hume on Religion*, ed. R. Wollheim (Fontana, 1963), p. 121.

demonstrate by your own reason and experience', and must, for our soul's sake, accept on decent authority what has not been clearly disproved (see *Works*, vi. 206). Second, in the field of practice, especially political: law is universal where 'men live in a state exalted above that of brutes' (vi. 27), and obedience to such law cannot be at our solitary pleasure. '. . . there is in every civil community, somewhere or other, placed a supreme power of making laws, and enforcing the observation of them.' (vi. 18) Even if a prince once had no 'right' to the crown, 'once [he is] in possession of it and you have sworn allegiance to him, you are no longer at liberty to inquire by what unrighteous steps he might have obtained it' ('Advice to the Tories': vi. 57).

Such absolute submission to sovereign authority is presented as an inviolable law of nature, or dictate of reason. '. . . the attainment of the greatest good, or deliverance from the greatest evil, that can befall any man or number of men in this life, may not justify the least violation of [this law].' (vi. 18) He sometimes argues for this conclusion on immediately consequentialist grounds, that 'the ills of rebellion are certain, but the event doubtful' (vi. 55; see vi. 41 f.). But the force of the law does not rest upon the likelihood of ill consequences: those usual evils are God's warning to us, and the act no less to be condemned because God in His mercy sometimes allows rebellions to succeed. We must learn from reason and experience together what God requires of us. Conformity to His will is our only stable happiness; His will must be directed to the good of all His creatures, not to any particular group;[26] He has shown us that we cannot hope to bring about such good except by concerted action, and general rules. Those are the rules, accordingly, to which He expects absolute conformity—the rules, that is, that can be conceived to be obeyed without contradiction.[27] 'Positive rules' may sometimes conflict, and must therefore always contain an implicit codicil relieving us of an impossible duty: 'negative rules' can be obeyed, though often in great hardship, without contradiction. Accordingly, we are forbidden to rebel against established authority, or to do anything that may weaken its power over human minds. We are not always required literally to obey (for example, when the sovereign wickedly orders us to break other absolute and negative rules that

[26] Cf. Pitcher, *Berkeley*, p. 236.
[27] J. Kupfer, 'Universalization in Berkeley's Rule-Utilitarianism', *Revue Internationale de Philosophie* 28 (1974), p. 528.

are, by custom and sound evidence, necessary for the well-being of God's creation). We are required not to rebel, even though it is 'a more heinous and inexcusable violation of (the law) for the persons entrusted with the supreme power to use that power to the ruin and destruction of the people committed to their charge' (*Works*, vi. 40).

To be a sovereign authority is to be one to whom citizens ought to submit; without such an authority there is no hope of civil liberty, for we are then 'an open prey to the rage and avarice of every wicked man on earth' (*Works*, vi. 44). 'Unbounded, universal liberty' is a contradiction (see *Alc.*, 215). '. . . our present impending danger is from the setting up of private judgment, or an inward light, in opposition to human and divine laws.' (vi. 217.) '. . . all political societies have found it necessary, to oblige each individual member, to conform his civil life and actions, to the will or decrees of the community, rather than leave him to be governed at his own pleasure.' (*Works*, vii. 131.) True civil liberty rests upon ancient law and prescription (*Alc.*, 211), and it is the general respect for law and the sovereign, and for the subjects, inculcated by the Christian religion that alone makes it possible (*Alc.*, 217).

In resisting those political theories that rest the duty of consent simply upon prior contract and voluntary association, Berkeley seemed to some to be opposed to the 'Glorious Revolution' of 1688, and was denied preferment as a result. He had himself been critical of earlier assertions of the absolute right of sovereigns. William I 'had the same title to the crown that a highwayman has to your purse. So that after all we are forced to place the right of kings in the consent and acquiescence of the people; whence it follows that whoever has the crown in possession, and the people or the representatives i.e. Lords and Commons consenting with him, the same is rightful king.'[28] On the one hand, the one to whom we should submit is the one that has the consent of the people; on the other, 'to represent the higher powers as deputies of the people manifestly tends to diminish the awe and reverence which all good men should have for the laws and government of their country' (*Works*, vi. 30). God requires us to follow common judgement—a requirement made clear by the dreadful consequences of rebellion—but the authority of the laws does not rest on majority vote. '. . . nothing is a [natural] law merely

---

[28] Rand, *Berkeley and Percival*, p. 62 (21. 10. 1709).

because it conduceth to the public good, but because it is decreed by the will of God.' (vi. 34.)

One of the arguments that Berkeley uses against the moral programme of individual autonomy is that Nature itself acts on general laws (vi. 23 f.)—or rather, God Himself does so, as a message to us to act accordingly. God also sends us a message in the manifold connectedness of natural events (*Alc.*, 63). Everyone must consider himself 'as the member of a great City, whose author and founder is God' (*Alc.*, 129), because we can see from what God shows us in nature that there are no self-sufficient, isolated entities. He has also set a principle of mutual attraction in our souls, analogous to the natural principle of gravitation, that draws us 'together in communities, clubs, families, friendships, and all the various species of society' (*Works*, vii. 226). 'This it is that inclines each individual to an intercourse with his species, and models every one to that behaviour which best suits with the common well-being.' (vii. 227.) We must not, of course, make such impulses of tenderness and benevolence of temper 'the sole rule of our actions' (*Works*, vi. 23). They are only guides, to be corrected and woven together by the use of reason, especially the sovereign's reason.

'The legislator's function is to achieve some harmony of interests from a cacophony of individual interests', since 'the public good may be distorted or hidden by a malicious egoism or a misguided altruism'.[29] The number and welfare of its subjects is the true strength of the crown, and its first step must be to feed and clothe its people (vi. 116). Piety, industry, sobriety of manners, and an honest regard for posterity are essential to public happiness (vi. 82), and honourable sovereigns must endeavour to encourage such virtues. The circulation of money is, as Lysicles said, the true life of business, so that industry may be promoted as well by speeding up the flow as by increasing the material stock of bullion (vi. 106). There is no need to try and explain away Berkeley's concern with paper money as a by-product of his digestive problems (as Wisdom: 'Faced with growing internal disorder, Berkeley was making a special effort to exercise control over the external world'[30]). Nor was he quite so original, or so

---

[29] F. Petrella, 'George Berkeley's theory of economic policy and classical economic liberalism', *Southern Economic Journal* 32 (1965–6), pp. 275 ff.

[30] J. O. Wisdom, *The Unconscious Origin of Berkeley's Philosophy* (Hogarth Press, London, 1953), p. 165.

Keynesian, as (for example) Johnston supposes.[31] John Law had taken the decisive step, in 1705, of identifying credit as the soul of commerce,[32] and Berkeley differed from other 'paper-money mercantilists' mostly in that he had the experience of living in a 'depressed economy, distressed area, under-developed country and an exploited colony'[33] all at once. The actual coinage used in Ireland 'consisted of a nondescript collection of the oldest and worst coins that would pass', and had it not been for Bankers' Notes domestic traffic would have been impossible to manage even half as well as it was.[34] Berkeley wished to correct this lack of decent currency by urging the foundation of a National Bank of Ireland that could improve the internal circulation of credit. Ireland was not allowed to compete with English manufactories, but there were other industries that could be cultivated if the obsession with bullion was forgotten.

Though Berkeley saw no need for bullion—he had remarked to Percival in 1713 that the export of cattle did more harm to Ireland than any good the import of pistoles did[35]—he was not therefore entirely Keynesian. Keynes regretfully (and his followers more single-mindedly) rejected the virtues of thrift and temperance. For Berkeley it was clear that 'frugality of manners is the nourishment and strength of bodies politic' (*Works*, vi. 74).[36] '. . . which is most likely to promote the industry of his countrymen, a virtuous married man with a healthy numerous offspring . . . or a fashionable rake about town? I would fain know whether money spent innocently doth not circulate as well as that spent upon vice?' (*Alc.*, 72.) It is wrong for the wealthy to hoard their cash, as it is also wrong for them to spend it upon fantastical pleasures. The Irish Commons of 1704: 'It will greatly conduce to the relief of the poor (reduced to extreme want and beggary by reason of the great decay of trade and discouragement of the manufacture of this Kingdom) and to the good of this Kingdom

[31] J. D. Johnston, 'Monetary manipulation: Berkeleian and otherwise', *Hermathena* 110 (1970), p. 34.

[32] E. F. Heckscher, *Mercantilism*, tr. M. Shapiro, ed. E. F. Soderlund (Allen and Unwin, London, 1955), p. 234.

[33] Hutchison, 'Berkeley's Querist', p. 52.

[34] J. D. Johnston, 'Irish Currency in the Eighteenth Century', *Hermathena* 52 (1938), pp. 4, 23; see his 'Berkeley and the abortive bank project of 1720-1', *Hermathena* 55 (1940), p. 111.

[35] Rand, *Berkeley and Percival*, p. 115.

[36] I. D. S. Ward, 'George Berkeley: precursor of Keynes or Moral Economist on Underdevelopment', *Journal of Political Economy* 67 (1959), p. 33; *pace* Hutchison, 'Berkeley's Querist', p. 70.

that inhabitants thereof should use none other than the manufacturing of this Kingdom in their apparal and the furniture of their houses'.[37] Berkeley agreed, and set himself to practise this device. If the rich should practise an Aristotelian liberality and munificence in hiring local talent to build their houses and clothe their backs, the poor should work. Berkeley shared the usual perspective of his age in reckoning that too many of the poor were 'lazy'. 'Among traditionalistic peoples, where a rigid standard of living, embracing not much more than the necessaries of physical subsistence, obtains, any increase in wages will result in an immediate diminution of labor hours.'[38] Other studies have suggested that a degree of 'irresponsible present-mindedness' (or trustful unconcern for the morrow?) is widespread in traditional society, and among the chronically poor, who prefer to spend any windfall on immediate consumption rather than increased productivity.[39] The solution was not to encourage vice, as Berkeley not unreasonably believed that Mandeville was advocating, but to make it possible for the poor to achieve an honourable competence. 'An inadequate level of employment and effective demand may be a serious problem which state action, by fiscal, monetary and other policies can and ought to deal with.'[40]

The leading men of the nation, including the Roman clergy (whom Berkeley wooed with increasing courtesy[41]), should aim to instil appropriate desires in their flock. Even temporary servitude is better than idleness and beggary (*Works*, vi. 136),[42] but the goal of an improved industry is to be a nearer equality (vi. 122). A National Bank, public works, and the issue of paper money on whatever security is generally acceptable, are specifically monetary measures, but they take their place in a general scheme of moral reform, a re-creation of public spirit. That spirit must move outwards by degrees: family and friends constitute our first cares, but we can also

---

[37] F. G. James, *Ireland in the Empire 1668–1770* (Harvard University Press, Boston, Mass., 1973), p. 59.

[38] E. S. Furniss, *The Position of the Laborer in a System of Nationalism* (Houghton Mifflin Co., Boston, 1920), p. 234.

[39] See M. Rothbard, *Towards a New Liberty* (Macmillan, New York, 1972), pp. 171 ff.; M. Sahlins, *Stone Age Economics* (Tavistock, London, 1972).

[40] Hutchison, 'Berkeley's Querist', p. 74; see D. Vickers, *Studies in the Theory of Money 1690–1776* (Peter Owen, London, 1960), pp. 158 f.

[41] Leyburn, 'Bishop Berkeley: the Querist', p. 79.

[42] For other advocates of temporary servitude see Furniss, *The Position of The Laborer*, pp. 80 f., P. W. Buck, *The Politics of Mercantilism* (Henry Holt & Co., New York, 1942).

recognize ourselves as parts of a single Kingdom, or of a wider unity (United Kingdom, or humankind, or—as I shall argue later—God's creation).

When Berkeley set himself to advance religion and sound learning in America, he hoped that Planters and Indians and slaves would discover something of a wider unity than their parochial concerns.

An ancient Antipathy to the *Indians*, whom it seems, our first Planters . . . imagined they had a Right to treat on the foot of *Canaanites* or *Amalekites*, together with an irrational Contempt of the Blacks, as Creatures of another Species, who had no Right to be instructed or admitted to the Sacraments, have proved a main Obstacle to the Conversion of these poor People. (*Works*, vii. 121 f.)

The discovery of our common humanity, our common creatureliness, rested on the recognition that 'as God is the common father of us all, it follows it cannot be his intention, that we should each of us promote his own private interest, to the wrong or damage of his neighbour' (vii. 130).

As members of that Great City whose Author and Founder is God (*Alc.*, 129), we must comport ourselves as that omnipotent legislator must be supposed to require, obediently to the laws and customs of an honourable tradition and for the greater good of all. We must so awaken our belief and desire for heaven as to defeat the endemic sloth and present-mindedness of our kind, and be wholly conformed to the divine will, 'our base nature renewed and assimilated to the Deity, our being made fellow-citizens with angels, and sons of God' (*Alc.*, 179). It was Berkeley's not unreasonable conviction that only such a story could have sufficient force to bring men's factious desires under control. How many would be moved to set aside their own private interest merely for the sake of an intuited 'moral beauty', or obey a self-appointed government if they could get away with disobedience? Fear of the magistrate is not enough to secure civil peace: 'what is it that renders this world habitable, but the prevailing notions of order, virtue, duty, and Providence?' (vi. 202.)

In this Berkeley once again follows ancient tradition: even atheistical moralists had regularly agreed that the great mass of the people would be better ordered if they thought that they acted 'in the eye of infinite wisdom, power, and goodness' (*Works*, vii. 196). Berkeley thought with the vulgar that there would indeed be much less reason to be 'good' if we did not believe. If what happens is the

result of 'blind, unthinking principle' (*Alc.*, 128), what reason could
we have to trust that our natural impulses or customary preferences
were worth following? And once the thought has occurred to us that
they are not, how can we create any rational reconstruction of belief
and morals? Must we not relapse upon immediate whim, and the
power of the strongest sword? '. . . all those who write either explicitly
or by insinuation against the dignity, freedom, and immortality of the
human soul, may so far forth be justly said to unhinge the principles
of morality, and destroy the means of making men reasonably
virtuous.' (*Alc.*, 23.) 'He who makes it his business to lessen or root
out from the minds of men [a religious awe and fear of God] doth in
effect endeavour to fill his country with highwaymen, house-
breakers, murderers, fraudulent dealers, perjured witnesses, and
every other pest of society.' (*Works*, vi. 219 f.) Once the lingering
credit of the old notions is exhausted, the 'age of monsters is not far
off' (vi. 221).

So Berkeley is one who founds moral decency not on individual
autonomy, but on our conformity to the will that sustains all things
with impartial generosity, as that will has made itself manifest in the
customs and laws of our several communities, up to and including the
whole world of nature. Of 'moral goodness' in the abstract, or
attempts to build up decency from rationally incontrovertible
premises, he thinks little. What we must do, all that we can do, is act
according to our highest ideal of how the world should be, and trust
that so we habituate ourselves to the air of heaven.

IV

There are, of course, a great many points in Berkeley's exposition on
which critical inquiry could focus. My object has been to expound his
system, in brief, and not to respond to any large-scale criticism. The
charge against all those who found morality in the will of God, that
God might be 'immoral',[43] I have sought to deal with in another
place. The particular charge with which I have most sympathy is
Pitcher's,[44] that Berkeley gives no reason to say that it is the greatest
good of humankind that God wills (*Works*, vi. 20, *Alc.*, 60), rather

---

[43] P. J. Olscamp, *The Moral Philosophy of George Berkeley* (Nijhoff, The Hague,
1970), p. 235; see my 'God's Law and Morality' in *Philosophical Quarterly* 32 (1982),
pp. 339 ff.

[44] Pitcher, *Berkeley*, p. 235.

than the good of all creation. The arguments he offers, indeed, lead rather to that conclusion, and he even expresses his thesis in terms of 'universal well-being'. His reason, no doubt, was that he was so far Cartesian as to think, sometimes, that animals were not spirits, but ideas: 'we see the Horse it self, the Church it self it being an Idea & nothing more' (*PC*, 427), whereas no one strictly sees a person, *qua* spirit (*Alc.*, 147). At other times, he speaks without qualms of the age of a fly as measured by its ideas (*PC*, 48), and of the happiness of moles and bats (*Alc.*, 86). Even if the non-human creation were an aggregate of ideas there might still be discoverable rules about how God wanted us to help order those ideas, but there could be no question of achieving the welfare of that creation. If we acknowledge that there are other spirits in the world than human or angelic spirits, it can no longer plausibly be claimed that we 'have no influence on the other orders of intelligences' (*Works*, vi. 20).

In expanding Berkeley's message, accordingly, it seems advisable to say that not the greater good of humankind, but of the created universe, is to be our criterion of moral truth.

We ought not therefore to repine at the dispensations of providence, or charge god foolishly. I say it becomes us with thankfulness to use the good things we receive from the hand of God, and patiently to abide the evil, which when thoroughly considered and understood may perhaps appear to be good, it being no sure sign that a thing is good, because we desire, or evil, because we are displeased with it. (*Works*, vii. 134)

The cultivation of that moral temper, in ourselves and in society, was Berkeley's goal, and, in some measure, his own achievement.[45]

[45] Other works on Berkeley's Moral and Economic Theory consulted for this paper were as follows. D. Berman, 'Mrs Berkeley's annotations in her interleaved copy of An Account of the Life of George Berkeley (1776)', *Hermathena* 123 (1977), pp. 15 ff. G. P. Conroy, 'George Berkeley on Moral Demonstration', *Journal of the History of Ideas* 22 (1961), pp. 205 ff. I. Hedenius, *Sensationalism and Theology in Berkeley's Philosophy* (Alonquist and Wicksells, Uppsala, 1936). J. D. Johnston: 'Commercial Restriction and Monetary Deflation in the Eighteenth Century', *Hermathena* 54 (1939), pp. 79 ff.; 'A synopsis of Berkeley's monetary philosophy', *Hermathena* 55 (1940), pp. 73 ff.; 'Locke, Berkeley and Hume as monetary theorists', *Hermathena* 56 (1940), pp. 77 ff.; 'Bishop Berkeley and kindred economic thinkers', *Hermathena* 59 (1942), pp. 30 ff.; *Berkeley's Querist in Historical Perspective* (Dundalgan Press, Dundalk, 1970). D. E. Leary, 'Berkeley's Social Theory', *Journal of the History of Ideas* 38 (1977), pp. 635 ff. P. J. Olscamp, 'Some suggestions about the moral philosophy of George Berkeley', *Journal of the History of Philosophy* 6 (1968), pp. 147 ff. J. Tussman, 'Berkeley as a political philosopher', in *George Berkeley*, ed. S. C. Pepper *et al.* (University of California Press, Berkeley, 1957), pp. 122 ff.

INDEX OF NAMES

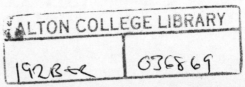